FANON

IN SEARCH OF THE AFRICAN REVOLUTION

Fanon: In Search of the African Revolution is different from other books on Fanon in that it approaches him as both a political philosopher and political sociologist of the African experience. It suggests that Fanon's political writings be viewed in terms of his concern with how relations are structured in colonial and post-colonial Africa and the implications of those structural arrangements for political conflict in Africa.

Fanon's attempt to explain the pathologies and contradictions of African politics in terms of class and the historical processes that influence and constrain class political behaviour is provocative and insightful. But the moral dimension that informs Fanon's theoretical perspectives is no less important, if only because it attests to his strong advocacy of the need for revolutionary change as a condition for the restructuring of African political systems.

I0894145

FANON

IN SEARCH OF THE AFRICAN REVOLUTION

L. Adele Jinadu

Routledge
Taylor & Francis Group
LONDON AND NEW YORK

First published in 2003 by
Kegan Paul Limited

Published 2014 by Routledge
2 Park Square, Milton Park, Abingdon, Oxfordshire OX14 4RN
711 Third Avenue, New York, NY 10017

First issued in paperback 2014

Routledge is an imprint of the Taylor & Francis Group, an informa business

ISBN 978-0-7103-0185-7 (hbk)
ISBN 978-1-1380-1070-3 (pbk)

British Library Cataloguing in Publication Data
A catalogue record for this book is available from the British Library.

Library of Congress Cataloging-in-Publication Data
Applied for.

For Gloria and MusRash
and also in memory of my father and grandmother,
Mama Campos

Contents

ACKNOWLEDGEMENTS

This study is a revision of my doctoral dissertation, *The Political Ideas of Frantz Fanon: Essay in Interpretation and Criticism,* submitted to the Graduate School of the University of Minnesota in November, 1973. I am grateful to Mulford Sibley, Ellen Pirro, August H. Nimtz, Jr. and Homer Mason, for their comments on initial drafts of the dissertation. For his comments on Chapter 6 of the present work, I am grateful to Vincent Ostrom. I have also benefitted from interminable discussion on Fanon with Emmanuel Hansen.

The revision of the dissertation was started and completed during a 10-month period I spent at Indiana University as a Fulbright Scholar in the Workshop in Political Theory and Policy Analysis and the African Studies Program there. I am grateful to Vincent Ostrom and Elinor Ostrom, Co-Directors of the Workshop and also to Patrick O'Meara, Director of the African Studies Program for making my stay both socially and intellectually rewarding.

The secretarial and research facilities placed at my disposal by the Workshop are particularly appreciated. I thank Patty Zielinski, Kathy Solt, and Cheryl Weir for typing the manuscript.

I

PROLOGUE

Chapter 1

INTRODUCTION

Frantz Fanon's Critical Spirit

This book is concerned with answering the question: How does Fanon aid our understanding of the nature of political processes in colonial and postcolonial Africa? In other words, the purpose is to offer a critical examination of the ideas about man and society in colonial and postcolonial Africa set forth in the political writings of Frantz Fanon.[1]

This is necessarily a two-fold task: first, there is the task of exposition, by means of which one aims at a better understanding of the man and his ideas, of the connection between his thought and the milieu or environment within which he wrote. Pertinent questions to ask, in this respect, include the following: What did Fanon mean? How did his ideas on colonialism and postcolonial African politics relate to one another? How did those ideas develop — what were the social, historical, biographical and intellectual contexts which determined and shaped their development? Second, there is the task of criticism and evaluation. To do this is to inquire about how valuable, valid, insightful and convincing those ideas are; it is to assess their explanatory power, to see if they will stand up to close scrutiny and withstand the weight of evidence that may be adduced against them. It is also to

[1] References will be made in this book to the American editions of the following published writings of Frantz Fanon: *Black Skin, White Masks,* 1967; *Studies in a Dying Colonialism,* 1967; *Toward the African Revolution,* 1967; and *The Wretched of the Earth,* 1968 — all of which are published by Grove Press.

evaluate the cogency and force of criticisms made of those ideas by other critics of Fanon.

Both tasks are indeed closely related, if only because it is by a critical assessment that one will come to have a sympathetic understanding and admiration for the thought of Fanon. Indeed, throughout much of this study critical remarks and evaluations are juxtaposed with the exposition of Fanon's ideas on man and society.

The portrait of Fanon that should emerge is that of a moralist and humanist. He had a passionate concern for, and commitment to humanity and the human condition; he felt uneasy in a hypocritical world where lip service was paid to the ideals of social justice, equality and freedom. He brought moral concerns and perspectives to bear on social and political questions.

Organization of the Book

In Part II, I offer a critical exposition of Fanon's views on man and society in a colonial milieu and examine Fanon's moral justification of violence and his theory of revolution. Part III is concerned with Fanon's analysis of politics and political change in postcolonial Africa and the policy implications that can be inferred from that analysis.

My argument is that there is a direct link between these parts of the dissertation. An analysis of colonial society and its heritage leads to an analysis of the conditions under which change can be effected. It is after all Fanon's contention that problems of modernization and nation-building in postcolonial Africa are directly tied to colonial rule and its heritage.

Fanon on Man and Society in a Colonial Milieu

Part II of this book is, then, concerned with the views of Frantz Fanon on man and society in a colonial milieu. The concern here is to raise and answer a number of questions:

What conception of human nature does Fanon entertain? How does this conception affect both his critique of colonial society and his conception of the ideal society? What criticisms of colonialism and colonial rule does he offer and how are the criticisms related to his conception of human nature and the ideal society? What is the connection, if any, between his thesis that violence is cleansing and purifying and his critique of colonial society, on the one hand, and his conception of human nature on the other hand?

In attempting to answer these questions I shall relate Fanon's political writings to a wider context of western and nonwestern social and political thought. The purpose of so relating Fanon's thought is neither to establish the "influence" of any particular social theorist or school of social theory on Fanon, nor to stake a claim for the "influence" of Fanon on some other social theorists. Skinner has brilliantly illuminated some of the methodological and conceptual problems involved in establishing "influence" in the history of political ideas.[2]

But to say that it is difficult or impossible to establish one social theorist's influence on another social theorist is not to deny that there is what Greenleaf has called an "affinity" between the speculations of two or more social theorists on a particular concept or social issue. In situations where this "affinity" of thought is present, so Greenleaf rightly observes, "no question of influence need arise: it is simply that there are certain similarities in manner of thought which appear to the mind of the observer."[3] For example, in the case of Fanon one wants to examine the "similarities in manner of thought," which might be said to exist between his conception of "violence" and that of Marx or Sorel or Sartre; or between his critique of colonialism and that of Césaire; or between his

[2] Quentin Skinner, "Meaning and Understanding in the History of Ideas," *History and Theory*, Vol. 8, No. 1 (1969), pp. 25-27.

[3] W. H. Greenleaf, "Hobbes: The Problem of Interpretation," in Maurice Cranston and Richard S. Peters, eds., *Hobbes and Rousseau: A Collection of Critical Essays* (Garden City, New York: Doubleday, 1972), p. 28.

speculations on revolution and those of Marx or Lenin or Mao; or between his conception of freedom and that of Rousseau or Marx or Sartre.

Part II is divided into four chapters. In Chapter 2, I state and assess Fanon's critique of colonialism and colonial rule. Chapter 3 is about the concept of alienation in Fanon's political writings: in this respect, focus will be placed on his discussion of what he considers to be the inherent violent nature of the colonial situation, and his thesis about the role of language as a form of cultural imposition. In Chapters 4 and 5, I examine the concepts of violence, liberation and revolution in Fanon.

The African Context of Fanon's Political Writings

In Part III, I place Fanon's political writings in a postcolonial African setting. I assess his contribution to the historiography of African politics in the period since 1957, the year of Ghana's independence. Having done that, I then discuss his analysis of social class behavior and political conflict in postcolonial Africa. Hopefully, the following questions should be answered: What moral considerations inform his assessment of political processes in colonial and postcolonial Africa: What model of political conflict in postcolonial Africa does Fanon offer us? What does the model tell us about the direction of social and political change in Africa? What policy recommendations can be reasonably drawn from the model?

A consideration of Fanon's analysis of postcolonial African politics raises two questions. First, is it meaningful to talk about African politics as such? Second, how credible is Fanon as an analyst of postcolonial African politics?

The first question is a pertinent one to ask insofar as Africa is not composed of uniform social, economic, and political units. My position, however, is that when one talks about

African politics and of a model of African politics, one is talking about underlying currents of politics on the continent, about political institutions and political "styles" which, while having local variations, are fundamentally the same from one country to another or one region to another. Such a focus is at least a starting point for an understanding of politics in postcolonial Africa. To say, therefore, that there is a pattern to African politics is neither to deny the heterogeneity of Africa nor to overlook limitations inherent in any model of African politics.

The second question is about the extent and reliability of Fanon's knowledge of postcolonial African politics. It would seem that Fanon was greatly handicapped in this connection. His "field" experiences in Africa were limited to North Africa and West Africa. He had no first-hand knowledge of East, Central and Southern Africa, and it is open to question how much he knew or could have known of those West African countries in which he lived or visited. My approach, however, is to look upon him as an analyst who brings a primarily normative or ethical perspective to bear on his concerns about the problems of nation-building in Africa. He relied on his impressions and intuitions. It is argued later on that it is a measure of the greatness of the man that, limited as his "field experiences" were, he offered us penetrating insights into the social dynamics of political conflict in postcolonial Africa.

Part III is divided into three chapters. Chapter 6 offers an assessment of Fanon's notion of commitment and how this affects his views on the role of the African intellectual as an agent of social change. Chapter 7 assesses Fanon's theory of African politics and underdevelopment. Chapter 8 discusses the policy implications of Fanon's political writings.

Some Methodological Questions

The task of interpreting and assigning meanings to political texts, or any literary texts for that matter, is not an easy one.

The problem is essentially one of providing a set of appropriate criteria of evidence one should follow in uncovering and assigning meaning to the text in question. If poetic, literary or philosophical interpretation is not to became a capricious affair the question posed by Skinner must be faced, namely, "What are the appropriate procedures to adopt in the attempt to arrive at an understanding of the work?"[4] Does one rely exclusively on either the text itself or the social milieu or context within which the writer is or was operating? Are these textual and contextual procedures for interpreting the work mutually exclusive? What constitutes "understanding" in the circumstances?

I have, however, employed two broad strategies, suggested by Cioffi,[5] in interpreting Fanon and assigning meaning to his political writings. First, I have relied on autobiographical and biographical facts about him. Second, I have also had to rely on empathy, on my intuitions and judgment.

The selection of autobiographical considerations to bring to bear on the interpretation of literary texts is a vexing one; for, as Cioffi points out, "it is difficult to know where the line should be drawn" between those considerations that are strictly relevant and those that are mere irrelevant "intrusions."[6]

In the case of Fanon, we know, as a relevant autobiographical fact about him, that he was concerned with colonialism, racism, and political development in Africa; we know also that this was one reason why he wrote *Black Skin, White Masks, A Dying Colonialism, Wretched of the Earth,* and *Toward the African Revolution.* His political writings, his explicitly stated concerns and interests, as borne out particularly in the last three of these four books, were chiefly about Africa.

[4] Skinner, "Meaning and Understanding," p. 3.

[5] Frank Cioffi, "Intention and Interpretation in Criticism," *Proceedings of the Aristotelian Society,* New Series, Vol. LXIV, (1963-1964), pp. 85-106.

[6] Ibid., p. 103.

These four books also define the context within which he wished to be interpreted and understood. We know that he was concerned about political leadership roles in Africa; we also know that he was concerned about, and interested in problems of nation-building, particularly those connected with the creation of political order and social justice, in Africa; we know he subscribed to the idea of Pan-Africa. These observations are no doubt truer of the Fanon of the late 1950's and early 1960's than of the Fanon of the early 1950's when *Black Skin, White Masks* was published.

To place Fanon in an explicitly African setting is not, however, to say that his concerns and interests, or that the "relevance" of his writings and message, were exclusively limited to Africa. One implication of this autobiographical approach is the denial of the textual-contextual dichotomy; instead it points to the interconnections between the text and the context in interpreting a piece of literature.

Reliance on one's own judgment of the intention of a writer is an important aspect of literary interpretation. This may involve one's making a leap of faith. No doubt some judgments are better than others; yet it is part of the problem one must face that it is never clear how one is to formulate the criteria of good judgment. As Cioffi admits, "though there are those whose judgment is better in such matters; and rules for determining this, these do not form a system and only experienced people can apply them. There are consequences which distinguish correct from incorrect judgment, but these are of a diffuse kind and like the rules incapable of general formulation."[7]

The connection between one's own intuitions and some autobiographical facts about a writer lies in the fact that "a conviction that a poet stands in a certain relation to his words conditions our response to them."[8]

[7] Ibid., p. 106.
[8] Ibid.

The Significance of Fanon

This book is different from others on Fanon in that it approaches Fanon as both a political philosopher and political sociologist of the African experience. It suggests that Fanon's political writings be viewed in the context of his concern with how power relations are structured in colonial and postcolonial Africa and the implications of those structural arrangements for political conflict in Africa.

It is perhaps to be expected that discussion of the work of such a polemical and didactic political philosopher as Fanon will usually be colored by political or ideological bias. As a result of this, interpretations of his ideas, particularly by hostile reviewers, have tended to be based on a careless or impressionistic reading of his writings. Those writings have not been viewed by most of these reviewers in their totality. Rather, this or that passage from *The Wretched of the Earth,* his most famous work, is taken as representative of his ideas generally. The result, not surprisingly, is a distortion of his meaning and message. What is offered here is therefore a measured, but sympathetic interpretation of various aspects of Fanon's life and work in the context of Africa.

But in what does Fanon's importance as well as his relevance lie? Fanon rode the crest of the wave of radicalism in North America — a radicalism that grew out of the civil rights movement and opposition to the war in Vietnam — in the late 1960s and early 1970s. However, to most on the right and to many liberal intellectuals in Western Europe and North America he was a villain, a perpetrator of a heinous myth, someone who glorified violence. Yet such denunciations invariably conveniently refused to place Fanon's discussion in the wider perspectives of his valid characterization of colonial and postcolonial Africa as well as the global system of power relations as inherently violent. In short, if Fanon was a hero to some in the 1960s and 1970s, he was also to many the purveyor of hatred. It is perhaps indicative of the importance attached to his work that he was both hated and admired with a burning, consuming passion.

By the mid-1970s one had begun to notice some decline in the popularity of Fanon in North America, something which was, perhaps, partly due to the deradicalization of North American politics. Within the heterogenous Black power movements in the United States there was, moreover, an increasing tendency to question the relevance of Fanon to the Black movement in the United States. The experience of some Black Panthers in Algeria had not helped much. Revolutionary rhetoric had been tamed by the harsh realities of life as well as the ability of the political system to contain subversive threats to its equilibrium.

It will, however, be facile to say that interest in Fanon had waned substantially. In the Caribbean and in Africa there is an increasing interest in Fanon. While much of this interest is confined to radical, leftist intellectual circles, the protracted wars of national liberation in Guinea-Bissau, Mozambique, Angola, Zimbabwe, and Southern African have continued to bring into sharp focus the practical and theoretical importance of Fanon's writings. Here is an opportunity to test and refine Fanon's theoretical underpinnings, a refinement that has been provided by Amilcar Cabral in particular, but also by Eduardo Mondlane and Samora Machel. It is usual in some circles to contrast Cabral and Fanon, so as to discredit the latter. The fact, however, is that there is no gulf separating the theoretical perspectives of both men.

The continuing interest in and relevance of Fanon since the mid-1970s should therefore be related to the evolving political situation in independent Africa and in Zimbabwe and Southern Africa. It is not only in the Caribbean and Africa that this interest has been sustained. In North America and Europe there is also a renewed interest in Fanon, an interest that reflects a concern with some of the moral issues that Fanon raised and posed unequivocally: commitment, the legitimacy of political authority, the banality and dehumanizing impact on individuals of certain types of political structures and institutions. Just as conservative and liberal intellectuals have shown increasing interest in the humanism of Marx, so also are they now showing an appreciation for Fanon's humanism. This itself testifies to the failures of conservatism and liberalism to resolve basic contradictions in capitalist societies and in their peripheries. Even in Christian circles, the relevance and appropriateness of defensive violence in reaction to oppression is now being conceded as being in the Christian tradition.

In a sense, much of the application of dependency theories to the analyses of political processes in contemporary Africa should be viewed as deriving in part from Fanon's *Wretched of the Earth.* There is reason to believe that, in spite of the tentative and sketchy nature of his discussion of postcolonial African politics, the inspiration for what has now virtually become the orthodoxy in the study of African politics comes from Fanon. African scholarship is therefore vindicating both Fanon's insight and his powerful conjectures about the direction in which African politics was inexorably moving. Fanon was of course no prophet, but his achievement was to have refused to be mystified by political forms and the self-serving rhetoric of political leaders in the first few years of political independence. He was among the few who pointed to the illusion of independence at that time.

Some liberal writers have sought to discredit Fanon by claiming either his ideas are not original or that he is a second rate thinker. This is, however, an academic question Not only is it open to question what it is to be original in this respect, but also it is not clear what will constitute acceptable criteria of listing political thinkers in rank order. What this book hopes to bring out, however, is that Fanon's political ideas are important and suggestive because they have affected and to some extent powerfully influenced, the historical situation in which we have found ourselves.

There is a force to Fanon's observations, particularly on the human predicament in Africa, that is captivating; one finds in his writings an insight into the nature of political developments in Africa that is not only significant in the senses already indicated, but also incomparable. There are three areas in which Fanon's writings have proved suggestive.

First, I have argued that Fanon looked upon *critical theory* as a practical, instrumental effort. Theory, on this view, is indispensable to the construction of viable political systems, particularly in the Third World. This also is why there is a strong connection between morality and politics in his writings.

Secondly, I have tried to direct attention to Fanon's delineation of the sociological structure and the social-psychological pathology of racism and colonialism. Fanon's notion of violence is important in this respect. For purposes of critical exegesis I have offered a three-fold categorization of his notion of violence into *physical, structural,* and *psychological* violence.

Thirdly, a major contribution of Fanon to the study of African politics, already mentioned with respect to dependency theories, is class analysis of African politics. In this respect, as I argue in Chapters 7 and 8, Fanon's analysis of African politics is primarily concerned with the conditions under which constitutional order can be maintained in Africa. The importance of this concern cannot be overemphasized particularly since the conditions Fanon suggests provide interesting criteria for assessing the chances for a "new" beginning in countries as varied as Nigeria, Ghana, and Zimbabwe.

Intellectual derivations are usually difficult to establish, but there can be little doubt that the work of a rapidly growing group of radical and committed African scholars bears the stamp of the reinterpretations of Marxism provided by Fanon. It used to be said in the 1960s that Fanon was "rediscovered" in Europe and North America. The implication was that he was little known and read in Africa. Some even argued that

Fanon did not write for Africa, but was essentially concerned with carrying on a dialogue with the European left. There might have been some point to this. Yet, if Fanon was not widely read in Africa, this was partly to be attributed to the apprehensions of colonial regimes and their successors; it was also partly due to the educational system whose curriculum was by and large devoted to justifying "la mission civilisatrice."

It is a sign of the changes that have taken place in Africa since the mid-1970s that Fanon is now being "resuscitated" within Africa by a group of African social scientists, most of whom are members of the African Association of Political Scientists. The work of these scholars offers a critical reassessment of the place and role of the social sciences, indeed of the academic and professional disciplines in Africa. Their basic concern, reflected in their writing and professional activities, is with the decolonization of the teaching of the social sciences in Africa. This orientation has also meant a reinterpretation of the developmental process and of the relevant variables that should provide the theoretical or organizing framework for the study of that process.

This is part of what was meant when it was claimed earlier that the application of dependency theories to the study of African politics owed its origins, in some respects, to Fanon. It should, of course, be pointed out that these African scholars have not sought to mystify or idolize Fanon. Rather, they have been sharply critical of him and have in the process sharpened and refined his analytical categories.

There is also a concern with policy matters by these scholars. Commitment in the sense in which Fanon used it cannot be separated from policy issues. It matters what policies are adopted and implemented by governments. The duty of the committed scholars is to influence the policy-making process. This also implies, of course, that the African social scientist, indeed the African intellectual as such, takes a critical though not necessarily antagonistic posture towards government and political regimes.

This critical posture that Fanon emphasizes again and again is now manifesting itself. The dissident intellectual is necessarily a threat to the political regime. In denouncing the excesses and chicaneries of postcolonial regimes in Africa, Fanon placed some hope in the radicalization and conversion of a faction of the African petty bourgeoisie. There is reason to believe that this has been happening, as the cases of Ghana and Nigeria have shown in recent years. The problem has been, however, to link the radicalization of the dissident intellectual to that of the proletariat and peasantry. How this link is to be provided has always been problematic in Fanon's writings. Yet what has now been accepted by the African intellectual is basically Fanon's thesis about the critical role of the committed individual in exposing and then transcending the contradictions of society. It is not unlikely that the more this dissidence is articulated, the more unsafe, and therefore the more repressive political regimes will tend to be.

Fanon died a young man. It is a moot question whether had he lived longer he would not have re-evaluated his main ideas. But the self-critical person that he was, he would certainly have shown a sensitiveness to the congruence of his ideas with concrete social reality. He was far from being dogmatic. He believed in the dialectical relationship of theory and practice with one another.

We can look back with the aid of hindsight and see in clearer perspectives problems and issues that Fanon only saw dimly. But this in fact serves to give us a better understanding and a more informed appreciation of the man. This understanding is now reflected in books and articles on Fanon: there is less and less of vitriolic attack on him. Racism, violence, colonialism, imperialism, freedom, human rights — these are global problems that threaten the prospects for world order. They constitute the themes of Fanon's writings and reflect his concerns for man *qua* man.

If discussion of Fanon is more informed now, there is nevertheless no lack of passion in that discussion. It is hoped that this book, while offering a reassessment of important aspects of Fanon's political ideas, will stimulate and generate further passionate, but informed discussion about the life, times, and work of a man who always believed in questioning received opinions.

II

THE POLITICAL SOCIOLOGY OF COLONIAL SOCIETY

Chapter 2

FANON'S MODEL OF COLONIAL SOCIETY - I

Introduction

A recurring concern that gives the writings of Frantz Fanon an underlying unity and substance is his attempt to understand and help in resolving what he once described as "the Black-White relation."[1] This expression refers basically to a particular type of culture and race contact which, in his view, is fostered by colonialism and colonial rule. The primary purpose of this chapter is an examination of Fanon's characterization and critique of certain aspects of colonialism.

There are three pertinent questions to raise in pursuing this purpose. First, what provides the model for Fanon's critique of colonialism and colonial rule? Secondly, how does he go about developing his critique? Thirdly, what does he mean by the colonial situation?

My thesis is the following. The uncompromising nature of Fanon's critique of colonialism is to be found, first, in his denial of the rationalization of colonialism as "the White man's burden"; secondly, in his denial of the progressive nature of colonialism; and thirdly in his reference to the boomerang effect of colonialism on the colonializing countries. Much of this critique of colonialism is to be found as well in such Black thinkers as Aimé Césaire.

It is sometimes argued that Fanon's work, particularly his concern with the Black-White relation, reflects the attempt of a disappointed *évolué* to work out "the solution to his personal

[1] Fanon, *Black Skin, White Masks*, p. 9.

drama in political action and philosophy."[2] Although psychological factors have their place in the interpretation of the work of a political thinker, one must resist the temptation to fall victim to a psychological reductionism that overly stresses psychological factors in the evolution of the ideas of political thinkers.

The problem is that, to be satisfactory, a psychological explanation must take note of such intervening variables as the socioeconomic and political context against whose background political thinkers are writing. There is also the problem of deciding the relevant psychological factors to focus on. In short, the psychological must be seen as part of other biographical data that are relevant to the development of a political thinker's work.

It is, however, important to reconcile any psychological interpretation of Fanon's work with his interest in issues and problems that extend beyond his personal dilemmas under racist and colonialist environments. Fanon would agree that one must face one's personal dilemmas squarely; he would also agree, as he repeatedly argued in *Black Skin, White Masks,* that one must attempt to achieve some virtue in one's own personal existence. He would also maintain, however, that it would be undesirable for one to do so in isolation from other people. For Fanon, man is defined by his social existence and the human predicament is pre-eminently social and interpersonal.

The Model for Fanon's Critique

There is necessarily a sense in which political thinkers are products of their social milieu. Their thought and writings are profoundly affected by the complex nature of the various social influences and forces to which they are exposed and

[2] Albert Memmi, in his review of Caute, *Fanon,* and Geismar, *Fanon,* in *The New York Times Book Review* (March 14, 1971), p. 5.

subjected. In the case of Fanon, his writings on colonialism are rooted in the socioeconomic and political milieu created by French colonial rule in Martinique and Algeria. His writings also derive from the experiences of *évolués* in France. Martinique, Algeria, and France therefore constitute the primary sources for his writings on colonialism and racism, although he also benefitted from discussions with colonial subjects from other parts of the colonial world, from what he read about colonialism and racism, and from his travels in countries other than France, Martinique, and Algeria.

In order to delineate the model for Fanon's critique, two questions must be answered: What is the theory or philosophy underlying French colonial rule? Is there a basis for generalizing from the nature of French colonial rule to the nature of colonial rule as such? To raise a question about the theory of French colonial rule is to examine the congruence between its principal propositions and socioeconomic and political reality in France and her overseas territories. To ask about the generalizability of Fanon's characterization is to ask about the relevance of the characterization in contexts other than France, Martinique, and Algeria.

The theory of French colonial rule, reflected in the French colonial policies of assimilation and association, is based primarily on the revolutionary doctrine of the equality of all peoples and the assumption of the superiority of French culture and civilization, an assumption that, as a corrollary, rests on the denial of the authenticity of indigenous culture. Of the two terms, assimilation and association, assimilation is commonly used to characterize French colonial policy. But it is also generally conceded that, even among Frenchmen at the peak of French imperialism and colonization, there were different strands of assimilationist thought and that differing and conflicting policy recommendations and options were put forward and debated.[3]

[3] Cf. Michael Crowder, *Senegal: A Study of French Assimilation Policy*,

Assimilation was, however, more than a constitutional fiction. The massive work of social and political transformation required of the attainment of its ideals were superficially and sporadically undertaken.[4] Rather, the official strategy was to create a gallicized or frenchified indigenous elite, separated from the mass of their peoples and used as instruments or agents of French colonial rule.[5] This gap between theory and practice adds force to Martin Deming Lewis's observation that the motivation behind the policy of assimilation was "less a generous urge to extend to benighted peoples the blessing of [French] civilization than the need to provide justification for the maintenance of French rule."[6]

Fanon's experiences in Martinique and France pointed to the gap between the theory and practice of assimilation. Although he had "assimilated" French values in Martinique, he discovered in Martinique and France that colonialist society was a rigidly stratified or racist society in which the color question was an overriding one that precluded his admission to, and mobility within, French society on equal socioeconomic and political terms with White Frenchmen.

There is, in this respect, a similarity between Fanon's experiences and those of such Black critics of the racist

rev. ed. (London: Methuen, 1967), pp. 2-4; Michael Crowder, "Indirect Rule — French and British Style," *Africa,* Vol. 39, No. 3 (July, 1964), pp. 202-203; Martin Deming-Lewis, "One Hundred Frenchmen: The 'Assimilation' Theory in French Colonial Policy," *Comparative Study in Society and History,* Vol. 4, No. 2 (January, 1962). Both Crowder and Lewis point to the difficulty of defining assimilation; but see Crowder, *Senegal,* p. 2 for a general statement of what a policy of assimilation entails.

[4] Thomas Hodgkin, *Nationalism in Colonial Africa* (New York: New York University Press, 1957), p. 38.

[5] On the nature of this strategy, see R. L. Buell, *The Native Problem in Africa,* Vol. 2 (London: Macmillan, 1928), pp. 77-85. At least this would seem to have been the practice at the center. For what amounts to an extension of indirect rule to French colonial administration, particularly at the periphery, see Donal B. Cruise O'Brien, *Saints and Politicians: Essays in the Organization of Senegalese Peasant Society* (London: Cambridge University Press, 1975), Ch. 3 particularly.

[6] Lewis, "One Hundred Frenchmen...," p. 151.

presuppositions of colonialism as René Maran, Aimé Césaire, and Jacques Roumain, among others. Their reaction against the denial of their African ancestry led them to an attempt to rediscover their African heritage and to an assertion of racial pride and consciousness.[7]

Fanon and these other Black critics of colonialism touch on a number of themes in their critique, as Hodgkin has pointed out.[8] First, they employ a form of dialectic reasoning in order to counter assimilationist positions and arguments. They assert the antithesis or contraries of assimilationist propositions. For example, the claim that colonialism substituted "civilized" institutions for "barbarous" ones is countered by the claim that colonialism had led to the destruction of authentic African civilizations and the substitution of European ones.

An important element in this formulation of the civilization/barbarism antithesis concerns the denial of the material benefits of colonial rule. This denial anticipated the basic thesis of contemporary underdevelopment theorists that colonialism was unprogressive, rapacious, exploitative, and above all had prevented colonized societies from developing by disrupting their history. This denial, which modifies the view of Marx, should be placed in the wider context of the identification by these Black critics of the racial element in colonialism. Although Marx and Engels indicted the moral basis of colonialism and regarded it as "actuated by vilest interests," they nevertheless saw redeeming features in

[7] F. A. Irele, "Literature and Ideology in Martinique: René Maran, Aimé Césaire, Frantz Fanon," *Research Review*, Vol. 5, No. 3 (Legon, Ghana: University of Ghana, Trinity Term, 1969), pp. 1-32; T. Hodgkin, "Some African and Third World Theories of Imperialism," in R. Owen and B. Sutcliffe, eds., *Theories of Imperialism* (London: Longman, 1972): Peter Worsley, "Frantz Fanon: Revolutionary Theories," *Studies on the Left*, Vol. 6,No. 3 (May/June, 1966), p. 32.

[8] Hodgkin, "Some African and Third World Theories of Imperialism."

colonial rule as "the unconscious tool of history in bringing about ... revolution."[9]

If it is argued, as Marx and Engels seem to be arguing, that colonialism could provide (or indeed provided) material benefits, the response of Fanon is that such benefits are inconsequential when compared with the present weak material base of colonized societies and the abject poverty of the generality of colonized peoples. Colonial rule was inherently unprogressive because it was incapable of releasing and generating productive forces that Marx and Engels had hoped would destroy the Asiatic mode of production.[10]

Another important element in Fanon's formulation of the civilization/barbarism antithesis is the claim that colonial rule was essentially preceded, inaugurated, and maintained by violence, particularly physical violence. This central theme in Fanon's discussion of colonialism is more extensively discussed in the next chapter. For him "colonialism is not a thinking machine nor a body endowed with reasoning faculties. It is violence in its natural state..."[11] In the concluding pages of *Wretched of the Earth,* he enjoins the colonized to "leave this Europe where they are never done of talking of Man, yet murder them everywhere they find them."[12]

The argument is that the imperative of maintaining colonial rule in the face of resistance or challenges to it by colonized peoples, led various colonial administrators to resort to the use of brute physical force. This law and order rationale for the use of physical violence to maintain colonialist

[9] S. Avineri, *Karl Marx on Colonization and Modernization* (Garden City: New York: Doubleday, 1969), p. 94. For an informed assessment of the views of Marx on colonialism, see Colin Leys, *Underdevelopment in Kenya: The Political Economy of Neocolonialism, 1964-1971* (London: Heinemann, 1975), pp. 1-8.

[10] C. Ake, *Revolutionary Pressures in Africa* (London: Zed Press, 1978), p. 70.

[11] Fanon, *Wretched of the Earth,* p. 61.

[12] Ibid., p. 311; Aimé Césaire, *Discours Sur Le Colonialisme,* Quatrè edition (Paris: Presence Africaine, 1955), p. 17ff; also emphasizes this point.

hegemony was aptly expressed by a Mr. George Wilson, British colonial administrator in Uganda, in 1879:

> Recently, I have been compelled to assert my authority in a manner that has caused serious loss of life and property. To allow uncivilized races to defy authority is a sure way of losing it, and my action therefore was imperative.[13]

A second theme, particularly evident in Fanon and Césaire, is that of the "boomerang" or corrupting effects of colonization on the colonizers. The claim is that the logic of colonial rule, exemplified in its violent methods and the attitudes and institutions sustaining it, inevitably dehumanizes the coloniser and can lead to the reimportation of those violent methods, attitudes, and institutions into their own countries by the colonizing bourgeois ruling class. This is why for Fanon and Césaire, Fascism and Nazism were internal manifestations of practices inherent in colonialism.[14]

A third theme is cultural relativism, the view that all cultures are equally valid and that moral standards are neither absolute nor universal. In Fanon's words, "universality resides in this decision to recognize and accept the reciprocal relativism of different cultures once the colonial status is irreversibly excluded."[15]

Is there a basis for generalizing from Fanon's experience of French colonialism to the nature of colonial rule as such? This question is concerned with the data base of Fanon's critique.

[13] Quoted in Tarsis B. Kabwegyere, "The Dynamics of Colonial Violence: The Inductive System in Uganda," *Journal of Peace Research*, Vol. 4 (1972), p. 305.

[14] Fanon, *Black Skins, White Masks*, pp. 90-92; Fanon, *Wretched of the Earth*, pp. 311-316; Césaire, *Discours*, pp. 12-13; 19-20.

[15] Fanon, *Toward the African Revolution*, p. 44. A more extended discussion of this aspect of Fanon is L. Adele Jinadu, "The Moral Dimensions of the Political Thought of Frantz Fanon," *Second Order: An African Journal of Philosophy*, Vol. 5, No. 1 (January, 1976).

Fanon himself is careful to concede that "since I was born in the Antilles, my observations and my conclusion are valid for the Antilles — at least concerning the Black man at home."[16]

Concerned with the "neurotic pathology" of colonialism as he saw it in Martinique and France, Fanon is, however, convinced that he could abstract, from the nature of colonialism in those specific contexts, generalizations about the nature of that pathology in other colonial contexts:

> I shall try to discover the various attitudes that the Negro adopts in contact with white civilization... I believe that the fact of the juxtaposition of the white and black race has created a massive psychoexistential complex. I hope by analyzing it to destroy it. Many Negroes will not find themselves in what follows. This is equally true of many whites. But the fact that I feel a foreigner in the worlds of the schizophrenic or the sexual cripple in no way diminishes their reality...[17]

This aspect of Fanon's critique will be discussed in another section of this chapter that will be devoted to his discussion of the colonial situation.

The Rationale for Fanon's Critique

What is Fanon's purpose in offering a critique of colonialism? How does he develop that critique? If it is legitimate to set much store by the declared purpose of a political thinker, we are lucky that Fanon is quite explicit about his purpose in writing about colonialism:

> Someone to whom I was talking about this book asked me what I expected to come of it. Ever since Sartre's decisive essay, "What is Literature?", ... literature has been committed more and more to its sole really contemporary task, which is to persuade the group to

[16] *Fanon, Black Skin, White Masks,* p. 14.
[17] Ibid., p. 12.

> progress to reflection and meditation: This book, it is hoped, will be a mirror with a progressive infrastructure, in which it will be possible to discern the Negro on the road to disalienation.[18]

The operative or key word in this quotation is "committed": it points to Fanon's belief in the social responsibility of the artist or political thinker. It is this belief that gives a programmatic or ideological bent to Fanon's writings. On this view of commitment, to *write* is to commit oneself to the imperative of acting. It is a view that can be traced back to Plato and one that was radically reintroduced and reinterpreted by Karl Marx when, in one of his theses on Feuerbach, he complained that although "the philosophers have only interpreted the world in various ways, the point is to change it."[19] The social critic or observer writes not only to understand and explain the functionings of society, but also to change it, especially in situations where there is a disjunction between his conception of human nature and social reality.

Fanon's purpose was therefore closely linked to his interest in the disalienation of the Black person.[20] This concern with disalienation reflects Fanon's faith in the ability of men to change their situations in life. As he puts it, "Man is what brings society into being. The prognosis is in the hands of those who are willing to get rid of the worm-eaten roots of the structure."[21]

What is at the root of this alienation? To answer this question one would have to take into account the structure of the colonial situation — a question to be considered in the next section. Suffice it to say that, based on his analysis of the social

[18] Ibid., pp. 183-184.

[19] Lloyd D. Easton and Kurt H. Guddart, *Writings of the Young Marx on Philosophy and Society* (Garden City: New York: Doubleday, 1967), p. 402.

[20] Fanon, *Black Skin, White Masks*, p. 8: "The black is a black man; that is, as the result of a series of aberrations of affect, he is rooted at the core of a universe from which he must be extricated."

[21] Ibid., p. 11.

psychology of colonialism, Fanon concluded that one banal effect of colonial rule is the enstrangement of the colonized from both himself or herself and others. Fanon's analysis points to the conclusion that the enstrangement is fostered by the social, economic, political, and cultural institutions of colonialism:

> The effective disalienation of the black man entails an immediate recognition of social and economic realities. If there is an inferiority complex, it is the outcome of a double process: primarily, economic: subsequently, the internalization — or better, the epidermilization — of this inferiority.[22]

How does Fanon go about developing his critique of colonialism? He disclaims any interest in methodological questions: "...I leave methods to the botanists and the mathematicians. There is a point at which methods devour themselves."[23] Yet he is not without method. Indeed, if he is explicit about his purpose in examining the colonial situation, he is even more explicit about how the study is to be pursued. He makes it clear "the analysis I am undertaking is psychological."[24] David Caute is right in pointing out that Fanon's method is to proceed by describing "the many techniques, some of them only semiconscious, by which the Black native is persuaded to feel and live his inbred racial guilt"; and that this method has an affinity with the existentialist— phenomenological perspectives of Sartre and Merleau-Ponty.[25]

Where Freud places emphasis on the ontogenetic, Fanon's emphasis is on the social environment. It is Fanon's thesis, for example, that "... every neurosis, every abnormal manifestation, every affective erethism in an Antillian is the product of

[22] Ibid.
[23] Ibid., p. 12.
[24] Ibid., p. 10; see also ibid., pp. 144-145.
[25] David Caute, *Fanon*, pp. 5, 9-10.

his cultural situation."[26] But what is the nature of the evidence adduced by Fanon to support his analysis?

One set of evidence is provided by the psychoneuroses.[27] Fanon finds in his professional knowledge of the inner psychic strains and stresses experienced by the colonizer and colonized a rich vein of information which he mines assiduously in his study of colonial societies. Another set of evidence is empathic, deriving in part from the fact that Fanon was a participant observer in the drama he was describing. He knew what it was to be Black, to live in a dominant White society and to wear a white mask.

This section has raised issues and themes, e.g., commitment and the structure of the colonial situation, that will be amplified in subsequent chapters. The main concern is rather with showing that, based on his acceptance of the notion of commitment, Fanon's rationale for looking at colonialism was to bring about social and political change, to "disalienate" both colonizer and colonized. The concern also is to suggest that his method in showing the alienation characteristic of colonial society was dialectical and phenomelogical, emphasizing the interaction between social structure and individuals.

What is the Colonial Situation?

The notion of the colonial situation is fundamental to Fanon's analysis of the nature of colonialism. What does he mean by the colonial situation? His characterization of the colonial situation bears striking resemblance to that of a group of British and French sociologists and social anthropologists, namely E. A. Walcker, H. Laurentie, R. Maunier, L. Wirth, and Georges Balandier.[28]

[26] Fanon, *Black Skin, White Masks,* p. 152.

[27] Ibid., pp. 204-209; *Wretched of the Earth,* pp. 249-310.

[28] On the analysis of the colonial situation by members of this group, see

Social systems can be viewed as artifacts deliberately created by human beings to provide a bridge between the individual and society. These social systems are necessarily buttressed and sustained by a network of reward and sanction that not only provides the coercive, but cooperative environment for, but also shapes, the pattern of human interaction. The nature of this network necessarily affects an individual's behavioral calculus.

For Fanon, the model colonial society, as a network of social interaction, is unlike others because access to its structure of reward and sanction is predicated quintessentially on race. This means that the dissolution of the individual into a racial category discriminated against, penalized, or favoured in terms of access to the structure of reward and sanction is more pronounced in the case of the Black individual. As Fanon argued in his discussion of Jean-Paul Sartre's *Anti-Semite and Jew:*

> The Jew can be unknown in his Jewishness. He is not wholly what he is.... His actions, his behaviour are the final determinant. He is a white man, and, apart from some other rather debatable characteristics, he can sometimes go unnoticed.... But in my case, everything takes on a new guise. I am given no chance. I am overdetermined from the outside. I am the slave not of the "idea" that others have of me but of my own appearance.[29]

It is therefore in the light of this attempt to view the individual in the context of his or her racial situation that Fanon's notion of the colonial situation must be viewed. For him the colonial situation involves a contact of races in which the numerically inferior alien race is actually the sociologically superior race. This dominant or sociologically superior

Georges Balandier, *The Sociology of Black Africa: Social Dynamics in Central Africa* (New York: Praeger, 1970), pp. 32-39.

[29] Fanon, *Black Skin, White Masks,* pp. 115-116.

position is due to the alien race's access to, and monopoly of, socioeconomic and political sources of power.

This control is maintained and facilitated by the sheer weight of the military superiority and laterial wealth of the alien race. Other mechanisms of control used by the alien race include racialist rationalizations of its presence and actions; legal and constitutional arrangements that primarily serve to protect and promote its interests; and the superimposition of its culture as a form of control.

What emerges from Fanon's position is a view of the colonial situation as a perverse form of racial contact, one that is based on the overwhelming economic and sociopolitical exploitation of the indigenous by the alien race. One aspect of this exploitation is the manichean nature of the colonial situation:

> The zone where the natives live is not complementary to the zone inhabited by the settlers. The two zones are opposed, but not in the service of a higher unity. Obedient to the rules of pure Aristotelian logic, they both follow the principle of reciprocal exclusivity....[30]

It should be pointed out, however, that Fanon and Césaire are not opposed to racial contact as such, only to the form it assumes in the colonial situation. Césaire, for example, has argued that a castigation of colonialism should not be construed as a rejection of race and culture contact as such.[31]

It was suggested above that Fanon was concerned with generalizing from the specific contexts of Martinique and France about the nature of colonialism in other contexts. What emerges from his attempts to do so is what can be described as a social psychology of colonial rule, which can be sketched out in the following way.

A basic assumption of colonial rule is the superiority of the

[30] Fanon, *Wretched of the Earth,* p. 38.
[31] Césaire, *Discours,* p. 10.

values and institutions of the metropolitan power over those of subject or colonial peoples. This assumption provides one rationalization for the acquisition of colonial territory usually by sheer military force, and the subsequent imposition of colonial rule. As a matter of conscious or unconscious policy, this imposition results in a process of imitation of, or adaptation to, European lifestyles and values by a large number of the colonized who come in contact with the colonizer.

The mechanisms of adaptation and imitation may be subtle, in which case the adaptation or imitation is due simply to the fact of contact. But the mechanisms of adaptation and imitation, as Fanon argues in *Black Skin, White Masks,* may also be overt and deliberately instituted, with appropriate inducements and sanctions stipulated for imitation and nomination, respectively. Assimilation is an example of this kind of imitation imposed by the colonizer. Whereas the first kind of imitation is spontaneous, the other is induced.[32]

One result of induced imitation of this process of adaptation is the emergence of marginal or doubly-socialized colonial subjects.[33] E. M. Forster's character, Dr. Aziz, in *Passage to India* as well as Okonkwo, the hero of Chinua Achebe's *Things Fall Apart,* illustrate the enormous dimensions of the existential problems of identity and acceptance — acceptance into both indigenous society and the world of the colonizer — that doubly-socialized colonial subjects characteristically have to face.

A corollary of this imitation is a partial, perhaps substantial and important rejection of indigenous values. The assimilated or doubly-socialized colonial subject, by definition, accepts the claim about the superiority of European values and in-

[32] See also R. Maunier, *The Sociology of Colonies,* Vol. 1 (London: Routledge and Kegan Paul, 1949), pp. 87-95.

[33] On "doubly-socialized" colonial subjects, see Antony D. Smith, *Theories of Nationalism* (London: Duckworth, 1971), p. 237. See also Edward Shils, *The Intellectual Between Tradition and Modernity: The Indian Situation* (The Hague: Mouton, 1961).

stitutions. It is this rejection of indigenous values that leads Fanon to assert that "white civilization and European culture have forced an existential deviation on the Negro,"[34] in an apparent reference to the assimilated colonial subject.

The urge to become "White" and "cultured" leads the aspiring "acculturated" colonial subject to despise his "less fortunate" brethren. Yet the attempt at imitation is necessarily self-defeating, given the racist structure and institutions of France and her colonial territories. The doubly-socialized colonial subject would in due course discover that, assimilationist promise notwithstanding, there were built-in and insuperable obstacles, based primarily on racial prejudices, to his or her upward mobility in a White-dominated or predominantly White society. It is a situation in which race as criterion for social stratification is used to consolidate the socioeconomic and political control of the colonizer:

> When you examine at close quarters the colonial context, it is evident that what parcels out the world is to begin with the fact of belonging to or not belonging to a given race, a given species. In the colonies the economic substructure is also a superstructure. The cause is the consequence; you are rich because you are white; you are white because you are rich. This is why Marxist analysis should always be slightly stretched every time we have to do with the colonial problem.[35]

The psychological shock attendant on this realization of the salience of race as a determinant of social stratification would lead to a soul-searching, in most cases compelling the doubly-socialized colonial subject to seek his primeval roots. The shock and the subsequent *rendezvous* with indigenous culture represent for the doubly-socialized individual the beginning of a change in consciousness, a turning point in the liberation of self and one's race.

[34] Fanon, *Black Skin, White Masks,* p. 14.
[35] Fanon, *Wretched of the Earth,* p. 40.

There is another dimension, already alluded to in the discussion of Fanon's critique of colonial rule, to Fanon's characterization of the social psychology of colonial rule. This is the alienation or depersonalization of the colonizer. Since colonialism is a corrupting, morally corrosive enterprise, it would in due course affect the outlook and behavior of the colonizer as well. This is what Fanon and Césaire refer to as the boomerang effect of colonialism.

How useful is Fanon's characterization of the colonial situation? On the credit side, it offers interesting and challenging perspectives on the nature of colonialism. Its focus on the relations between a colonizing race and a colonized one as a variety of race contact points to the need to distinguish between colonial rule and other forms of foreign or alien rule. The essence of the colonial situation created by colonial rule is racial polarization guided by what Fanon regards as "the principle of reciprocal exclusivity."

Secondly, as used by Fanon, the notion of the colonial situation avoids the equation of colonization and colonial relationships with merely territorial expansion and annexation. Thus some analysts have borrowed Fanon's concept of the colonial situation in describing Black-White, or minority-majority relationships in the United States of America.[36] On this view, therefore, any conception of colonization rooted primarily in terms of territorial expansion and settlement is likely to ignore such cases of internal colonialism as South Africa.

Moreover, to look upon colonization as essentially the outward movements of peoples to conquer and settle in new lands is to miss the force of Fanon's reference to the boomerang effect of the colonial situation on the metropolitan or colonizing society. This is because such a conception regards

[36] Stokely Carmichael and Charles V. Hamilton, *Black Power: The Politics of Liberation* (New York: Random House, 1967), Robert L. Allen, *Black Awakening in Capitalist America* (Garden City, New York: Doubleday, 1972), pp. 6-20.

colonization as a one-way process and thereby overlooks the feedback impact of the colonial experience on the mother-country. In other words, there is a necessarily organic relationship between what a colonizing or imperial power does abroad and what it is subsequently likely to do or has always done at home.

Thirdly, the chief merit of Fanon's characterization of the colonial situation lies in its attempt to construct a general sociology or, more appropriately, a social psychology of colonial relationships. His merit in this respect lies less in his offering us a full-blown or systematically thought-out theory than in his providing a potentially insightful perspective for looking at certain aspects of racial domination. For example, the proposition that we look upon colonialism as a clash of races and cultures is an intriguing one. If one accepts its appropriateness, it becomes interesting to study how, in the colonial context, this clash is managed or resolved, e.g., what socio-economic, political, and legal instrumentalities prop it up and what conflicts it generates; how the process of cultural diffusion takes place; and how the diffusion affects indigenous political institutions and systems.[37]

On the debit side, there are limitations to Fanon's characterization of the colonial situation. First, there is a sense in which it glosses over the nature of potential racial conflict in a colonial situation. This is because he tends to talk as if there are only two major racial protagonists, mainly Blacks and Whites, in such a situation. Yet as it has been pointed out with respect to East Africa, it is more appropriate, perhaps, to talk of a mode of stratification in which there are sociologically

[37] Some of these problems have been the concern of social anthropologists. See for example, Isaac Schapera, *Tribal Innovators: Tswana Chiefs and Social Change, 1795-1940* (New York: Humanities, 1970); Hilda Kuper, *The Uniform of Colour* (Johannesburg, South Africa: Witwatersrand University Press, 1947).

dominant racial minorities (Whites and Asians) and a sociologically inferior racial majority (Blacks).[38]

With respect to the Caribbean, the situation is even more complex than the structure that Fanon paints in *Black Skin, White Masks*. Philip Mason's notion of "the standard Creole structure" is instructive in this respect, in that it points to the extremely complex array of racial gradations in the Caribbean.[39]

Philip Mason's "standard Creole structure" also points to a problem that, though arguably implied in Fanon, is not given much attention by him. This is the problem created by the place of attitudes or beliefs in our understanding of the dynamics of race relations. In other words, the objective structures of race, i.e., skin pigmentation, and socioeconomic and political institutions must be placed in the context of the subjective interpretations which social actors use to categorize one another. This can be instructive in looking at the dynamics of intraracial as opposed to interracial relations; it is a perspective that may lead to the provocative suggestion that plural relations is a more preferable term to use than race relations.[40]

Secondly, the colonial situation is not a closed system from which Whites other than those from the colonizing society are excluded. Mercantilist assumptions, particularly in matters of trade, define the relationship between such Whites often referred to as foreigners and Whites from the metropolitan country. As George Balandier has pointed out, such foreigners "constitute a minority in the full sense of the word, both numerically and sociologically; though their economic status

[38] Donald Rotchild, *Citizenship and National Integration: The Non-African Crisis in Kenya* (Denver, Colorado: Centre on International Relations, 1969-70), p. 8.

[39] Philip Mason, *Patterns of Dominance* (London: Oxford University Press, 1970), Ch. 12; Philip Mason, *Race Relations* (London: Oxford University Press, 1970), pp. 123-130.

[40] Cf. M. G. Smith, *The Plural Society in the British West Indies* (Berkeley, California: University of California Press, 1965).

may be high, they are nevertheless subject to administrative restrictions...."[41]

Thirdly, Fanon's characterization assumes that each racial group in the colonial situation is a monolith. But this is not the case. In his portrait of the colonizer, Memmi distinguishes between "the colonizer who refuses" and "the colonizer who accepts."[42] As for the colonized Balandier has pointed to the fact that a colonized society is both "ethnically split" and "spiritually divided;" so much so that these divisions "determine not only the relations of the various peoples with the colonizing society but also their attitude toward the imported culture."[43]

If Fanon overlooks these considerations in his characterization of the colonial situation, particularly in *Black Skin, White Masks,* he takes them into account in his analysis of the postcolonial situation, or rather of postcolonial politics. He realizes that with the attainment of independence, the nationality question is crucial in the sense that problems of nation-building are not to be, and should not be, defined purely in racial and ethnic terms. Thus, in his discussion of the place and role of Algeria's European minority and Jews in independent Algeria, he points out that:

> For the F.L.N., in the new society that is being built, there are only Algerians. From the outset, therefore, every individual living in Algeria is an Algerian. In tomorrow's independent Algeria it will be up to every Algerian to assume Algerian citizenship or to reject it in favor of another.[44]

In *Wretched of the Earth,* the chapter on "The Pitfalls of

[41] Balandier, *Sociology of Black Africa,* p. 36.

[42] Albert Memmi, *The Colonizer and the Colonized* (Boston, Massachusetts: Little, Brown and Co., 1967), pp. 19-76.

[43] Balandier, *Sociology of Africa,* p. 38.

[44] Fanon, *A Dying Colonialism,* p. 152.

National Consciousness" includes an extended discussion of the ethnic factor in postcolonial Africa.

Before this section is concluded, mention should be made of an objection raised by Elie Kedouri against Fanon's characterization of the colonial situation as a Manichean one. Kedouri's main argument is that the picture of colonial Algeria that Fanon draws "is not one which obtains only where 'white people' and 'niggers and dirty Arabs' live side by side"; that it "may be equally observed in racially and culturally homogeneous societies whose placid, self-contained agricultural economy was brutally disrupted by industrialization and urbanization."[45]

Kedouri's objection is well-founded to some extent. It is arguable that to the extent to which Manichean social structures exist in other than colonial situations, then such social structures are not defining characteristics of the colonial situation. At best, they should be viewed as accompanying characteristics. Yet it must be emphasized that what Fanon offers us is a stipulative definition or characterization.[46] He so characterizes the colonial situation that, by its very nature and existence, it is structurally Manichean. To point to other situations where Manichean structures exist is not to invalidate Fanon's position.

The force of Fanon's position on this issue is that he stresses the racial factor as a crucially determining one in colonial situations. He is not talking about societies in general, but about a particular type of society in which race is the overriding central structural and organizing criterion of socioeconomic and political control. That is what, in Fanon's view, distinguishes the social injustice of a colonial situation from social injustice in other contexts.

[45] Elie Kedouri, *Nationalism in Asia and Africa* (New York: The World Publishing Co., 1970), p. 141.

[46] On defining and accompanying characteristics as well as stipulative and reportive definitions, see John Hospers, *An Introduction to Philosophical Analysis*, 2nd ed. (New York: Prentice Hall, 1967), pp. 28-34.

It does not require a critique like Kedouri's, however, to remind Fanon that social injustice exists in other than colonial contexts. Fanon's concern with what he calls true decolonization or liberation is to be interpreted in the light of his desire to see that the social evils of colonialism are not perpetuated in postcolonial Africa. Hence, his uncompromising condemnation of the successor regimes to colonial rule. More apt is his observation that,

> the people who at the beginning of the struggle had adopted the primitive Manicheism of the settler — blacks and whites, Arabs and Christians — realize as they go along that it sometimes happens that you get blacks who are whiter than the whites.... The people find out that the iniquitous fact of exploitation can wear a black face or an Arab one.[47]

Summary

Fanon's model of colonial society is abstracted from Martinique, France, and Algeria. Realizing situational variations, he nevertheless suggests a social psychology characteristic of colonial societies in general. Viewed as a total system colonial society is, by the very logic inherent in its theoretical foundations and socioeconomic and political structures, a violent and dehumanizing one. The purpose of his analysis, deriving from his notion of commitment, is to transform colonial society and help "disalienate" both the colonizer and the colonized.

His critique of colonialism utilized the civilization/barbarism antithesis to deny the rationalization of colonialism as a civilizing mission to confer material benefits and other alleged indices of civilization on the colonized. To support his denial

[47] Fanon, ***Wretched of the Earth***, pp. 144-145.

of this rationalization, he pointed to the weak material base of African societies and the psychoneuroses of colonial rule.

The next chapter is devoted to a more detailed examination of Fanon's claim concerning the violent nature of the colonial situation and some other themes in his critique of colonialism.

Chapter 3

FANON'S MODEL OF COLONIAL SOCIETY — II

Two Major Themes in Fanon's Critique of Colonialism

This chapter examines two major themes in Fanon's critique of colonialism. The first theme concerns his conception of the role of violence in the colonial situation; the second is about the connection he draws between language and culture, and can be viewed as an extension of his characterization of the colonial situation as inherently violent. Focus on these two themes should lead to a more elaborate formulation of aspects of the more general account of the colonial situation offered in the last chapter.

The purpose of Fanon's discussion of these two themes is to explain the consequences of a particular kind of race and culture contact that obtains in a colonial situation. His assessment of that contact is the negative one that the coming of the European meant not only political and economic, but also psychocultural exploitation. This negative assessment implies two related claims.

First, it implies that traditional patterns of life from which the colonized derived or could have derived a sense of self-worth and integrity were disrupted and destroyed by colonial rule. Fanon has an implicit notion of what life was in traditional or precolonial African societies. He does not make clear, however, what the nature of those societies was; nor is this problem resolved by his failure to offer a paradigm of the precolonial African society; nor does he seriously consider differential responses to the colonial factor in various African societies. However, it may be useful to look at Fanon's claim less as an anthropological or historical one than as a logical reconstruction which is then used as a standard to point to the negative impact of colonial rule on African societies.

Secondly, Fanon's negative assessment implies denial of the claim that colonialism was a modernizing factor. Rather, as it was pointed out in the last chapter, he asserts the contrary or antithesis of this claim — namely that colonialism had acted as a brake on the process of social change in precolonial Africa.

It should be pointed out again that Fanon's condemnation of colonialism in this regard is partly predicated on his psychological contention that political and socioeconomic structures powerfully condition and influence the behavior of the individual. Thus, neurotic behavior by both colonizer and colonized has its primary sources in the violent or hostile environment of the colonial situation. There is need to realize the casual relationship between psychopathology and social phenomena. As he asserts in his remarkable letter of resignation as Head of the Psychiatry Department of the Blida-Joinville Hospital in Algeria, "the social structure existing in Algeria was hostile to any attempt to put the individual where he belonged."[1]

Violence and the Colonial Situation

What does Fanon mean by violence? The problem of violence is an important one in Fanon's thought. It is one that calls for a distinction between his thesis that the colonial situation is an inherently violent one and his ethical justification of violence as a potent instrument of liberation.

Failure to make this distinction, or to emphasize it, is a major defect in much of the discussion of this aspect of Fanon's thought.[2] One reason for this is that much of the discussion is

[1] Fanon, *Toward the African Revolution*, p. 53.

[2] This is especially true of Caute, *Frantz Fanon*, and Geismar, *Fanon*. See my review of both books in *Review of Politics*, Vol. 34, No. 3 (July, 1972), p. 436. For a statement about this one-sided treatment of violence in the Fanon

that the concept of violence is an essentially contested concept.[4] It is not unlikely therefore that one's reaction to as well as one's definition of violence is a function of one's ideological or ethical biases.[5]

Fanon further complicates the problem because of his characteristic tendency to employ terms and concepts without giving explicit definitions of them. He assumes, perhaps, that his readers know what he is talking about. But to say that he does not define "violence" explicitly is not to say that he does not have a conception of violence. To discover what his conception of violence is, one must necessarily focus on how he uses the word and what analytic framework he provides for a study of violence in a colonial setting.

This strategy will proceed in two directions. First, leaving aside definitional questions, a useful approach is to focus on social and political phenomena delineated by Fanon as constituting violence. Secondly, the question whether these phenomena help us gain a better understanding of the nature of colonialism is posed. In other words, is his use of the concept in any sense nontrivial?

What Fanon offers, with respect to the first question, is a three-fold categorization of violence, which helps to shed more clarity or light on those sociopolitical phenomena that, in his view, constitute violence in the colonial situation. In short, a reading of *Black Skin, White Masks* and *Wretched of the Earth* suggests that Fanon makes a distinction, similar to that made by John Galtung in a 1969 article,[6] between *physical, structural,* and *psychological* violence.

Physical violence involves somatic injury inflicted on

[4] W. B. Gallie, "Essentially Contested Concepts," *Proceedings of the Aristotelian Society 1955-1956*, pp. 167-198.

[5] Robert Paul Wolff, "On Violence," *The Journal of Philosophy*, Vol. 19 (1969), pp. 601-616; Jukka Gronow and Jorma Hilppo, "Violence, Ethics and Politics," *Journal of Peace Research*, Vol. 4 (1970), p. 331.

[6] John Galtung, "Violence, Peace and Peace Research," *Journal of Peace Research*, Vol. 3 (1969), pp. 167-191.

human beings, the most radical manifestation of which is the killing of an individual. Thus, when Fanon claims that "colonialism...is violence in its natural state," part of his meaning is that colonial rule was usually preceded, inaugurated, and maintained by the use of physical violence. To "pacify" indigenous peoples and force them to accept the new alien order, the colonizer often found it necessary to wage wars against them.

This was especially true of instances when indigenous people resisted the establishment of colonial rule. Part of Fanon's meaning in claiming that "colonialism... is violence in its natural state" is, therefore, a variation of the gun and Bible theory of colonial rule — the argument that challenges the claim that colonial expansion was an evangelizing mission or that it occurred reluctantly and in a bit of absent-mindedness. As Fanon puts it, "...the foreigner coming from another country imposed his rule by means of guns and machines."[7] This conception of violence as involving the killing or wounding of human beings is reflected in many passages in *Wretched of the Earth.*

Fanon deduces his advocacy of the use of physical violence to replace the colonial situation precisely from his thesis that the colonial situation, together with the social roles and institutions that define it, rests on a basis provided by physical violence: "...It is obvious here that the agents of government speak the language of pure force."[8] When Fanon, therefore, claims that "colonialism is not a thinking machine nor a body endowed with reasoning," his thesis is partly that appeals to the conscience of the colonizer are, in certain contexts, misplaced and misdirected. This is because such appeals cannot bring about the termination of colonial rule. The liberal illusion is to assume that the state reconciles interest and that this can come about through "rational" discourse. The whole

[7] Fanon, *Wretched of the Earth,* p. 40.
[8] Ibid., p. 38.

point of Fanon's characterization of the colonial situation is that the colonial state does not function to reconcile, but to polarize colonizer and colonized.

Structural violence is what Fanon refers to as the manicheism of the colonial situation. Used in this sense, structural violence is a condition of social injustice. The abject poverty of the colonized is in stark contrast to the superfluity of the colonizer:

> The colonial world is a world divided into compartments. It is probably unnecessary to recall the existence of native quarters and European quarters, of schools for natives and schools for Europeans: in the same way we need not recall apartheid in South Africa.[9]

The purpose of colonialism, indeed the essence of the colonial situation, is the perpetuation of this condition of social injustice.

Structural violence reflects the fact of exploitation and its necessary institutional forms and props in the colonial situation. Underlying Fanon's notion of structural violence is the assumption that the colonizers are less concerned with bridging the gulf that separates them from the colonized than with sapping the colony of its economic wealth. This assumption runs counter to the view that colonies were economically unprofitable and therefore burdensome to the colonizer. According to Fanon, "in a very concrete way Europe has stuffed herself inordinately with the gold and raw materials of the colonial countries."[10] It is, moreover, because colonialism involved economic exploitation that Fanon calls upon the colonizing and capitalist countries to make economic reparations to their former colonies.[11]

Is there any connection between physical and structural violence? One answer to this question involves yet another

[9] Ibid., p. 37.
[10] Ibid., p. 102.
[11] Ibid., pp. 95-106.

reference to Fanon's belief in the influence of socioeconomic and political structures on the behavioral calculus of individuals. For example, Fanon's thesis is also partly that structural violence as a condition of social injustice invariably drives men to desperate ends and to the conviction that one way to redress or remove the condition is to resort to the use of physical violence. This is indeed "one of those laws of the psychology of colonization" to which Fanon refers in *A Dying Colonialism.*[12] The point is that the privileged position of the colonizer is envied by the colonized who, as a result, is likely to turn to radical political action to change the situation once his consciousness has been raised:

> The look that the native turns on the settler's town is a look of lust, a look of envy; it expresses his dreams of possession — all manner of possession...[13]

Fanon's position on this link between physical and structural violence is substantially reflected in Ted Gurr's notion of relative deprivation and its potential for explaining collective action.[14]

Psychological violence is injury or harm done to the human psyche. It includes brainwashing, indoctrination of various kinds and threats, all of which not only serve to decrease the victims' mental potentialities, but also constitute, in Galtung's words, "violence that works on the soul."[15]

Fanon's discussion of psychological violence in the context of the colonial situation is his way of dramatizing and emphasizing the alienation of the colonized. This psychological violence represents the attempt, conscious or unconscious, by the colonizer to create alienated colonized individuals who reject indigenous values and institutions because they are

[12] Fanon, *A Dying Colonialism,* p. 47.

[13] Fanon, *Wretched of the Earth,* p. 39.

[14] Ted Gurr, *Why Men Rebel* (Princeton, New Jersey: Princeton University Press, 1970).

[15] Galtung, "Violence, Peace and Peace Research," p. 169.

deceived or brainwashed into believing that those values and institutions are inferior to those of the colonizer.

The colonized subject, victim of psychological violence inflicted by the colonizer, apes the language and social mannerisms of the colonizer; he or she also wears "white masks." Psychological violence then becomes a form of cultural imperialism in the context of the colonial situation. Its victim is an alienated person, in the strong Marxian sense of man becoming a stranger to himself. To the extent that the brainwashed colonized individual defines himself or herself in terms of the Other, i.e., the White man, he is also not free. This is the sense in which Fanon characterizes psychological violence as preventing its colonized victim from achieving self-realization:

> In the man of color there is a constant effort to run away from his own individuality, to annihilate his own presence.[16]

Again and again in *Black Skin, White Masks* Fanon gives examples, cites case studies of victims of psychological violence, what he also calls "psychic alienation." It is familiarity with these cases that leads him to the conclusion that

> When the Negro makes contact with the White world, a certain sensitizing action takes place. If his psychic structure is weak, one observes a collapse of the ego. The black man stops behaving as an *actional* person. The goal of his behavior will be the Other (in the guise of the white man), for the Other alone can give him worth. That is on the ethical level: self-esteem.[17]

It should be pointed out that in developing his thesis on

[16] Fanon, *Black Skin, White Masks*, p. 60; cf. also ibid., p. 8: "At the risk of arousing the resentment of my colored brothers, I will say that the black man is not a man."

[17] Ibid., p. 154 (Emphasis in original).

psychological violence or psychic alienation, Fanon owes more to Sartre than to Marx.[18] Sartre's basic argument is the existentialist one that a person, in this case the Jew, is defined by the gaze of the Other, namely the Anti-Semite. The mistake of the "inauthentic" Jew is to have allowed himself to be poisoned by the stereotype that the Other has of him. It is in this sense that the action of the "inauthentic" Jew is overdetermined from the inside.[19]

Similarly, according to Fanon, the alienated colonized individual accepts the stereotypical view that equates Black with evil; he or she becomes the object of the Other's view that denies him or her of any authenticity. Fanon, however, goes further than Sartre. Fanon's argument is that the Black person is overdetermined from both the inside and, more importantly, on account of color, the outside. As he puts it, "Jean-Paul Sartre had forgotten that the Negro suffers in his body quite differently from the white man. Between the white man and me the connection was irrevocably one of transcendence."[20]

Is there any relationship between psychological and structural violence? Fanon thinks that the nature of the relationship is to be found in the fact that the attempt to become White reflects the superior socioeconomic and political status of the colonizer. As Fanon observes, "historically, it must be understood that the Negro wants to speak French because it is the key that can open doors which were barred to him fifty years ago."[21]

Is there any relationship between psychological and

[18] Paul Nursey-Bray, "Marxism and Existentialism in the Thought of Frantz Fanon," *Political Studies,* Vol. 20, No. 2 (June, 1972), p. 160; Gendzier, *Fanon,* pp. 30-35; Caute, *Fanon,* pp. 12-13.

[19] Jean-Paul Sartre, *Anti-Semite and Jew,* trans. by G. J. Becker (New York: Shocken Books, 1965), p. 90.

[20] Fanon, *Black Skin, White Masks,* p. 138; see also pp. 115-116: "The Jew is disliked from the moment he is tracked down. But in my case everything takes on a *new* guise. I am given no chance. I am overdetermined from outside. I am the slave not of the 'idea' that others have of me but of my own appearance." (Emphasis in original).

[21] Ibid., p. 38.

physical violence? Again, Fanon thinks so. His thesis is that the "effective disalienation" of the Black person demands the use of physical violence, the extent and scale of which should be viewed situationally: "If need be, the native can accept a compromise with colonialism, but never a surrender of principle."[22] Thus Fanon looks upon physical violence which, when utilized under certain conditions and not just indiscriminately, should free the colonized from their inferiority complex and confer on them again their self-respect.[23]

This section has so far been taken up with a restatement of socio-economic and political phenomena analyzed by Fanon as constituting violence in the colonial setting. How useful or nontrivial is his three-fold categorization of violence?

First, the categorization is useful for heuristic purposes. This is particularly so with the distinction between physical and psychological violence. It makes sense to say that violence has been done to one's soul or humanity in more than a metaphorical sense. This is an important dimension of violence in the colonial situation and elsewhere for that matter; it focuses on all kinds of indoctrination to which the colonized are exposed without their necessarily suffering physical or bodily harm.

Although useful for heuristic purposes, the categorization may give rise to confusion or ambiguity when it comes to employing it for empirical purposes. Thus, the dividing line between the three types of violence may be a tenuous one. For example, how do we classify the action of a government that secures compliance to its orders by threatening, without really intending to do so, to use force to disperse a group of protesters? To take another example, is the denial of access to certain privileges, say access to good schools, an example of structural or psychological violence?

Secondly, it can be argued that violence, in all its three

[22] Fanon, *Wretched of the Earth*, p. 143; also ibid., pp. 58-59, 70.
[23] Ibid., p. 93.

forms, is necessarily a feature of historical societies as opposed to some ideal or essential societies. However, demands for the removal of structural violence as a condition of social injustice need not be couched in terms of the creation of a Platonic Ideal Form. What matters is how glaring and abominable any condition of social injustice is, what efforts the sociologically dominant sections of society make to redress it. With respect to the colonial situation, the force of Fanon's analysis of structural violence, for example, lies in his identification of, and emphasis on, its racial basis, and on the fact that the colonizers are not responsible, i.e., not accountable to the colonized, which is to say that the question of redressing or equalizing the structural polarization was hardly posed.

Thirdly, Fanon's references to structural violence raises interesting questions about intentionality and motivations. It is one thing to claim that a structure performs certain functions. It is another thing to say that it was specifically set up to perform these functions. Thus, it is not clear whether Fanon is referring to the objective consequences of the colonial situation or to the subjective intentions of the colonizer; or even to both. This distinction can be a useful one to make because it is not always the case that there is a congruence between A's intentions in doing Y and the consequences of A's doing Y. This is why it makes sense to talk of unintended consequences of A's action and to suggest that on the basis of that fact, that A is not blameworthy or is only partially blameworthy.

Fourthly, it can be objected that Fanon's categorization makes no distinction between violent and nonviolent behavior. Acts of civil disobedience are manifestations of physical violence, yet they may not involve as much bodily harm or injury as armed resistance. But this objection, which also raises a definitional problem, can be too easily stretched. Is self-immolation violent or nonviolent behaviour? Ordinarily it is viewed as the ultimate sacrifice in nonviolent behaviour; yet it involves the killing of oneself. A fast-unto-death, similarly, can involve doing harm to one's body. Although it can be argued that violence is always inflicted by X on Y, i.e., for an action to constitute violence two or more agents must be involved, this need not be so.

Language, Culture and the Colonial Situation

This section examines one aspect of Fanon's discussion of alienation or psychological violence in the colonial situation, namely his discussion of the relationship of language to culture. Fanon's discussion of this relationship should be viewed as part of his wider interest in the process of cultural diffusion in the colonial situation. His basic thesis is that, viewed as a cognitive system, language is one medium through which the colonized suffer alienation or psychological violence.

Fanon makes it clear that he attaches "a basic importance to the phenomenon of language.... For it is implicit that to speak is to exist absolutely for *the other*."[24] He views language as a transmitter and conservator of learning from one generation to the other, particularly about one's society. Precisely because it transmits learning intergenerationally, language has important consequences for behavior and action.

Put differently, if language is viewed as a system of symbols and conserver of intergenerational experience, then it has great potential for influencing thought and action. Language then becomes a great facilitator that, while allowing one to function in society, also regulates one's interaction with other persons. As Fanon puts it:

> a man who has a language consequently possesses the world expressed and implied by that language. What we are getting at becomes plain: Mastery of language affords remarkable power.[25]

[24] Fanon, *Black Skin, White Masks*, p. 17 (Emphasis in original).
[25] Ibid., p. 18.

What, then, does Fanon take the relationship between language and culture in the colonial situation to be? His argument is that in adopting and using the language of the colonizer, colonized individuals not only assume the colonizer's culture, but also reject their own culture. This argument is a variation of the linguistic *Weltanshauung* hypothesis that can be traced back to Herder's philosophy of history and which is also usually referred to as the *Whorf, Whorf-Lee,* and *Sapir-Whorf Hypothesis.*[26]

Linguistic relativists like Whorf and Sapir argue that the diversity of languages in the world has also led to a diversity of cultures — namely the totality of such institutions as religion, kinship, social stratification, and ideology — closely tied to languages. Two basic assumptions of this position are first, that one's identity is tied up with one's language and secondly, that language is central to one's psychological character.[27]

This identification of language with culture in the linguistic relativist position has some bearing, although not an unproblematic one, on the colonial situation. If language is an expression of a particular culture, the implication, as Fanon argues, is that the colonized persons who speak the language of the colonizer are *ipso facto* assuming the latter's culture. A primary function of language in the colonial situation is, in other words, to facilitate and promote cultural and political domination:

> To speak means to be in a position to use a certain syntax, to grasp the morphology of this or that language, but also to assume a culture, to support the weight of a civilization .... Every colonized people — in other words,

[26] Dell Hymes, "Linguistic Aspects of Comparative Political Research," in Robert T. Holt and John E. Turner, eds. *The Methodology of Comparative Research* (New York, New York: The Free Press, 1970), p. 298; John B. Carroll, *Language and Thought* (Englewood Cliffs, New Jersey: Prentice-Hall, 1964), p. 106; ID. *Language, Thought and Reality: Selected Writings of Benjamin Lee Whorf* (Cambridge, Massachusetts: M.I.T. Press, 1956), pp. 212-214.

[27] Hymes, "Linguistic Aspects of Comparative Political Research," p. 298.

> every people in whose soul an inferiority complex has been created by the death and burial of its local cultural originality — finds itself face to face with the language of the civilizing nation; that is, with the culture of the mother country. The colonized is elevated above his jungle status in proportion to his adoption of the mother country's cultural standards.[28]

Fanon's observations derive partly from his experiences as a child and young man growing up in Martinique where "the Negro ... will be proportionately whiter ... in direct ratio to his mastery of the French language."[29] But in what sense can one say, or what does it mean to assert that "to speak a language is to take on a world, a culture?" The argument I want to develop in answer to this question is the following. Although there is something in the claim that one's language affects or influences one's perception of the world, it is a completely different thing to say either that those perceptions would be different were one to speak another language or that to speak another language was *ipso facto* to subscribe to a different world view or culture. Language serves other functions apart from being a vehicle or transmitter of cultural imposition in the colonial situation.

Part of the problem in examining the question about the status of Fanon's thesis is that of assigning meanings to "language" and "culture." Vocabulary, i.e., the list of words to be found in a language, is one aspect of language that Fanon identifies. Another aspect he identifies is the mode of inflection as well as the syntax, i.e., the manner of sentence formation of a language: "to speak means to be in a position to use a certain syntax, to grasp the morphology of this or that language."[30]

Fanon seems to have emphasized the verbal transmission of language while overlooking its nonverbal aspects. A narrow

[28] Fanon, *Black Skin, White Masks*, pp. 17-18.
[29] Ibid., p. 18.
[30] Ibid., p. 19.

focus on verbal usage and structure can therefore be misleading. Dell Hymes has pointed out that language is allocated differently in different societies; it is

> but one of the communicative resources available. There is the accompanying code of vocal gesture in intonation ...; manual gesture; visual art; dance; instrumental music; and the genres built partly or wholly out of the resources of language, but organized at levels not necessarily reflecting its internal structure, such as song, myth and drama. As a selectively utilized resource, language is never the adequate expression of the whole thought of a people.[31]

The question of what constitutes culture is even a much more vexed one. To raise it is to enter a thicket of anthropological and social psychological controversy.[32] Although it may be easy to study language and its structure with some precision, it is a much more formidable task to define culture, study its structure, and delineate its content.

In 1956 Fanon proposed that "... culture is a combination of motor and mental behavior patterns arising from the encounter of man with nature and with his fellow man."[33] This conception of culture looks upon it as an attribute of man in society. When broadly defined, as Fanon does, it is inclusive of the totality of man's phenomenal experience and developments, providing a superstructure for economic and sociopolitical institutions.[34] To view culture in this way is necessarily to include language in the definition of culture ("We witness the destruction of cultural values, of ways of life.

[31] Hymes, "Linguistic Aspects of Comparative Political Research," pp. 311-312.

[32] Leslie A. White and Beth Dillingham, *The Concept of Culture* (Minneapolis, Minnesota: Burgess Publishing Co., 1973), esp. pp. 1-31 reviews contending theories and definitions of culture in anthropology.

[33] Fanon, *Toward the African Revolution*, p. 32.

[34] L. Adele Jinadu, "Some African Theorists of Culture and Modernization: Fanon, Cabral and Some Others," *African Studies Review*, Vol. 21, No. 1 (April, 1978), pp. 122-124.

Language, dress, techniques are devalorized").[35] If this is indeed the case, then Fanon's thesis is tautological.

It may be the case that Fanon, through using culture in a broad or all-inclusive sense, is actually concerned with investigating the relationship between language as one aspect of culture and such other aspects as social stratification, ideology, and geophysical environment. If viewed in this way, there is some evidence to support Fanon's contention.[36] But as Hockett has also pointed out, "it is here that we find the most reliable and dullest correlations between the rest of culture and language."[37]

A fundamental objection against Fanon, however, is that it is not necessarily true, even within the colonial situation, that to speak the colonizer's language is to assume the colonizer's culture or embrace his civilization. The colonizer's language has many uses in the colonial situation. It may have been introduced for reasons of communications and efficiency. The colonizer probably found it easier to use French or English as a *lingua franca* for administrative, military, and economic purposes. It was, of course, an example of cultural arrogance to have imposed French or English and not to have developed one of a number of possible local languages.[38]

[35] Fanon, *Toward the African Revolution*, p. 33.

[36] Benjamin L. Whorf, "The Relation of Habitual Thought and Behavior to Language," in Carroll, *Language, Thought and Reality*, pp. 134 -159; Harry Hoijer, "Cultural Implications of Some Navajo Linguistic Categories," *Language*, 27 (1951), pp. 111-120.

[37] C. F. Hockett, "Chinese Versus English: An Exploration of the Whorfian Thesis," in Harry Hoijer, *Language in Culture*, American Anthropological Association, Memoir No. 79 (1954), p. 108.

[38] If it is argued that the theory and practice of indirect rule represented respect for the language and culture of the indigenous peoples, Fanon's answer is that "this pseudo-respect in fact is tantamount to the most utter contempt, to the most elaborate racism .... The constantly affirmed concern with respecting the culture of the native populations accordingly does not signify taking into consideration the values borne by the culture, incarnated by men. Rather, this behaviour betrays a determination to objectify, to confine, to imprison, to harden." *Toward the African Revolution*, p. 33.

Another use of the colonizer's language was that of upward mobility. The educated colonial subject might have learned how to speak and write French or English not with a view to becoming "white" or "whiter" or to assuming the colonizer's culture. He or she might have learnt the language primarily for the opportunity it presented for personal advancement in the rigidly stratified colonial situation. In Fanon's words, "historically the Negro wants to speak French because it is the key that can open doors which were still barred to him fifty years ago."[39] While this fact links language with one aspect of culture, it does not follow that it also involves a rejection of one's culture and the corresponding acceptance of the colonizer's culture. Clyde Mitchell's study of African workers in the Zambian copperbelt utilizes the concept of reference group behavior to describe how African workers use European lifestyles and mannerisms as criteria of prestige ranking.[40] What is involved is imitation rather than acceptance of European lifestyles or a rejection of the workers' African background.

Language also served in the colonial situation to protest colonial rule. As Caute has observed, "apprentice literature (respectful toward the colonizer) does not always involve assimilation of the occupying culture and language."[41] The colonizer's language becomes simultaneously a symbol of protest and rejection of Western culture. Fanon's discussion of the role played by sound radio and the French language in the Algerian nationalist struggle confirms this protest and symbolic function of the colonizer's language. This would seem to undercut his categorical assertion that "to speak a language is to take on a world, a culture." According to him:

> the broadcasting in French of the programs of *Fighting Algeria* was to liberate the enemy language from its

[39] Fanon, *Black Skin, White Masks*, p. 38.

[40] C. Mitchell, *The Kalela Dance* (Manchester, England: Manchester University Press, 1956), pp. 12-15.

[41] Caute, *Fanon*, p. 28.

> historic meanings.... The French language lost its accursed character, revealing itself to be capable also of transmitting, for the benefit of the nation, the messages of truth that the latter awaited. Paradoxical as it may appear, it is the Algerian Revolution... that is facilitating the spread of the French language in the nation... Expressing oneself in French, understanding French, was no longer tantamount to treason or to an impoverishing identification with the occupier. Used by the *Voice of the Combattants,* conveying in a positive way the message of the Revolution, the French language also becomes an instrument of liberation.[42]

Even if the colonized were able to speak French or English as fluently as the French or English, objective conditions in the colonial situation precluded their assimilation into French or English culture. Apart from contacts at the workplace, there was little other contact between colonizer and colonized. Each had his own circle of friends and clubs that he frequented. The colonized *évolué* hardly gained entrée into the world of the colonizer. This situation is consistent with Fanon's thesis about the nature of social polarization in the colonial situation. What is worthy of note, in other words, is that merely to speak a language is not to be equated with belonging to the culture of the native speakers of the language, particularly where the culture concerned is defined in racial or ethnic terms.

What the foregoing critical analysis points to is this: though scarcity is part of the human predicament, yet man, as a social engineer or architect, has access to potential variety. This is to say that he is characteristically involved in an on-going process of selection to organize his experience, generate new life, and adapt to the phenomenal world and contend with constraints. Part of his engineering or architectural implements is language. In other words, man's ability to recognize and deal with constraints, modify behavior in response to constraints can be reflected in the use of language. The function of the

[42] Fanon, *A Dying Colonialism*, pp. 89-90.

colonizer's language in the colonial situation, when viewed in this light, becomes a two-edged one: it enables the colonized to adjust to it and creates opportunity for transforming or terminating the colonial situation. From this perspective the revolutionary use of French by the FLN should not appear paradoxical. Similarly, the behavior of the workers in Zambia's copperbelt is an attempt to deal with perceived restraints.

The linguistic relativity thesis is a variation on the theme of ethical and cultural relativity. It can be objected against it that there is always a human basis and background that all cultures hold in common, in spite of their distance in time and space from one another. Fanon's own desire "to discover and to love man, wherever he may be"[43] is an attempt to establish a universal morality. His emphasis on the particular is therefore problematic in view of his desire for the universal in human relations.

Other objections can be raised. For example, the direction of the causal chain is unclear. Is it language that influences culture, or is it the other way?; or is the question misplaced, the relationship being a dialectical one? To one who attributes a causal power to language, it can be objected that language is the effect and expression of a certain world view or cultural milieu.

Fanon's discussion of the role of language in the colonial context is, nonetheless, a powerful demonstration of one particular type of alienation, of the kind of neurotic behavior manifested in attempts to speak French or English with deliberately exaggerated affectation. This is why Fanon characterizes "the problem of language" as "evidence of a dislocation, a separation."[44] His discussion of this phenomenon should be placed within the perspective of the general nature of the colonial situation as a socioeconomic and

[43] Fanon, *Black Skin, White Masks,* p. 231; Fanon, *Wretched of the Earth,* pp. 311-316.

[44] Fanon, *Black Skin, White Masks,* pp. 18-22.

political system premised on utter disregard for local values and institutions even where, as in the case of indirect rule, such institutions are utilized by the colonizer.

Indeed, an overall impression one gets from Fanon is that what he condemns is not the adoption of an alien language as such. His condemnation is best viewed as being directed at the manner of its imposition as well as at one kind of attitudinal or psychological response it generates. What is, therefore, deplorable about the imposition of the colonizer's language is, as Fanon contends, the assumption that "it is the intervention of the foreign nation that puts order into the original anarchy of the colonized country. Under these conditions, the French language, the language of the occupier, was given the role of *Logos*, with ontological implications within Algerian society."[45]

The criticism of Fanon's position offered in this section is not therefore a denial of claims such as Gendzier's that "not only does Fanon explode the myth of the neutrality of language, he offers an astute elaboration of what it means to speak the language of the dominant class."[46] The point of the criticism is to point to limitations in Fanon's linguistic relativity thesis.

While it is true that one's language influences one's world-view or thought-patterns, it is not necessarily true that, were one to learn or speak other languages, one's world-view or thought-patterns would automatically change. To hold otherwise is to confer a false autonomy on each language and culture, to assume that language and culture are closed systems, to deny that there is something called cultural diffusion or interdependence and to underestimate the impact of bilingualism on cultural development.

Thus, in his classic study of Indian intellectuals, Shils clearly shows that, in spite of a mastery of the English language and literature, the Indian intellectual is "quite firmly rooted in

[45] Fanon, *A Dying Colonialism*, p. 91.
[46] Gendzier, *Fanon*, p. 47.

India, in its past and its present."[47] On another level, Hymes has referred to the study by Bright and Bright of Indian peoples in Northwestern California. The Brights conclude that even though these Indian peoples speak quite distinct languages, the contents of their folk taxonomies are similar. "The case has provided a stock instance of noncongruence between culture and language."[48]

Language and Politics in Postcolonial Africa: A Digression and Some Observations

In *Black Skin, White Masks,* Fanon discussed the salience of language in the colonial situation. He did not pursue this question in his analysis of postcolonial African societies. Yet the discussion of that question in *Black Skin, White Masks* is relevant to the political sociology of contemporary Africa. This section anticipates aspects of Fanon's analysis of postcolonial African politics to be offered in subsequent chapters. The purpose of this digression is to explore some of the implications of the language problem for our understanding of contemporary African politics. The language problem has not been a critical issue in postcolonial African politics in the sense in which it has been in India, for example.[49] It is nevertheless one about which concern has been expressed by Africans of varying shades of ideological orientations, some viewing it as of critical importance while others see it as epiphenomenal and diversionary — an issue thrown into political discourse to hide and distract attention from the basic class contradictions of African societies.

A glaring legacy of colonial rule in contemporary Africa is

[47] Shils, *Intellectual Between Tradition and Modernity,* p. 61.

[48] Hymes, "Linguistic Aspects of Comparative Political Research," pp. 312-313.

[49] On the language issue in Indian politics, see W. H. Morris-Jones, *The Government and Politics of India,* 2nd ed. (London: Hutchinson, 1967), Ch. 3, esp. pp. 97-106.

the continued use of the colonizers' languages, particularly French, English, and Portuguese, as *lingua franca.* In North Africa, where Arabic is widely spoken, French is also widely spoken and, in most cases, is the *lingua franca* as well as the language of the western-educated intelligentsia. In Tunisia and Algeria, there are experiments in bi-lingualism. In East Africa where Swahili is widely spoken, English is nevertheless the *lingua franca.* In West Africa where, perhaps with the exception of Hausa, there is no language to compare with the status of Arabic in North Africa or Swahili in East Africa, French or English is the *lingua franca.*

One reason for the resilience of French and English in post-colonial Africa, particularly in sub-saharan Africa, is the ethnic factor. The point is that, particularly with respect to tropical Africa, Balandier's claim that Africa is "ethnically split" is an apt description of Africa's ethnic mosaic. Since ethnicity is often drawn along linguistic lines in Africa, there is bound to be little agreement about which language should replace either French or English.

The selection of an ethnic group's language is likely to be interpreted as another form of colonialism by other ethnic groups, or at least as threatening to the survival of their language and culture. The potential of such a selection for social and civil strife and unrest is amply illustrated by the controversy over the choice of Hindi as the *lingua franca* in India. African countries like Rwanda, Burundi, Botswana, Somali, Lesotho, Tanzania, and Central African Republic that are ethnically homogeneous, or almost so, have, with differing degrees of success, attempted to adopt African languages as their *lingua franca.* Yet in all of them, French or English is the principal medium of higher education and contact with the outside world.

To say, however, that language has not been a critical issue in postcolonial African politics is not to say that Fanon's thesis about the function of language as a subtle form of colonialism is irrelevant to an analysis of political processes on the continent. His thesis is highly relevant and illuminating in at least three ways.

First, it can be argued that the acquisition and mastery of the languages of the colonizing powers have created a form of social stratification or class system based on one's ability to communicate in French or English. From a Fanonian standpoint, a crucial criterion used by colonizing powers in deciding which group or class of Africans to hand over power to was fluency in French or English. This is part of the reason why Fanon looks upon the process of decolonization in much of tropical Africa as a conspiracy between a national bourgeoisie and a colonizing bourgeoisie to perpetuate colonial rule.

It may be objected that, given the state of the modern world, its scientific and technological sophistication, the colonizing powers had no choice but to hand over power to a national bourgeoisie fluent in French or English. But this is precisely Fanon's point that French and English have been used to co-opt the national bourgeoisie of hitherto colonial territories into a world-wide imperialist network whose primary aim is the cultural, economic, and sociopolitical exploitation of these countries. According to him, this was the primary purpose of the colonial educational setup.

Secondly, Fanon's discussion of language can be placed in the context of his discussion of center-periphery relations in post-colonial Africa.[50] Thus it can be argued that there is a communication gap between the national center and the local periphery. In the one, French or English is used to conduct administrative business as well as exchange in the political market-place; in the other the currency of exchange is constituted by the various local languages. This communication gap undermines and obstructs the processes of incorporating the periphery into the national political system and of transmitting instructions from the center to the

[50] Aspects of Fanon's discussion of center-periphery relations in Africa are discussed in Chapter 6. But see also Jinadu, "African Theorists of Culture and Modernization."

periphery. It also tends to create suspicion of the center's purpose.by the periphery. While there is necessarily a tension between the center and periphery in any political system, Fanon suggests that the language problem further complicates the relationship in the African context: "the country people are suspicious of the townsman. The latter dresses like a European; he speaks the European's language, works with him, sometimes even lives in the same district..."[51]

Thirdly, it can be argued that much of Africa is in the grips of neocolonialism and that French and English are subtle forms of cultural imperialism. From this, the argument will maintain, it follows that African countries are not really free, though politically free.

Summary

This chapter has offered a critical exegesis of Fanon's conceptions of the role of violence and language in the colonial situation. The chapter suggested that, though problematic from both a conceptual and an empirical standpoint, Fanon's categorization of colonial violence into physical, structural, and psychological violence sheds some interesting light on the colonial situation.

Although it is conceded that Fanon's thesis on the ideological function of language in the colonial situation has some merits, the chapter argued that language also serves other than an ideological function. Fanon's analysis of the uses to which Algerian nationalists put the French language suggests that he is not opposed to the adoption of the colonizer's language as such. His condemnation, it seems, is directed at the manner of its imposition and particular psychopathological behavioral responses it generated among some of the colonized.

[51] Fanon, *Wretched of the Earth,* p. 112.

Chapter 4

THE MORAL JUSTIFICATION OF VIOLENCE

Introduction

It is now time to move away from analysis to prescription. Fanon, of course, does not think analysis is separable from prescription. To analyze or describe is, in his view, necessarily to prescribe. His concern with analyzing and characterizing the colonial situation is to suggest the imperative of action to terminate the colonial situation and the network of social relations it has given rise to. This position implies a rejection of the fact/value dichotomy; indeed the assumption is that what constitutes a "fact" in this respect is value-ladden.

The concern in this chapter is, therefore, to assess some of Fanon's prescriptions for terminating the colonial situation. To do this is to examine critically his notion of liberation and how this is related to his notions of physical and psychological violence. Put differently, the concern here is with Fanon's moral justification of physical violence as, *in certain cases,* a necessary and desirable means for individual and social liberation.

Fanon's moral justification of violence will be placed in the wider perspective of his discussion of the Hegelian master/slave paradigm. The problem posed for his moral justification of violence by the case studies at the end of *Wretched of the Earth* are also examined.

Fanon's Notion of Liberation

An underlying dimension of Fanon's political thought is the view of colonized man as liberated man. This liberation is but one phase in the continuous struggle of the colonized to attain the good life. The unenviable task, according to Fanon, is that of "the liberation of the man of color from himself."[1] Ignorance, prejudices, hate, and exploitation are some of the basic obstacles that would have to be removed if the colonized were to be liberated: "I seriously hope to persuade my brother, whether black or white, to tear off with all his strength the shameful livery put together by centuries of incomprehension."[2]

What does Fanon mean by liberation? Ordinarily to liberate means to release from restraint or bondage or to be set free. This definition implies that there are certain impediments, not necessarily external or physical, that stand in the way of one's realizing one's potentialities as a morally autonomous agent. If one is to be free, these impediments must be removed. It may be the case either that one is unaware of those impediments or that one internalizes them.[3]

Fanon's conception of liberation involves much more than spiritual freedom or the Stoic internalization of impediments. It implies the removal of a whole arsenal of socioeconomic, cultural, and political restrictions imposed on colonized man — restrictions that limit the area of choices and opportunities that are available and open to him. Fanon's position is that the extent of one's freedom is a function of sociopolitical institutions and practices; in other words, these institutions and practices can have either a liberating or a constraining impact on individuals. In a colonial situation their impact on the individual is negative.

Fanon, however, points out that one's freedom is a function of one's determination to act in order to remove obstacles that stand in one's way. This is an important aspect of Fanon's notion of liberation, because Fanon looks upon liberation in

[1] Fanon, *Black Skin, White Masks*, p. 8.

[2] Ibid., p. 12.

[3] Sir Isaiah Berlin, *Four Essays on Liberty* (London: Oxford University Press. 1969), p. xxxviii.

the sense of freedom as an opportunity and a willingness to act. More importantly, it is a particular kind of action itself. One's freedom, with this view, is incomplete if one does not consciously or deliberately act to make good the opportunities and possibilities open to one. It is partly this view that Fanon has in mind when he asserts that he has "one duty alone: that of not renouncing my freedom through my choices."[4]

Fanon's strategy is to define liberation in terms of the assumed or anticipated consequences or results of particular kinds of action. His discussion of decolonization illustrates quite well his adoption of this strategy in talking about liberation.

In one sense Fanon uses liberation to refer to decolonization, the termination of formal colonial rule and the transformation of the colonial situation in such a way that the numerically superior, but sociologically inferior race is now both numerically and sociologically superior. On this view, liberation and decolonization are synonymous with political independence or freedom from alien rule:

> In decolonization there is therefore the need of a complete calling in question of the colonial situation. If we wish to describe it precisely, we might find it in the well-known words: "The last shall be the first and the first last." Decolonization is the putting into practice of this sentence. That is why, if we try to describe it, all decolonization is successful.[5]

In another sense, however, liberation means more than political independence for Fanon. As is shown in the next section where his thesis that decolonization is necessarily a violent phenomenon is discussed, Fanon makes a distinction between "true" and "false" decolonization or liberation. In the former case, the colonial relationship is actually replaced,

[4] Fanon, *Black Skin, White Masks,* p. 229.
[5] Fanon, *Wretched of the Earth,* p. 37.

whereas in the latter case, colonial rule is carried on by more surreptitious means because "there is nothing save a minimum of readaptation, a few reforms at the top."[6] This distinction is related to Fanon's conception of freedom as a particular kind of action. True liberation is achieved only when one fights for it. False liberation occurs or obtains where freedom is granted or conceded by the alien power.

Fanon's notion of liberation points to an interconnection that he posits between it and the concept of revolution. In this sense, liberation is inextricably bound up with the social and political revolution that is yet to come. Liberation is part of a continuing process in which man's potentialities are forever enlarged. Liberation is thus constituted by a perpetual search for the "truth." Once that truth has been discovered, conditions of alienation will no longer exist. This is what is usually referred to as the utopian, romantic, or chiliastic aspect of Fanon's thought.[7]

The perjorative connotation of "romantic" should not be allowed to detract from the merit of Fanon's position. By focusing on liberation as a continuous process, one is able to examine the shortcomings of one's society and demonstrate how that society is incompatible with freedom as self-fulfillment. It therefore matters less that Fanon's conception of liberation is romantic or utopian than that it provides one possible yardstick for assessing social reality.

This conception of liberation is again implied in Fanon's call for the creation of a new man.[8] It is this concern with the creation of a new man that gives Fanon's notion of liberation, as well as his writings, a universalist perspective. Both the colonized and the colonizer should be encouraged to release themselves from their ignorance if they are to become free. This is why Fanon is concerned with the imperative of

[6] Ibid., p. 147.

[7] Aristide Zolberg, "Frantz Fanon: A Gospel for the Damned," *Encounter,* 27 (November, 1966), p. 58.

[8] Fanon, *Wretched of the Earth,* p. 316.

establishing love, justice "as the basic values that constitute a human world."[9]

Fanon's discussion of liberation is premised on the theme of Promethean bifurcation. He believes man is as capable of good as of evil. But he places his ultimate faith in the ability of man whether colonized or colonizer to conquer evil. This is the liberation that most concerns him, one that frees man from the shackles of prejudice and ignorance:

> I said in my introduction that man is a *yes*; I will never stop reiterating that. *Yes* to life. *Yes* to love. *Yes* to generosity. But man is also a *no*. *No* to scorn of man. *No* to degradation of man. *No* to exploitation of man. *No* to the butchery of what is most human in man: freedom.[10]

This is why he sees in the Algerian war of liberation a precursor of things yet to come, an "oxygen which creates and shapes a new humanity."[11] What is important here is not that the course of events in Algeria has not led to the creation of a new man[12] — a debatable claim in itself — but that Fanon incorporates into his conception of revolution the notion of regeneration or recreation at the individual and collective levels.

One weakness of such a conception, however, is the time dimension. When do we know that a new man has been created? Can it ever be too late to create a new man? In other words, can the opportunity be missed? The latter questions are important because of Fanon's distinction between demanding and merely being granted freedom. Yet, and paradoxically, this weakness is also its main strength. It offers a challenge. The fact that we do not know at precisely what point in time a

[9] Fanon, *Black Skin, White Masks,* p. 222.

[10] Ibid., p. 222 (emphasis in original).

[11] Fanon, *A Dying Colonialism,* p. 181.

[12] On the claim that contemporary events in Algeria have falsified Fanon's "prophecy," see W. B. Quandt, *Revolution and Political Leadership: Algeria, 1954-1968* (Cambridge, Massachusetts: The M.I.T. Press, 1969), p. 11.

new man will be created is not an excuse for our not persevering in our efforts to create him.

Another weakness of this conception of liberation is that it is never clear what will constitute a new man. What is he going to look like? To say that he is not going to look like extant man is not very helpful. For logically it is possible to have a man who is even worse than extant man. How do we know that the new man is an improvement?

Fanon's position can be defended, however. It can be argued that to say that we do not know what our new man will look like is not to say that we can never create him or have an idea of him. To the extent to which the development of the new man depends on tampering with and transforming socioeconomic structures, then the notion of the new man is inextricably bound up with development of those structures. If we can establish that structures have changed, then there is some basis for assuming that their impact or effect will alter social relations and facilitate the emergence of our new man. The strategic issue then becomes one of determining the nature of the new structures and fashioning them accordingly.

One underlying problem that emerges from these questions is that of giving meaning to "humanity," "new man," and kindred terms. For surely to say that extant man is not free or truly liberated is not to make a logical point, but to make a moral one; it is to set up negative criteria of humanity that do not necessarily follow from the mere use or meaning of the word, man.[13]

There is, in short, an Hegelian/Marxist flavor to Fanon's notion of liberation and revolution as involving the creation of a new man. Like Hegel and Marx, what Fanon offers us is a theodicy in that man is pictured as reaching out and progressing towards higher and higher horizons that, perhaps when the highest horizon is attained, must eventually terminate. It is

[13] Cf. Eugene Kamenka, *Marxism and Ethics* (New York: St. Martin's Press, 1969), pp. 25-26, for a critique of Marx along these lines.

then and only then that harmony will be established, that man will become truly human and will be able to pursue his interests unencumbered by prejudice and hate. This is Fanon's ultimate goal, based on his firm belief that "no attempt must be made to encase man, for it is his destiny to be set free."[14]

The Problem of Physical Violence and Liberation in Fanon

Fanon has been described as "the most eloquent panegryst of ... violence, a writer who celebrates it with savage lyricism."[15] This one-sided criticism fails, like Albert Camus' condemnation of the Algerian nationalist fighters,[16] to take into account the defensive nature of the physical violence prescribed by Fanon and used by the F.L.N. It is defensive in the sense that it is necessitated by the essentially violent nature of the colonial situation. Kedouri's criticism also overlooks Fanon's own equivocation about the inevitability of physical violence as a means of liberating the colonized. It should also be pointed out that Fanon is not "celebrating" violence as an end in itself. It is precisely this equivocation as well as Fanon's moral justification of violence as necessary for a higher moral end — liberation — that constitutes the problem of physical violence and liberation in Fanon.

Fanon draws on his knowledge of sub-Saharan Africa and his experiences in Accra, Ghana, as Ambassador of the Algerian Provisional Government to conclude that there are different types of political regímes in liberated or independent Africa. The difference is due primarily to the means or strategy used in the process of liberation. The sense in which he uses

[14] Fanon, *Black Skin, White Masks,* p. 230.

[15] Kedouri, *Nationalism in Asia and Africa,* p. 139.

[16] Connor Cruise O'Brien, *Albert Camus of Europe and Africa* (New York: Viking Press, 1970), pp. 88-92. "Despite his revulsion from the methods of repression his position was necessarily one of support for repression since he consistently opposed negotiation with the actual leaders of the rebellion, the F.L.N.," p. 90.

liberation in this respect is that of decolonization or the formal transfer of political power to an indigenous elite.

This perspective leads him to suggest that the strategy employed by colonized peoples in their struggle for liberation (political independence) has implications extending beyond the struggle itself:

> In the colonial countries where a real struggle for independence has taken place, where the blood of the people has flowed and where the length of the period of armed warfare has favored the backward surge of intellectuals towards bases grounded in the people, we can observe a genuine eradication of the superstructure built by these intellectuals from the bourgeois colonialist environment.[17]

Fanon points out, on the other hand, that

> Without that struggle, without that knowledge of the practice of action, there is nothing save a minimum of readaptation, a few reforms at the top, a flagwaving; and down there at the bottom, an undivided mass, still living in the middle ages, endlessly marking time.[18]

It should be pointed out that Fanon is relating the strategy adopted not only to sociopolitical structures and processes emerging in the postcolonial period, but also to psychological or behavioral orientations towards government and governing. An aspect of this perspective is the crucial importance Fanon attaches to organizational imperatives, particularly leadership and mobilizational ones, created by the different strategies.[19]

Fanon's experiences in Algeria, as a partisan of the Front for National Liberation (F.L.N.) led him to see in the resort to physical violence the "true" means of achieving true liberation. He was also equally willing to concede that other

[17] Fanon, *Wretched of the Earth*, p. 46.

[18] Ibid., p. 147.

[19] Ibid., p. 59. Talking of the national political parties, Fanon argues that "their objective is not the radical overthrowing of the system."

means short of physical violence might be appropriate if the situation or context dictated it. As he observed, "if need be, the native can accept a compromise with colonialism, but never a surrender of principle."[20] Yet, at other times he gives the impression he was not sure which was the true strategy to employ:

> Because the various means whereby decolonization has been carried out have appeared in many different aspects, reason hesitates to say which is a true decolonization and which a false one.[21]

He also seems to have adopted what can be described as a domino-theory of decolonization:

> The uprising of the new nation and the breaking down of colonial structures are the result of one of two causes; either of a violent struggle of the people in their own right, or of action on the part of surrounding colonized peoples which acts as a brake on the colonial regime in question.[22]

How is this problem to be resolved? Is it possible to reconcile Fanon's enthusiastic prescription of physical violence with his equivocation? It is arguable that the problem is more apparent than real. On this view, the resolution of the problem lies in distinguishing between Fanon the political sociologist and Fanon the moralist or ideologist. Thus, if one accepts the thesis that to describe is not necessarily to prescribe or recommend, one will look upon Fanon as a sociologist of African politics concerned primarily with describing the various ways in which formal political independence has been achieved as well as their consequences for political processes in postcolonial Africa.

But if one views Fanon as a moralist or ideologist then one

20 Ibid., p. 143.
21 Ibid., pp. 58-59.
22 Ibid., p. 70.

will look upon him as being less concerned with describing than with deriving certain conclusions and recommendations from his analysis of the various patterns and strategies of decolonization. On this view, the point of his examination of the various patterns is to show and emphasize his preference of a particular type, exemplified in the Algerian war of national liberation. This position also rejects the fact/value dichotomy implied in the distinction between Fanon the political sociologist and Fanon the moralist.

A political sociologist is, however, not necessarily averse to asserting his or her preferences. But it seems to me that there is an acute awareness on Fanon's part that the strategy used must depend on situational conditions. If this is so, then one important reason for Fanon's apparent inconsistency lies in the special colonial situation of Algeria with its sizable and politically powerful White settler community — one that exercised and exerted a power far out of proportion to its numerical size and geographical location over successive French governments during the Third and Fourth French Republics.[23]

Fanon and his compatriots in the F.L.N. saw no other way than the use of physical violence of persuading successive French governments and administrations as well as the French settler community in Algeria to concede and grant Algeria self-determination and autonomy as an independent entity. In fact, a common feature of French rule in Algeria, particularly from about 1950 onward, was the use of large-scale physical violence under the guise of maintaining law and order.[24] To

[23] Philip M. Williams, *Wars, Plots and Scandals in Post War France* (London: Cambridge University Press, 1970), p. 169, observes of the wealthy white settlers in Algeria: "conscienceless reactionaries, clinging to every privilege and fighting every measure to improve the Moslems' lot... As skillful lobbyists with large funds, great experience, and a powerful influence on the Algiers' administration, they were usually able to impose their wishes on the weak and timid ministries which theoretically ruled Paris."

[24] Pierre Vidal-Naquet, *Torture: The Cancer of Democracy: France and Algeria, 1954-1962*, translated by Barry Richard (London: Penguin 1963);

those, especially on the French Left, who claimed that the use of torture by the French occurred only in exceptional circumstances, Fanon's rebuttal is that "torture is not an accident, or an error, or a fault. Colonialism cannot be understood without the possibility of torturing, of violating, of massacring. Torture is an expression and a means of the occupant-occupied relationship."[25]

It is partly against this background of a politically powerful settler community and a French colonial administration apparently irrevocably committed both to the perpetuation of French hegemony and to the subversion of any French government that appeared willing to concede self-determination to Algerians that Fanon's discussion of physical violence as a strategy of decolonization should be read. The virulence and acerbity of the *Wretched of the Earth* and Fanon's incisive perception of the exploitative colonial situation in Algeria could hardly have been possible without his deep concern for the human condition of the colonized. In short, given the objective situation in Algeria, Fanon concluded that dialogue between settler and Arab was impossible. But Fanon cautions against extrapolating from the Algerian situation. As he puts it "We know today that in Algeria the test of force was inevitable. But other countries through political action and through the work of clarification undertaken by a party, have led their people to the same results."[26]

Regenerative Violence, Recognition, Conflict and Liberation

Fanon's equivocation about the inevitability of physical violence as a strategy of decolonization is one aspect of the problem of violence in his political thought. Another aspect of

Henri Alleg, *The Question,* translated by John Calder (London: J. Calder, 1958); David Gordon, *The Passing of French Algeria* (London: Oxford University Press, 1966).

[25] Fanon, *Toward the African Revolution,* p. 64.

[26] Fanon, *Wretched of the Earth,* p. 193.

this prob[illegible] be found in his thesis concerning the regenerat[illegible] physical violence under certain conditions. There are two dimensions to this thesis. First, there is the empirical dimension — does the use of physical violence lead to regeneration? Secondly, there is the methodological dimension, arising from the attempt to deduce generalizations about social wholes or categories from statements about individual behavior. Underlying both dimensions is, of course, what meaning is to be attached to regeneration.

Fanon maintains that the violent confrontation between the colonized and the colonizer in Algeria gave rise to the emergence and acquisition of a new social and political consciousness among native Algerians. To be regenerated then is to assume this new consciousness. But what it, this new consciousness? Fanon apparently means by it psychological reorientation towards social and political relations. It is an attitudinal change that has implications for social and political action in that it sees social and political processes in a new light. It points, in other words, to the contradictions in society and, more importantly, to the imperative of acting to remove the contradictions.

Fanon lucidly describes the attitudinal or psychological changes involvement in the national liberation war effected on individual Algerians. *A Dying Colonialism* is incomparable in its portrayal of the regenerated Algerian, transformed by the experience of revolutionary action. Typical of the regenerated Algerian is "the unveiled Algerian woman, who assumed an increasingly important place in revolutionary action, developed her personality, discovered the exalting realm of responsibility."[27] This same theme is developed in *Wretched of the Earth:*

> But it so happens that for the colonized people this violence, because it constitutes their only work invests their character with positive and creative qualities.[28]

[27] Fanon, *A Dying Colonialism,* p. 107.
[28] Fanon, *Wretched of the Earth,* p. 93.

> At the level of individuals, violence is a cleansing force, it frees the native from his inferiority complex and from his despair and inaction; it makes him fearless and restores his self-respect.[29]

This regeneration does not operate at the individual, psychological level only. Fanon links individual to social regeneration, a term Fanon uses to refer to organizational and mobilizational structures developed as a result of the war of liberation. The transformation of society, at both the infrastructural and superstructural levels, will result mainly from the violent confrontation between the colonizer and the colonized:

> The mobilization of the masses, when it arises out of the war of liberation, introduces into each man's consciousness the ideas of a common cause, of a national destiny, and of a collective history. In the same way the second phase, that of the building-up of the nation, is helped on by the existence of this cement which has been mixed with blood and anger.[30]

Fanon's thesis on regenerative violence is based on his other thesis, particularly in *Black Skin, White Masks* and, deriving from Hegel, that mutual recognition is intrinsic to respect in human relationships:

> Man is human only to the extent to which he tries to impose his existence on another man in order to be recognized by him. As long as he has not been effectively recognized by the other, that other will remain the theme of his actions. It is on that other being, on recognition by that other being, that his own human worth and reality depend.[31]

If mutual recognition is important, so also is "absolute reciprocity," whose relevance is described by Fanon as being

[29] Ibid., p. 94.
[30] Ibid., p. 93.
[31] Fanon, *Black Skin, White Masks*, pp. 216-217.

constituted by "the degree to which I go beyond my own immediate being [to] apprehend the existence of the other as a natural and more than natural reality."[32]

Another notion highly relevant to Fanon's thesis on regenerative violence is his notion of conflict or struggle. Fanon's argument is that the slave, in this case the colonized, is cheated of recognition and denied respect by his master when freedom is given to him by, and not demanded from, the master, i.e., the colonizer. The slave must, by his own struggle or effort, seize freedom from his master. The slave must, in other words, work for his freedom.

> Thus human reality in-itself — for itself can be achieved only through the risk that conflict implies. This risk means that I go beyond subjective certainty of my own worth into a universally valid objective truth.[33]

This notion of work in Fanon is different from that of Hegel.[34] Hegel had suggested that the reciprocal basis of the master-slave relationship was due to its symbiotic nature. Master and slave depended on each other and recognized each other's consciousness. Work or labor in the narrow sense of economic activity or productivity becomes a vehicle for the liberation of the Hegelian slave; this is because the master depends on the slave's productivity, which is why he does not annihilate the slave. Fanon, however, argues that the colonial situation is such that there is neither reciprocity nor recognition in the Black-White relationship:

> For Hegel there is reciprocity; here, [the colonial situation] the master laughs at the consciousness of the slave. What he wants from the slave is not recognition but work. In the same way, the slave here is in no way

[32] Ibid., p. 217.
[33] Ibid., p. 218.
[34] Zahar, *Fanon: Colonialism and Alienation*, pp. 78-31; Gendzier, *Fanon*, pp. 25-26.

> identifiable with the slave who loses himself in the object and finds his work the source of his liberation.
>
> The Negro wants to be like the master. Therefore he is less independent than the Hegelian slave. In Hegel the slave turns away from the master and turns toward the object. Here the slave turns toward the master and abandons the object.[35]

Work in the sense in which Fanon uses it means violent revolutionary action to transform the colonial situation. According to him:

> The militant is also a man who works.... The group requires that each individual perform an irrevocable action. Each one was personally responsible for the death of that victim. To work means to work for the death of the settler.[36]

Fanon's critique of Hegel raises two related problems. First, does Hegel's notion of work rule out revolutionary action? Secondly, does Fanon's emphasis on the psychological dimensions of revolutionary praxis neglect economic alienation?

Gendzier criticizes Fanon's narrow interpretation of Hegel's notion of labor, pointing out that the Hegelian conception involves much more than economic productivity.[37] Yet the issue is not to be posed in terms of the scope of the Hegelian conception; rather it is whether violent struggle or revolutionary activity advocated by Fanon in both *Black Skin, White Masks* and *Wretched of the Earth* is consistent with the Hegelian system. Part of the problem is that Hegel is ambiguous and inconsistent on the question of revolution.[38]

[35] Fanon, *Black Skin, White Masks*, pp. 220-221, footnote 8.

[36] Fanon, *Wretched of the Earth*, p. 85.

[37] Gendzier, *Fanon*, p. 26.

[38] J. F. Sutter, "Burke, Hegel and the French Revolution," in Z. A. Pelczynski, ed., *Hegel's Political Philosophy: Problems and Perspectives, A Collection of New Essays* (London: Cambridge University Press, 1971); John

This problem is about interpretation. Like much else in Hegel, the master-slave paradigm is not easy to understand.[39] On the question of revolution, however, there is much force in the Marxian critique that, under the Hegelian system, the elevation of the status quo, of existing political institutions as emanations of the Idea has the practical implication of uncritical acceptance of the status quo.[40] Hegel's parochialism and Protestant bias led him to see in the Prussian state of his time a realization of the Idea or Spirit.[41] He therefore forecloses any attempt to alter the economic and social relations of production, or to replace the colonial situation.

If one looks at the master-slave paradigm and disregards Hegel's political bias and parochialism, there is much more to the paradigm than Fanon concedes. As Plamenatz argues, Hegel's "assertion that the future belongs to the oppressed is altogether in the spirit of Marxian philosophy"[42]; it is also in the spirit of the closing pages of *Wretched of the Earth* where the "wretched" are proclaimed as inheritors and saviors of the world. Hegel's thesis that, in recognizing the limitations of their conditions, the oppressed act to terminate their servile status is also similar to Fanon's thesis that it is the manicheism of the colonial situation that ultimately prompts the colonized to revolutionary action. Hegel's claim that the community of the future is one in which everyone recognizes everyone else as his brother's keeper is also in the spirit of Fanon's invocation to the "wretched" to help set afoot a new man.

P. Plamenatz, *Man and Society*, Vol. 2 (London: Longman, 1963), pp. 168-169, 192-195).

[39] George A. Kelly, "Notes on Hegel's 'Lordship and Bondage'," in Alasdair McIntyre, *Hegel: A Collection of Essays* (New York: Doubleday, 1972), p. 191.

[40] R. N. Berki, "Perspectives in the Marxian Critique of Hegel's Political Philosophy," in Pelczynski, ed., *Hegel's Political Philosophy;* Jean Hyppolite, *Studies on Marx and Hegel* (New York: Basic Books, 1969).

[41] Plamenatz, *Man and Society*, Vol. 2, pp. 204-205, 209-211.

[42] Ibid., p. 156. For a critique of Plamenatz's and the Marxian interpretation of this aspect of Hegel, see Kelly, "Hegel's 'Lordship and Bondage'," pp. 193-194, 216.

Does Fanon's emphasis on the psychological dimensions of revolutionary praxis neglect economic alienation and the conditions for its removal? Zahar argues that, by devoting too much attention to the first phase of violence, identified as the removal of "the psychological torpor and alienation of the colonized," Fanon fails to address himself adequately to the second phase of violence when the capitalist colonial structures that give rise to alienated behavior should have been altered.[43]

It is hard to accept Zahar's criticism. Fanon realizes the paramount important of the problem of transition. But he sees an organic link between the psychological and structural elements in the decolonization process. It is precisely because of his concern that economic and social relations of production inherited from the colonial situation are not perpetuated in postcolonial Africa that he rejects a two-phased strategy of socialist revolution:

> The theoretical question that for the last fifty years has been raised whenever the history of underdeveloped countries is under discussion — whether or not the bourgeois phase can be skipped — ought to be answered in the field of revolutionary action, and not by logic.[44]

This is also why Fanon emphasizes the place of ideology and organization for consciousness-raising without which "there is nothing save a minimum of readaptation, a few reforms at the top, a flagwaving."[45] Pertinent in this respect is his observation that that "for my part, the deeper I enter into the cultures and the political circles, the surer I am that the great danger that threatens Africa is the absence of ideology."[46]

Fanon regards physical violence used by the colonized in certain contexts and under certain conditions as constituting the praxis of decolonization. This is to suggest in effect that if

[43] Zahar, *Colonialism and Alienation*, pp. 78-81.
[44] Fanon, *Wretched of the Earth*, p. 175.
[45] Ibid., p. 147.
[46] Fanon, *Toward the African Revolution*, p. 186.

physical violence is adapted to a rationally-planned collective revolutionary action and given social direction, it will assume a new dimension, it will serve towards removing psychological and structural violence. It is not a question of his emphasizing one phase at the expense of the other.

True and False Decolonization: A Misleading Dichotomy?

How valuable is Fanon's distinction between true and false decolonization? This distinction is a variation of Fanon's distinctions between being set free and struggling to free oneself. Fanon's preference is for one's struggling to free oneself because when one is set free one "knows nothing of the cost of freedom for [one] has not fought for it."[47] There is also the assumption that when one is set free, one's freedom of action, one's ability to pursue an independent course of action is compromised to the extent to which one feels indebted to whoever grants one one's freedom. No gift is ever unconditional.

There is, however, some validity in the objection that it does not necessarily follow from the fact that if freedom is granted to the slave, for example, that the slave will not appreciate the value of his or her newly-acquired freedom or work hard to preserve it. While there may be some basis for the claim that to be indebted is to compromise one's freedom to act, the claim is by no means self-evident. Fanon's mistake is in confusing two different issues. It is one thing to state a preference for struggling to free oneself; it is another thing to claim that where freedom is achieved without struggle, people will not appreciate or will eventually compromise their newly-won freedom.

Does a particular strategy guarantee *ab initio* the success or failure of the various experiments in nation-building in Africa?

[47] Fanon, *Black Skin, White Masks*, p. 221.

Is there reason to believe that the pattern as well as strategy of decolonization can help to explain differences between political regimes?

If, as was argued earlier in this chapter, Fanon equivocated on the question of the inevitability of physical violence, then it will appear that he is undecided about the connection between means and end. Yet he does not want to maintain this position because it is clear to him that there are significant differences between the organizational and mobilizational structures developed in the course of a war of national liberation and those developed by nationalist movements that did not engage in violent confrontations with the colonial powers. This is why Fanon contends that "violence alone, violence committed by the people, violence organized and educated by its leaders, makes it possible for the masses to understand social truths and gives the key to them."[48]

Let us now return to our concern with Fanon's distinction between true and false decolonization. What, for example, is true decolonization? Fanon is not of much help in this respect. He does not state clearly what he means by true decolonization, although he attempts to characterize what he means by false decolinization:

> Without that struggle, without that knowledge of action, there is nothing but a fancydress parade and the blare of trumpets. There is nothing save a minimum of readaptation, a few reforms at the top, a flagwaving; and down there at the bottom an undivided mass, still living in the middle ages, endlessly making time.[49]

This way of putting the distinction between true and false decolonization is problematic in at least two respects. First, it is arguable why "struggle" or "action" should be restricted to physical violence or armed resistance. Sorel, for example,

[48] Fanon, *Wretched of the Earth,* p. 147.
[49] Ibid., p. 147

regards "violence" in the form of the general strike as a sharp struggle in that the proletariat withholds its labor in order to extract concessions from producers or established authorities.[50] This conception of violence is similar to Mahatma Gandhi's method of nonviolence and Kwame Nkrumah's notion of positive action. It would be misleading to talk as if no struggle or action was involved in those African countries where there was gradual devolution of political power to the indigenous bourgeoisie.

Whether the action or struggle was enough to prevent a "deal," such that political or formal independence was handed over to the bourgeoisie on a "platter of gold" is a different matter. Nkumah's operationalization of his notion of positive action is, for example, in another sense compatible with revolutionary action — at least to the extent to which there is a continuing debate among Marxist-Leninists about the appropriateness of violence or nonviolence as a strategy for achieving socialism.

In this respect, Cabral has expressed his appreciation of Nkrumah's contribution to the African Revolution.[51] Fanon's position, it seems to me, is due less to disagreement with the strategy adopted as to what he views as reactionary policies pursued by the various regimes in sub-Saharan Africa and the opportunities afforded to the national bourgeoisie to entrench themselves in power.

The second respect in which Fanon's distinction is problematic is that it is possible that a state of affairs in which "there is nothing save a minimum of readaptation" can exist even in countries where the independence struggle was "mixed with blood." Winning formal independence by whatever means is one thing; consolidating a new regime on that

50 Georges Sorel, *Reflections on Violence*, translated by T. E. Hulme (New York: Collier, 1961), p. 77.

51 P.A.I.G.C., *Cabral on Nkrumah*, Speech delivered at Symposium in Memory of Nkrumah, May 13, 1972 (Newark, New Jersey: Jihad Productions, [n.d.]).

independence is another thing, requiring and depending on such resources as economic and natural resource endowment, manpower, and leadership resources, among others.

Yet it is not that Fanon was unaware of the problems of nation-building. Drawing on her conversations with him, Simone de Beauvoir suggests that Fanon knew about dissensions, liquidations, and intrigues within the F.L.N.[52] He was not oblivious to the rivalry and recriminations arising from the dynamics of a revolutionary situation. But these were questions to be settled after the war.

There are some hard epistemological questions that must be asked, if not resolved. How does one determine whether violence is the only means left open? Can one guarantee success in the circumstances? Can one in fact talk of the success or failure of a strategy before it is used? In a sense these questions are academic because the question of the success or failure of violence in terminating the colonial situation is quite distinct from the question whether the resort to violence is necessary and inescapable.

While revolutions are not a trivial matter, that is to say that it may be desirable to count the cost of waging them, one must also resist the temptation to adopt the Burkean position that revolutionaries are reckless adventurers. To adopt this position is to forget that revolutionaries do not create the situations in which they act.

Fanon's position on the "means-success" question is reductionistic. Impressed by the apparent unity of the F.L.N. in the presence of a common foe, Fanon tends to attribute that unity as well as the inevitability of success to one cause — the application of physical violence by the F.L.N. A *post hoc* examination of how independence was won in Algeria shows that, at best, the claim is not the whole of the matter and that more than the mere occurrence of violence is needed. The role

[52] Simone de Beauvoir, *Force of Circumstances* (London: André Deutsch and Weidenfeld and Nicholson, 1965), p. 595.

of General Charles de Gaulle is important in this respect. It is indeed one of the ironies of the Algerian war of liberation that the Algerians or rather the F.L.N., did not "seize" independence from France and that the terms of, and conditions for, Algerian independence were negotiated at Evian.

Is the true-false decolonization dichotomy then misleading? While it is problematic in the sense identified in this section, there is nevertheless some validity to it. As Fanon and Cabral have argued, the development of a revolutionary culture produces a political leadership with a radical orientation. A war of national liberation by its very nature necessarily forges strong links between this leadership and the masses, thereby facilitating political mobilization, as studies of Mozambique by John Saul and Yoweri Museveni have shown.[53] The development of revolutionary culture also gives a different dimension to the dependent status of such countries as Algeria, Angola, and Mozambique in that, unlike most other African countries, they are able to exercise their political control to direct and restrict the activities of multinational companies, for example. This is to suggest that there is, perhaps, something in the logic of a war of national liberation that minimizes the emergence of a comprador bourgeoisie.

Rejuvenation and Fanon's "Economy of Violence"

Is physical violence as rejuvenating as Fanon claims? A number of objections can be raised against Fanon's thesis about the transformation brought about at both the individual and societal levels by revolutionary violence. An objection is that from an observation of behavioral and attitudinal changes

[53] John Saul, "Mozambique: Peasants and Revolutions" (mimeo); Yoweri T. Museveni, "Fanon's Theory of Violence: Its Verification in Liberated Mozambique," in Nathan Shamuyarira, ed., *Essays on the Liberation of Southern Africa* (Dar-es-Salaam, Tanzania: Tanzania Publishing House, 1971), pp. 1-24.

effected in individuals during involvement in concrete revolutionary situations, one cannot validly deduce the nature and structure of the socioeconomic and political system that will evolve thereafter.[54] There are two aspects or variations of this criticism.

One variation is that revolutionary violence can be dysfunctional or disorientational, as Fanon's case studies at the end of *Wretched of the Earth* clearly show. The other variation of the criticism holds that it is questionable whether the use of violence, even where functional or cathartic, is primarily responsible for the change in individual perception or consciousness. What alternative explanations can there be for the change in consciousness? It is arguable, for example, that it is the need for status change, induced by a change in social consciousness, that leads to the resort to violence as a means of bridging the gap between what ought to be and what is.

Another set of objections against the processes of social change that Fanon lucidly portrays, particularly in *A Dying Colonialism,* is directed at their permanence and validity. Nghe and Rohdie both claim that Fanon's analysis lacks sociological dimensions. David Gordon contests the validity and permanence of Fanon's account of the changes that participation in the war of liberation brought about in the social roles and position of the Algerian womanhood.[55]

Fanon's assertion that physical violence is rejuvenating should, however, be viewed as a contingent and not an analytically true proposition. In other words, if there is evidence in Fanon's writings to support the thesis that physical violence is rejuvenating, there is also strong evidence to the contrary in his writings; witness the case studies at the end of *Wretched of the Earth.* Indeed, in the light of these case studies

[54] Nguyen Nghe, "Fanon et les problemes de l'Independance, " *La Pensée* (January/February, 1963); S. Rohdie, "Liberation and Violence in Algeria," *Studies on the Left,* Vol. 6, No. 3 (May/June, 1966).

[55] David C. Gordon, *Women of Algeria: An Essay on Change* (Cambridge, Massachusetts: Harvard University Press, 1968).

and Fanon's involvement with them, it is seemingly difficult to explain why Fanon holds that physical violence is rejuvenating.

Can it be that Fanon thinks certain kinds of physical violence are preferable to others? It is interesting that his discussion of rejuvenating physical violence is limited to its use by the colonized. Does this mean that the physical violence of the colonizer is neither rejuvenating nor cleansing when used against the colonized? Fanon's answer would be in the negative since such physical violence negated freedom.

It was not only the physical violence of the colonizer that Fanon condemned for its negation of freedom. His discussion of "the well-known behaviour patterns of avoidance" and "collective autodestruction" among the indigenous peoples shows his disapproval of this type of physical violence.[56] As he states:

> All these patterns of conduct are those of the death reflex when faced with danger, a suicidal behaviour which proves to the settler (whose existence and domination is by them all the more justified) that these men are not reasonable human beings.[57]

If, however, this manifestation of physical violence is adapted to a rationally planned collective revolutionary action, it will assume a new dimension compatible with the collective liberation of the colonized:

> The native discovers reality and transforms it into the pattern of his customs, into the practice of violence and into his plan for freedom.
>
> We have seen that this same violence, though kept very much on the surface all through the colonial period, yet

[56] Fanon, *Wretched of the Earth,* pp. 54-58.

[57] Ibid., p. 54. For a critique of Fanon's position on this issue, see Norman A. Klein, "On Revolutionary Violence," *Studies on the Left,* 4 (May/June, 1966), pp. 62-82.

> turns in the void.... When formerly it was appeased by myths and exercised its talents in finding fresh ways of committing mass suicide, now new conditions will make possible a completely new line of action.[58]

Fanon also condemns the physical violence used by the ruling groups in postcolonial Africa to maintain and perpetuate their accumulation of wealth. Fanon is less concerned with the question whether any government can sustain itself without some form of physical violence. Rather, he is concerned with the use of physical violence to sustain the socioeconomic distance between the few at the top and the vast mass of African peoples:

> In the same way that the national bourgeoisie conjures away its phase of construction in order to throw itself into the enjoyment of its wealth, in parallel fashion in the institutional sphere, it jumps the parliamentary phase and choses a dictatorship of the national-socialist type....
>
> In these poor, underdeveloped countries, where the rule is that the greatest wealth is surrounded by the greatest poverty, the army and the police constitute the pillars of the regime.[59]

What this reconsideration of Fanon's thesis about rejuvenating physical violence points to is the importance Fanon attaches to the nature of the context in which it is utilized. In this respect, Sheldon Wolin's discussion of Machiavelli's economy of violence[60] can be usefully applied to Fanon's discussion of violence. Machiavelli has pointed out

[58] Fanon, *Wretched of the Earth*, p. 58.
[59] Ibid., p. 172.
[60] Sheldon S. Wolin, *Politics and Vision: Continuity and Innovation in Western Political Thought* (Boston, Massachusetts: Little, Brown and Co., 1960), pp. 220-224.

that "it is the man who uses violence to spoil things, not the man who uses it to mend them, that is blameworthy."[61]

This concern with drawing a distinction between political creativity and political destruction is quite explicitly expressed by Fanon. Just as Machiavelli had argued that violence was the only means of arresting decadence under certain circumstances,[62] Fanon also regards physical violence as a means of arresting the continued dehumanization of the colonized in certain colonial contexts.[63] His condemnation of the African one-party regime, characterized in its empirical manifestations by the use of physical violence to suppress opposition, is premised on his belief that it cannot sustain itself indefinitely without active and popular support in such circumstances:

> Such exploitation and such contempt for the state, however, inevitably gives rise to discontent among the mass of the people. It is in these conditions that the regime becomes harsher. In the absence of a parliament it is the army that becomes the arbiter: but sooner or later it will realize its power and will hold over the government's head the threat of a manifesto.[64]

This is also why he cautions some of his F.L.N. colleagues to be judicious in their use of physical violence. The use of the instruments of physical violence to attain a revolution may represent a mirror image of the racist and oligarchic structures of authority against which the F.L.N. is struggling. However, while the use of physical violence is justified in this sense, Fanon is also concerned that once the revolution is successful, the basic elements and structures that the F.L.N. is opposing

[61] Quoted in Wolin, *Politics and Vision: Continuity and Innovation in Western Political Thought*, p. 221, note 90.

[62] Wolin, *Politics and Vision: Continuity and Innovation in Western Political Thought*, p. 221.

[63] Fanon, *Wretched of the Earth*, p. 36.

[64] Fanon, *Wretched of the Earth*, p. 174.

and trying to destroy are not incorporated into an independent Algeria under the rule of the F.L.N.:

> Because we want a democratic and renovated Algeria, we believe one cannot rise and liberate oneself in one area and sink in another. We condemn with pain in our hearts, those brothers who have flung themselves into revolutionary action with the almost psychological brutality that centuries of oppression give rise to and feed.[65]

It is important to emphasize that what has been described as Fanon's equivocation about the positive functions of physical violence might usefully be regarded as a concern with "the economy of violence," with a judicious use of violence. Fanon was an "empiricist" who based his generalizations about a rejuvenating violence on his Algerian experiences It is doubtful, as he himself makes explicitly, clear, whether those generalizations can be applied to revolutionary struggles in general. My argument is that Fanon was merely describing as accurately and as best he could a process of liberation he was witnessing as a participant observer. He was, to use an oxymoron, a chronicler of the sweet horror of violent conflicts, but one who also showed an acute awareness of the need to separate the existential from the macrosociological dimensions of physical violence.

Fanon, Sorel and Sartre on Violence

This section offers a comparison of certain aspects of the conceptions of violence entertained by Fanon, Sorel, and Sartre. While the attempt is to show similarities and dissimilarities in their conceptions of violence, the aim is not to establish Sorel's or Sartre's influence on Fanon.

[65] Fanon, *A Dying Colonialism*, p. 25.

The question of Fanon's indebtedness to Sorel's *Reflections on Violence* has been discussed by a number of critics. On the one hand, there are those like Zolberg, Arendt, and Bienen who claim that Fanon's thesis about regenerating violence derives from, or bears striking similarity with, Sorel's position in his *Reflections on Violence*.[66] On the other hand, there are those like Caute and Gendzier who not only deny that Fanon's thesis is derived from Sorel, but also maintain that their conceptions of violence are substantially different.[67] What merits are there to either of these contentions?

Arendt claims that Fanon "was greatly influenced by Sorel and used his categories even when his own experiences spoke clearly against them."[68] But was Fanon greatly influenced by Sorel? Part of the problem in answering this question relates to what is to constitute evidence for Arendt's claim. Arendt seems to have based her claim on the fact that both Fanon and Sorel refer to the regenerative and cleansing functions of violence. But the fact that there is this similarity does not necessarily mean that Fanon was influenced by Sorel. Nor does it establish that they defined violence in the same way.

There are, however, two areas of similarity in Fanon and Sorel's discussion of violence. First, both men condemn liberal illusions about, and prejudices against, physical violence. On liberal prejudices against violence, Sorel has observed that "in the eyes of the contemporary middle class everything is admirable which dispels the idea of violence."[69] In a similar vein, Fanon derides reformist, liberal ideas, asserting instead that "I do not carry innocence to the point of believing that appeals to reason or human dignity can alter reality."[70]

[66] Zolberg, "Fanon: a Gospel for the Damned"; Hannah Arendt, *On Violence* (New York: Harcourt, Brace, and World, 1969), p: 71; Henry Bienen, *Violence and Social Change, A Review of Current Literature* (Chicago, Illinois: University of Chicago Press, 1968), p. 72.

[67] Caute, *Frantz Fanon*, pp. 93-94; Gendzier, *Frantz Fanon*, pp. 203-204.

[68] Arendt, *On Violence*, p. 71.

[69] Sorel, *Reflections on Violence*, p. 104.

[70] Fanon, *Black Skin, White Masks*, p. 224.

Secondly, Fanon and Sorel believe in the regenerative role of physical violence. Sorel argues that through revolutionary action the proletariat assumes a new moral force and vitality and becomes the savior of humanity. In his words, "it is to violence that Socialism owes those high ethical values by means of which it brings salvation to the modern world."[71] Fanon also argues in a similar vein when he hypothesizes that "for the colonized people this violence ... invests their characters with positive and creative qualities."[72]

In their attempt to deny that Fanon "was greatly influenced" by Sorel's concept of violence, Caute and Gendzier overlook these similarities in the two theorists' discussion of violence. It seems that Caute and Gendzier's strong denials arose out of their desire to counter the misleading attempt by Arendt and Zolberg to read fascist overtones into Fanon by linking him to Sorel.

There are, however, fundamental differences between Fanon and Sorel's concept of violence. One difference is in Sorel's equation of physical violence, i.e., the general strike, with myth.[73] Fanon is not opposed to myths as such. But violence is more than a myth for him. It is something concrete aimed at the overthrow of existing structures. A second difference, therefore, is to be found in Sorel's equation of violence with general strike. The impression one gets from reading Sorel's discussion of the general strike is that, unlike Fanon, he does not think that violence necessarily has to involve physical force. For Sorel, violence is more like a sharp struggle in which, for example, the proletariat withholds its labor in order to extract concessions from producers or established authorities.

A third difference lies in the fact that Sorel views violence as part of the "irrational" nature of man, becoming an end in itself. On the other hand, Fanon places violence within the

[71] Sorel, *Reflections on Violence*, p. 249.
[72] Fanon, *Wretched of the Earth*, p. 93.
[73] Sorel, *Reflections on Violence*, p. 126.

context of an oppressive environment, specifically that of the colonial situation. Moreover for Fanon, violence is not an end in itself and it has to be used judiciously or "economically." It is this concern with "the economy of violence" that sets apart Fanon's thesis about a rejuvenating violence from that of Sorel.

While much has been written about Fanon's indebtedness to Sartre, there has been little, if any, attempt to investigate one important area of similarity between them. This is Sartre and Fanon's conception of violence as a bond around which a group coalesces. Both men posit a solidary function for violence. But what maintains a group is not only the fear of an opposing group, but also the knowledge by every member that violence will be used against him or her if he or she breaks the pledge that binds the group together. In other words, if a group is not to disintegrate and become a "series" it must maintain itself by terror.

Sartre argues that what makes men form groups is the fact of scarcity. It is indeed scarcity that makes human relationships intelligible. Since scarcity can never be eliminated, it becomes imperative for men to coalsce in collaborative groups to deal with the scarcity problem. Although scarcity makes us all rivals, it also makes collaborators out of us.[74] As for the relationship between scarcity and violence, Sartre declares that

> thus we consider, at the very level of need and through need, that scarcity lives itself, in practice, through manichean activity, and that the ethical reveals itself as a destructive imperative: evil must be destroyed. It is at this level, too, that one must define violence as a structure of human action under the sway of manicheanism and in the context of scarcity. Violence claims also to be a counter-violence, that is, retaliation to the violence of the other.[75]

[74] Jean-Paul Sartre, "Critique de la Raison Dialectique," in Robert D. Cumming, ed., *The Philosophy of Jean-Paul Sartre,* (New York: Random House, 1965), p. 440.

[75] Ibid., p. 441.

Fanon does not explicitly use the notion of scarcity. What is important however, is his notion of conflict. One consequence of scarcity for Sartre is conflict between groups for scarce resources. In the colonial situation the colonized are denied access to resources enjoyed by the colonizer. Presumably, if these resources were not scarce, it would be unnecessary to use race as a criterion of access to those resources. In order to protect and preserve their privileged access, the colonizer resorts to violence against the colonized and those colonizers who attempt to weaken the solidarity of their race by siding with the colonized. Similarly, the colonized constitute a group whose solidarity must depend on the sanction offered by violence.[76]

It is appropriate at this juncture to consider Sartre's preface to *Wretched of the Earth.* Sartre has always been excited at the idea of violence, as his novels and plays make clear. It is not surprising, however, that he endorses wholeheartedly, to the point of distortion, Fanon's thesis about revolutionary violence; witness his Preface to Fanon's *Wretched of the Earth:*

> Make no mistake about it, by this mad fury, by this bitterness and spleen, by their ever-present desire to kill us by their permanent tensing of muscles, which are afraid to relax, they have become man .... Hatred, blind hatred which is as yet an abstraction, is their only wealth...[77]

This reference to hatred by Sartre is plainly a misrepresentation of Fanon, who unmistakably makes it clear that his purpose in analyzing the colonial situation is "to persuade my brother, whether black or white, to tear off with all his

[76] Fanon, *Wretched of the Earth,* pp. 84-86.
[77] Jean-Paul Sartre, "Preface," in Fanon, *Wretched of the Earth,* p. 17.

strength the shameful livery put together by centuries of incomprehension."[78] More pointedly, Fanon observes that

> you do not carry on a war nor suffer brutal and widespread repression, nor look on while all other members of your family are wiped out in order to make racialism or hatred triumph. Racialism and hatred and resentment ... cannot sustain a war of liberation.[79]

Summary

Fanon was not an advocate of the indiscriminate use of physical violence as an instrument of liberation. To the extent to which he equivocated in his espousal of physical violence he was at heart an "empiricist" who not only based his generalizations on his experiences in Algeria, but also emphasized the imperative for a judicious or "economical" use of violence.

His distinction between true and false decolonization raises important problems that are linked to the basic distinction between being set free or struggling to set oneself free. Yet there is some validity to Fanon's distinction when viewed in the light of organizational and mobilizational structures generated by a war of national liberation.

[78] Fanon, *Black Skin, White Masks*, p. 12; see also Ibid., pp. 228-232.
[79] Fanon, *Wretched of the Earth*, p. 139.

Chapter 5

TOWARD A FANONIAN THEORY OF REVOLUTION

Fanon as a Theorist of Revolution

It is suggested in Chapter 4 that, in one sense of the word, Fanon regards liberation as being inextricably bound up with the notion of revolution. According to this view revolution is not merely a political act aimed at transforming the colonial situation. Both notions give expression to a continuing process through which man's potentialities are continuously enlarged. It is a process that spans time, giving direction to social and political life.

On what does the claim that Fanon is a theorist of revolution rest? This question poses some problems. Should one regard him as writing on behalf of the F.L.N.? If one should so regard him, to what extent is he representative of that movement? He was at one stage involved in editorial work on *El Moudjahid,* the F.L.N. newspaper. He also served as ambassador of the Algerian Provisional Government to Accra, Ghana. Moreover, his major work, *Wretched of the Earth* was partly inspired by the Algerian war of national liberation.

It might be doubted whether Fanon's views on revolutionary change were representative or an adequate reflection of those of the F.L.N.[1] His status as a theorist of revolution nevertheless rests simply on the fact that his speculations on revolution belong to what Sheldon Wolin has characterized as "a distinct tradition of revolutionary writings, flourishing, for

[1] Gendzier, *Frantz Fanon,* pp. 140-85; 231-260.

the most part, outside academic and scholarly communities..."[2] Fanon was in this respect an *engagé* writer, a pamphleteer whose primary purpose was to evoke an attitude and response favorable to the cause he was promoting. As he puts it, "scientific objectivity was barred to me, for the alienated, the neurotic was my brother, my sister, my father."[3]

Fanon and the Marxist-Leninist Theory of Revolution

What does Fanon mean by revolution?[4] Nowhere does he explicitly define what he means by revolution. Yet he has a certain conception of revolution which, although peculiarly his own and deriving from his Algerian experiences, is, broadly speaking, within the Marxist-Leninist tradition.

Marcuse has argued that the concept of revolution in Marxian theory is a dialectical concept that derives its vitality and dynamism from the fact that it needs to be re-examined from time to time so that it will reflect and not dominate the vicissitudes of the class struggle.[5] What Fanon has done is to adopt Marxist-Leninist conceptions of society, state, and revolution to the concrete historical reality of Algeria and, by

[2] Sheldon Wolin, "The Politics of the Study of Revolution," *Comparative Politics,* Vol. 5, No. 3 (April, 1973), p. 345.

[3] Fanon, *Black Skin, White Masks,* p. 225.

[4] The contemporary literature on revolution is profuse, dealing with such things as the causes and consequences of revolution, revolutionary leadership, comparative studies, and definitions of revolution. Useful reviews and surveys can be found in Lawrence Stone, "Theories of Revolution," *World Politics,* Vol. 18, No. 2 (January, 1966), pp. 159-176; Isaac Kramnic, "Reflections on Revolution: Definition and Explanation in Recent Scholarship," *History and Theory,* Vol. 2, No. 2 (1972), pp. 22-63; Michael Freeman, "Review Article: Theories of Revolution," *British Journal of Political Science,* Vol. 2, Part 3 (July, 1972), pp. 339-359; Perez Zagorin, "Theories of Revolution in Contemporary Historiography," *Political Science Quarterly,* Vol. 88, No. 1 (March, 1973), pp. 23-53; Wolin, "Politics of Study of Revolution."

[5] Herbert Marcuse, "Re-Examination of the Concept of Revolution," in Raymond Klibansky, ed., *Contemporary Philosophy,* Vol. 4 (Firenze: La Nuova Italia, 1968-1971), pp. 424-432.

extension, the rest of Africa and the colonized world.[6] As Fanon also maintains:

> When you examine at close quarters the colonial context, it is evident that what parcels out the world is to begin with the fact of belonging to a given race, a given species. In the colonies the economic substructure is also a superstructure. The cause is the consequence; you are rich because you are white; you are white because you are rich. This is why Marxist analysis should always be stretched every time we have to do with the colonial system. Everything up to and including the very nature of precapitalist society, so well explained by Marx, must be thought out again.[7]

Fanon's adaptation of the Marxist-Leninist theory should be placed within the general context of the appeal of communist models of modernization to intellectuals in the Third World. John Kautsky has argued that this appeal is due to the revolutionary character of Marxism as an ideology of modernization and the rejection of the evolutionary nature of what Kautsky calls the western model.[8] It is therefore necessary to examine the presuppositions of the Marxist-Leninst concept of revolution in order to gain an understanding of Fanon's indebtedness to it.

Marxism-Leninism sets great store by action and practice. This is why Marxists-Leninists subscribe to a theory of knowledge which presents the evolution of man's cognition from ignorance to knowledge; social action is the motor of this cognitive process. This theory of social action places a high

[6] Tony Martin, "Rescuing Fanon from the Critics," *African Studies Review,* Vol. 13, No. 3 (December, 1970), p. 385; Nursey-Bray, "Marxism and Existentialism in Fanon," pp. 152-160.

[7] Fanon, *Wretched of the Earth,* p. 40.

[8] John H. Kautsky, "The Appeal of Communist Models in Underdeveloped Countries," in Williard A. Beling and George D. Totten, *Developing Countries: Quest for a Model* (New York: Van Nostrand, 1970), pp. 101-115.

premium on the uniquely universalist role of the proletariat in bringing about revolution.[9]

This universalist role should be placed and makes sense only within the context of the Marxist-Leninist theory of the state. According to Marxism-Leninism, both the nature of the state and the course of social and political development are determined primarily by the economic structure of society, itself composed of forces of production and productive relations.[10] The Marxist-Leninist conception of the relationship between the state and political power follows from this analysis: the state is viewed as the agent for the furtherance of class interests, a function necessitated by the exigencies of the productive relations between a class of exploiters and a class of the exploited.[11]

The Marxist-Leninist theory of revolution is therefore a theory about the seizure of the mechanisms of state coercion by the proletariat as a first step towards as well as a precondition for the establishment of socialism. The task of correctly diagnosing the revolutionary situation is of supreme importance. This raises the question of strategy and brings together two important aspects of the Marxist-Leninist theory of revolution: the indispensability of political leadership and the necessity of mass support for the revolutionary movement.[12]

In short, the concept of revolution in Marxist-Leninist theory revolves around the following. The revolution is to be

[9] Karl Marx, "Toward the Critique of Hegel's Philosophy of Rights," in Lewis S. Feuer, *Marx and Engels: Basic Writing on Politics and Philosophy* (London: Collins, Fontana Library, 1969), pp. 305-306.

[10] There is controversy among critics of Marxism as to whether Marx regards the technique of production or the economic structure as the factor determining the general character of social life. See Plamenatz, *Man and Society*, Vol. 2, pp. 274-279.

[11] F. Engels, "The Origin of the Family, Private Property and the State," in Feuer, *Marx and Engels: Basic Writings on Politics and Philosophy*, p. 431; Karl Marx and F. Engels, *The Communist Manifesto*, with an introduction by A. J. P. Taylor (London: Penguin, 1967).

[12] V. I. Lenin, *Left-Wing Communism: An Infantile Disorder*, revised translation (New York: International Publishers, 1937), pp. 35, 65.

triggered by an economic crisis that both weakens and undermines the established order. It is to be carried out by large-scale mass action of the proletariat underpolitical leadership provided by a vanguard party.

The Leninist Reinterpretation of Marxism

This outline of the Marxist-Leninist theory of revolution in its application to nonwestern, nonindustrial societies is to be viewed in the light of the Leninist reinterpretation of Marxism.[13] That reinterpretation raises two important questions that are pertinent to Fanon's views on revolution. First, what is the place of developing countries in the overall strategy for a world-wide Marxist-Leninist revolution? Secondly, what kind of revolution should it be and which class should lead it?

Lenin's discussion of the place of developing countries in the world Marxist revolution arose in the context of his theory of imperialism.[14] Marx and Engels had seen economic and political development as unfolding themselves in definite sequential stages that were controlled by historical forces. Both men considered it a remote possibility that this pattern could be violated or "skipped." In spite of the equivocation of Marx in later life, as evidenced by his observation while discussing Imperial Russia, that the developmental sequence might vary owing to "different historical surroundings,"[15] it is fair to say that he substantially held, especially in *Das Kapital,* to his thesis of historical inevitability and developmental sequences.

An implication of this thesis was that developing countries would have to pass through the internal strife of bourgeois capitalism. This explains Engels' defence of "progressive

13 Herbert Marcuse, *Soviet Marxism: A Critical Analysis,* (New York: Vintage Books, 1961), p. 15.

14 V. I. Lenin, *Imperialism: The Highest Stage of Capitalism,* (New York: International Publishers, 1939).

15. Karl Marx, "Russia's Pattern of Development," in Feuer, *Marx and Engels,* pp. 476-479.

imperialism."[16] If stretched further, an implication of this position would be that preindustrial societies were revolutionary inert.[17] Lenin's reinterpretation thus provided theoretical support for the view that the colonial world could and would play an important role in the world Marxist revolution. It was the inadequacy of Marxist programs in western Europe that suggested to Lenin the relevance of applying Marxism, albeit in a modified form, to developing countries.

One reason that Lenin advanced to explain the revolutionary impotence or embourgeoisement of the western proletariat was the controversial thesis that surplus value derived from colonial expansion was being used to "bribe" the proletariat. The relevant distinction to make was between exploiting and exploited nations. However, to assign an active revolutionary role to the developing countries was essentially to assign to the peasantry, by far the predominantly single, largest social category, an important role in the revolutionary process.[18] This aspect of Leninist thought was later emphasized and developed by Mao tse-Tung, Debray and Fanon, among others.

The Leninist shift of emphasis away from the proletariat to the peasantry, however, raised the important question of what kind of revolution it should be and which class should lead it. Lenin was of the view that the revolution would have to be in two stages — a bourgeois, nationalist revolution in which the proletariat would offer tactical support to the national bourgeoisie, followed by a socialist revolution after independence had been won. The two-stage strategy assumes that a coalition of various classes was necessary and indispensable to the success of the revolution. Though resting on

[16] Friedrich Engels, "Defence of Progressive Imperialism," in Feuer. *Marx and Engels*, p. 489.

[17] David Mitrany, *Marx Against the Peasant* (New York: Collier, 1961).

[18] M. Zaninovich, "Socialist Models and Developing Countries," in Beling and Totten, *Developing Nations: Quest for a Model*, pp. 116-151.

the support base of the proletariat and peasantry, the revolution should be spearheaded by a revolutionary party committed to the theory of democratic centralism.

Fanon's Indebtedness to Marxism-Leninism

What, then, is Fanon's indebtedness to the Marxist-Leninist theory of revolution? Has he departed from or modified that theory? To put it differently, what is his contribution to that theory? His indebtedness lies in his discussion of the role of political leadership in arousing revolutionary consciousness; of the necessity for a coalition of various social groups to oppose colonial rule; and in his analysis of imperialism. His basic divergence from Marxism-Leninism is in his analysis of the role of social classes in the revolutionary process.

Fanon places a high premium on the right kind of political leadership if the latent discontent of the colonized was to be channeled into revolutionary action. He emphasizes the social role of the political leader and educator in effecting the transition from individual to group liberation. The transition is therefore to be brought about by revolutionary praxis, which is to say that it must be carried out within the context of an organization.

The existence of an organization is, however, not enough in itself. The direction and orientation of the organization are crucial in that they bring into sharp focus the purpose of the organization. It is this that the revolutionary or socially committed individual relates to. It offers him or her a cognitive map in the search for social action and the liberation that constitutes the end and leitmotif of social action. What is even more important for Fanon is that an organization, such as the F.L.N., animated with a social purpose or ideology, becomes a vehicle for the social and political mobilization that is a *sine qua non* for raising the political and social consciousness of the masses. The role of political leadership is precisely to formulate and articulate the ideology of the organization.

Fanon seems unclear about the organizational structure or hierarchy that should be adopted by the revolutionary movement. His repeated emphasis on openness and access to information suggests that he is opposed to the Leninist organizational theory of decision making. Relevant in this connection is his analysis of political party organizations in sub-Saharan Africa as ineffective vehicles of mobilization.

If Fanon, therefore, characterizes the task of the political educator as that of mobilizing the masses for political action, he does not view the relationship as a one-sided one. A viable, enduring polity, particularly one in which the masses are not to regard government as an extraneous force, requires a two-way communication flow between leadership and followership:

> The men coming from the towns learn their lessons in the hard school of the people; and at the same time these men open classes in military and political education.[19]

Fanon is quite firm in his recommendation of decentralization as one aspect of this two-way communication:

> ...The people must understand what is at stake. Public business ought to be the business of the public. So the necessity of creating a large number of well-informed nuclei at the bottom crops up again. Too often, in fact, we are content to establish national organizations at the top and always in the capital.... But if one takes the trouble to investigate what is behind the office in the capital, if you go into the inner room where the reports ought to be, you will be shocked by the emptiness, the blank spaces and the bluff. There must be a basis; there must be cells that supply content and life. The masses should be able to meet together, discuss, propose and receive directions. The citizens should be able to speak, to express themselves, and to put forward new ideas. The

[19] Fanon, *Wretched of the Earth,* p. 127.

> branch meeting and the committee meetings are liturgical acts. They are privileged occasions given to a human being to listen and speak. At each meeting, the brain increases its means of participation and the eye discovers a landscape more and more in keeping with human dignity.[20]

Fanon seems, therefore, to have rejected the Leninist notion of centralized decision making. Yet it is not that Leninism is against participation in public affairs or in decision making by the masses. To the extent to which there is this concern with centralized decision making and participation in Leninism, there is an apparent contradiction. But, as David Lane has suggested, "the contradiction in Lenin's thought was between what was practical and necessary, given various forms of political and social constraints, and what was desirable and possible under ideal conditions."[21] The key to partly resolving this contradiction lies in Lenin's vague distinction between bureaucracy, which he condemns, and management which he thinks is indispensable to the functioning of any organization.[22]

One should, therefore, not too readily read authoritarian implications into Lenin's thought. Viewed in this light, the problem becomes one of how to prevent oligarchic structures dictated by the exigencies of a war of national liberation, and reflected in the authority structures of the regime against which the revolutionaries are struggling, from becoming perpetuated in the new regime.[23] It seems to me that this is indeed Fanon's concern. In any case, his discussion of the role of the political educator places him in the Marxist-Leninist tradition, for that tradition from Marx to Mao and Che

[20] Ibid., pp. 194-195.

[21] David Lane, "Leninism as an Ideology of Soviet Development," in Emmanuel de Kadt and Gavin Williams, *Sociology and Development*, (London: Tavistock Publications, 1974), p. 31.

[22] Ibid., p. 30.

[23] For a discussion of aspects of this problem, see Milovan Djilas.

Guevara has always seen in the peasantry an extremely important revolutionary force that, on account of its incapacity for independent revolutionary action, would necessarily fall under the influence of middle-class revolutionaries or the proletariat.

Fanon's call for a coalition of various social groups in the colonies to oppose colonial rule is also in the Marxist-Leninist tradition. He realizes that none of the social groups in the colony, acting by itself, can transform the colonial situation. This is why he suggests a coalition of disenchanted elements of the national bourgeoisie, the peasantry, and the lumpen-proletariat. But, as has been made clear above, the coalition must find its base at the grassroots level. Régis Debray's view on this issue in the Latin American context is similar to that of Fanon. Debray argues that it is inevitable that the national bourgeoisie should be integrated with the anti-imperial movement.[24]

Fanon's position in this respect must be emphasized if one is not to confuse or equate, as Jack Woodis has done,[25] Fanon's analysis of the political behaviour of the African middle class and proletariat with a denial of their revolutionary *potential* as a force for revolutionary social change in postcolonial Africa. Fanon realizes that in the scheme of things, and particularly in the nation-building process, the middle class (usually intellectuals, teachers, lawyers, technocrats, bureaucrats, engineers, medical doctors, journalists, and students), must and should play an important part. Fanon condemns the middle class because of its failure "to put at the people's disposal the intellectual and technical capital it has snatched when going through the colonial universities."[26]

[24] Régis Debray, *Strategy for Revolution: Essays on Latin America* (New York: Monthly Review Press, 1970), pp. 71-81.

[25] Jack Woodis, *New Theories of Revolution: A Commentary on the Views of Frantz Fanon, Regis Debray and Herbert Marcuse* (New York: International Publishers, 1972), pp. 84-100.

[26] Fanon, *Wretched of the Earth,* p. 150.

Fanon's discussion of the imperative of a coalition of forces raises the question of a two-phased strategy of socialist revolution to which reference was made above. Lenin had suggested and the Second International had favored a two-phased strategy. Fanon's position runs counter to that of Lenin:

> In underdeveloped countries, the bourgeoisie should not be allowed to find the conditions necessary for its existence and its growth. In other words, the combined effort of the masses led by a party and of intellectuals who are highly conscious and armed with revolutionary principles ought to bar the way to this useless and harmful middle class. The theoretical question that for the last fifty years has been raised whenever the history of underdeveloped countries is under discussion — whether or not the bourgeois phase can be skipped — ought to be answered in the field of revolutionary action, and not by logic.[27]

Fanon rests his position on his analysis of the national bourgeoisie as "a sort of little greedy caste, avid and voracious... only too glad to accept the dividends that the former colonial power hands out to it."[28] This is why the bourgeois nationalist revolution, led by revolutionary-conscious elements of the middle class, must be simultaneously a socialist revolution. Debray, again with the Latin American context in mind, seems to support Fanon's position:

> to say that it has fallen to the proletariat and to the peasantry to accomplish the historic task of the bourgeoisie is to say that the alternative today is not between [peaceful] bourgeois revolution and [violent] socialist revolution... but between revolution *tout court* and counter-revolution.[29]

[27] Ibid., pp. 174-175.
[28] Ibid., p. 175.
[29] Debray, *Strategy for Revolution*, p. 147.

As to whose views are more plausible, Fanon and Debray's or Lenin's, this is to be settled at the empirical, not theoretical, level. But the empirical evidence available is not very helpful in that it tends to support both views. There is, however, much plausibility to the observations of David Caute that, on balance, wherever the national bourgeoisie has acquired political power in the developing world it has tended to consolidate that power.[30] Jack Woodis, for example, supports the two-phased strategy, arguing with respect to Peru that

> there can be a phase, under bourgeois nationalist leadership, during which positive steps are taken to weaken imperialism and its semi-feudal and bourgeois allies, and which gives the working class and its allies a certain breathing space in which they can consolidate their forces, strengthen their organization and political influence, and so prepare the way for their assuming leadership of the revolution.[31]

The problem with the observation of Jack Woodis is that he does not confront the issue whether the bourgeoisie is also consolidating itself by its control of the state and the instruments of state coercion.

Fanon also draws upon the Marxist-Leninist theory of imperialism in developing his notion of revolution. His discussion of the necessity for a coalition of various social groups in the colonies is, for example, predicated on the Marxist-Leninist assumption that imperialist rule would bring normally hostile groups and classes together in the common pursuit of ending colonial rule. His indebtedness to Marxism-Leninism in this respect is reflected in his analysis of the attitude of the French Left in general to the Algerian war of national liberation. Not only did the French Left benefit from the surplus value extracted from the colonial relationship, but

30 Caute, *Fanon.*
31 Woodis, *New Theories of Revolution*, p. 244.

it also, like other Frenchmen, saw the war as essentially a national issue: "...it is no longer possible to back the colonized without at the same time opposing the national solution. The fight against colonialism becomes a fight against the nation."[32]

Fanon's Divergence from Marxism-Leninism

Let us now examine Fanon's contribution to the Marxist-Leninist theory of revolution. One way to approach this question is to indicate the extent of Fanon's divergence from that theory. The mere fact of divergence does not in itself indicate that Fanon rejects Marxism-Leninism. Reference was made above to Marcuse's observation that Marxism derives its vitality from the need to re-examine it from time to time, so that it will reflect and not dominate the vicissitudes of the class struggle. This was essentially what Lenin and Mao did. Fanon does not reject Marxism-Leninism, as his emphasis on the need to "stretch" Marxism in analyzing the colonial relationship shows. The relevant issue to raise, therefore, is about whether his modifications are so fundamental and radical as to constitute a virtual rejection of Marxism-Leninism.

Fanon diverges from Marxism-Leninism in his discussion of class political behaviour, particularly in terms of the class basis and composition of the revolutionary struggle in the Third World. An extended discussion of Fanon's analysis of class political behaviour is given in Chapter 7. The highly relevant issue of the relevance of class categories to the analysis of African politics is also discussed in that Chapter. The concern here is to indicate the nature of his divergence from Marxism-Leninism as well as the force of certain objections against him.

Fanon has been sharply attacked by a number of apparently Marxist-Leninist critics for assigning an in-

[32] Fanon, *Toward the African Revolution*, p. 78; Gendzier, *Frantz Fanon*, pp. 151-169, offers an interesting discussion of this aspect of Fanon's writings.

significant role to the proletariat in the revolutionary process. Similarly, he has been attacked by this group of critics for assigning revolutionary capability to both the lumpen-proletariat and the peasantry. These objections are on both theoretical and empirical grounds.

From a theoretical angle, one must distinguish between Fanon's thesis that the African peasantry constitutes the backbone, the main force of the African revolution, and his thesis that, since it is a privileged and pampered class, the African proletariat lacks revolutionary consciousness and therefore should have no place or, at best, a secondary one in the coalition of social groups to carry out the revolution. While some of his critics like Nguyen Nghe are prepared to accept the first thesis, they find his second thesis heretical.

On an empirical level, Fanon's rejection of the proletariat as a revolutionary force is based on his analysis of its involvement with the colonial and neocolonial economic system and his conclusion that the advantages it thereby derives from its involvement have led to the embourgeoisement of the African proletariat. This is Fanon's version of the "labor aristocracy" thesis. Fanon's assessment is similar to that which can be implicitly deduced from the work of scholars such as Eric Wolf and Barrington Moore who have studied the role of various classes in socioeconomic and political changes. Wolf's study of the Mexican, Chinese, Cuban, Vietnamese, Algerian, and Russian revolutions assigns an insignificant role to the proletariat while the attempt of Moore to chart three historical routes to modernization focuses on coalitions and alliances between the bourgeoisie, the landed aristocracy, and the peasantry, with little again said about the proletariat.[33]

Nguyen Nghe challenges Fanon's assessment on a number of points. First, he rightly points out that Fanon's discussion is

[33] Eric Wolf, *Peasant Wars of the Twentieth Century,* New York: Harper and Row, 1969); Barrington Moore, *Social Origins of Dictatorship and Democracy,* (Boston, Massachusetts: Little, Brown and Co., 1966).

vitiated by a failure to distinguish between types of proletariat. Fanon should have distinguished genuinely proletarian elements like dockers and miners from petite-bourgeois ones like interpreters, taxi drivers, and clerks. Secondly, he denies Fanon's labor aristocracy thesis and contends that if the proletariat is privileged at all, it is in the sense that by virtue of its being an oppressed and exploited class, it is well-placed to overturn the colonial system:

> La classe ouvrière dans les colonies ne constitute pas une classe privilégiée au sens on l'entend Fanon, c'est-à-dire choyée par les colons; elle est privilégiée au sens revolutionnaire du mot, par le fait qu'elle est la mieux placée pour voir de près les mecanismes de l'exploitation coloniale, pour consevoir le chemin de l'avenir pour l'ensemble de la societé.[34]

Nghe, therefore, affirms the revolutionary potential and role of the proletariat in Asia and Africa. It is his claim that if left to themselves, the peasantry would not develop revolutionary consciousness, a task which is the duty of the urban-based militant to carry out by instigating the peasantry to revolutionary political action. Nghe's criticisms have been expressed and further developed by Jack Woodis, Romano Ledda, and Emile Braundi, among others.[35] How weighty are these criticisms?

Let us consider the issue of the alleged privileged and "pampered" position of the African proletariat. Jack Woodis provides impressive documentary and statistical evidence to show that the African working class is economically and socially depressed. But Woodis, Nghe, and Ledda do not

[34] Nguyen Nghe, "Frantz Fanon et les Problèmes de l'Indépendance," p. 31.

[35] Woodis, *New Theories of Revolution,* pp. 101-175; R. Ledda, "Social Classes and Political Struggle," *International Socialist Journal,* No. 22 (August, 1967); E. Braundi, "Neocolonialism and the Class Struggle," *International Socialist Register,* No. 1 (February/March, 1964).

address what Fanon regards as the more important question, i.e., whether the proletariat, in virtue of the nature of its involvement with the colonial and neocolonial economy, enjoys a higher standard of living than the peasantry.

Fanon's proposition is not that all is a bed of roses for the African proletariat. Rather, his thesis is that to the extent to which the urban areas are developed at the expense of the countryside, the African proletariat stands to gain more in a material sense than the peasantry. The point is that, as is argued in the next chapter, Fanon does not define class simply in terms of relation to productive forces.

It is not enough to argue that the African proletariat is socially and economically depressed. It also has to be shown that it is worse off as a general social category than the peasantry. It is, of course, a long road from the fact of immiseration to its awareness by either the proletariat or peasantry and then to revolutionary action. The transition as Fanon and his critics will argue is to be effected by political organization.

Two important critical observations should be offered at this juncture. Nghe is right in suggesting that Fanon should have distinguished genuinely proletarian from petty-bourgeois elements of the African working class. Fanon can also be criticized for overlooking the factor of labor migration and the existence of a peasant labor force in Africa. This oversight is, perhaps, due to his setting up the urbanized union worker as his model. The second critical observation is that Fanon should have distinguished between trade union leadership and its followership. Such a distinction should make clear middle-class infiltration of the upper echelons of African trade unions. On the basis of such a distinction, one can perhaps suggest that if the African proletariat is a revolutionary inert mass, a class-in-itself, the reason is partly that it has not been provided with revolutionary political leadership.

Fanon's thesis about the proletariat is partly based on his distinction between political and revolutionary consciousness.

In refuting Fanon, Woodis points to the important role played by the African proletariat in the independence struggle in most African countries. Yet, Fanon does not deny the involvement of the African proletariat in nationalist politics. In fact, in discussing the role of African trade unions in pressuring colonial and postcolonial administration for political and constitutional reforms, Fanon refers to their political consciousness.[36]

It seems that what Fanon means by "political consciousness," is the suggestion that by engaging in reformist, constitutional politics, the working-class leadership, like the middle class, is forced to compromise with the colonial administration. He further argues that the confrontation between the trade unions and ruling regimes in the postcolonial period is concerned *not* with altering productive relations and modes of production of the neocolonial system, but with how much benefit each class is to derive from it. This analysis of the status quo orientation of the trade union movement is also linked to its failure to establish links with the peasantry:

> These little islands of the mother country which the towns constitute in the colonial structure are deeply conscious of trade-union action; the fortress of colonialism which the capital represents staggers under their blows. But the "interior" — the mass of country dwellers — knows nothing of this conflict.[37]

Reference has already been made to the problem of the peasantry in Marxist-Leninist thought. This is another area where Fanon has taken an unorthodox Marxist-Leninist position. By elevating the peasantry as a potential revolutionary force he, in effect, rejects the notion of a proletarian vanguard.

[36] Fanon, *Wretched of the Earth*, pp. 121-123.
[37] Ibid., p. 122.

The concept of the peasantry in Fanon derives basically from the peasantry's economic position in the colonial and neocolonial economic systems. The concept also derives from two qualities which Fanon identifies in the peasantry — peasant authenticity and peasant radicalism. Yet Fanon also realizes the limitations of these two qualities. In particular peasant authenticity can give rise to reactionary, conservative political action.[38] One, therefore, finds in Fanon an awareness of the paradoxical nature of peasant society, the coexistence of conservatism and radicalism.[39]

Fanon's emphasis on the peasantry as a revolutionary force raises the question of strategy, namely what constitutes the setting, the battlefield for a socialist revolution? Fanon's answer, based on his Algerian experience, is that the revolution will begin and structure itself militarily in the countryside from where it will filter into the towns through uprooted peasants, disgruntled intellectuals and the lumpenproletariat.[40]

It seems, therefore, that Fanon accepts the Marxist-Leninist model of a small, dedicated, trained, and politically organized corps of revolutionaries, leading their followers in the revolutionary struggle. His departure from the Marxist-Leninist position lies in his equivocation about the need for a vanguard party and whether such a party necessarily has to be a political party, more specifically a Communist party. He shares an identity of views in this respect with Debray.

Woodis has criticized Fanon for failing to distinguish between "a *main* force" and "the *leading* force or principal revolutionary force" in the revolutionary process.[41] Although he grants that the peasantry is a "main" force, Woodis rejects the claim, which he attributes to Fanon, that the African

[38] Ibid., pp.109-113.

[39] Marie B. Perinbam, "Fanon and the Revolutionary Peasantry: The Algerian Case," *Journal of Modern African Studies,* Vol. 2, No. 3 (September, 1973).

[40] Fanon, *Wretched of the Earth,* p. 129.

[41] Woodis, *New Theories of Revolution,* p. 63 (emphasis in original).

peasantry is *the* leading revolutionary force. The same criticism is to be found in Nghe and Ledda, both of whom emphasize the need for political leadership provided by the urban proletariat. As Ledda states: "the present situation in rural areas is such that... only an *outside* force will be capable of carrying out the absolutely essential but difficult job of mobilizing and organizing the peasant masses."[42]

But, *pace* Woodis, Nghe and Ledda, one ought to read Fanon carefully on the question of the peasantry. Fanon's concern about the paradox of peasant society was noted above. He was not so naïve as to think that the peasantry, acting alone, could effect or lead a revolution. Political and economic power as well as the control of the state apparatus necessarily requires political and organizational skill and resources that Fanon realizes are lacking in the peasantry. This is why he underlines the need for a political educator:

> To hold a responsible position in an underdeveloped country is to know that in the end everything depends on the education of the masses, on the raising of the level of thought, and on what we are too quick to call "political education."[43]

If Fanon is unorthodox from a Marxist-Leninist perspective in assigning revolutionary potential to the African peasantry, he is even more so in also ascribing it to the lumpenproletariat. The lumpenproletariat provides the "urban spearhead" of the revolution and comprises "the pimps, hooligans, the unemployed and the criminals..."[44] Belonging to neither town nor country, the lumpenproletariat are rootless; they are yet to find their bearings in the city. This is why they are dangerous. But they also constitute a potential source of recruits for the revolution.

42 Ledda, "Social Classes and Political Struggle," p. 575 (emphasis in original).

43 Fanon, *Wretched of the Earth*, p. 197.

44 Ibid., p. 130.

Fanon, however, recognizes that, like the peasantry, the lumpenproletariat can be reactionary:

> In Algeria, it is the lumpenproletariat which provided the harkis and the messalists; in Angola it supplied the road openers who nowadays precede the Portuguese armed columns... while at Leopoldville the Congo's enemies made use of it to organize "spontaneous" mass meetings against Lumumba.[45]

Fanon's prescription for this reactionary aspect of the behaviour of the lumpenproletariat is that the political educator, i.e., the revolutionary leadership must pay "the fullest attention" to it so that its potentiality can be channeled to revolutionary action. Fanon's position is therefore contrary to that of Karl Marx, who dismissed the lumpenproletariat of his day. Peter Worsley has suggested that, in this respect, Fanon's position is similar to that of nineteenth-century anarchists like Bakunin, who believed in the potential of the lumpenproletariat to destroy the social order.[46]

Woodis vigorously denies Fanon's claim about the revolutionary potential of the lumpenproletariat. He claims that Fanon's assertion is unsupported and that the few examples offered by Fanon point to the reactionary nature of the lumpenproletariat.[47] It is, however, tendentious for Woodis to claim that Fanon offers no examples to back up his assertion.

First, Fanon's thesis about the revolutionary potential of the lumpenproletariat is based on his experience of Algers.[48] Secondly, Fanon explicitly refers to Kenya and the Belgian Congo (now Zaire) as examples of colonial territories where the colonial administration had to enforce "intimidatory

[45] Ibid., p. 137.

[46] Peter Worsley, "Frantz Fanon and the 'Lumpenproletariat'," in Ralph Miliband and John Saville, *The Socialist Register, 1972* (London: The Merlin Press, 1972), p. 207.

[47] Woodis, *New Theories of Revolution*, pp. 79-81.

[48] Worsley, "Fanon and 'Lumpenproletariat'," p. 211.

measures against the lumpenproletariat," presumably because of its "disturbing the social order."[49] Thirdly, even if it is correct that Fanon fails to provide concrete examples of the revolutionary activities of the lumpenproletariat, it can still be argued that Fanon's point is precisely that the lumpenproletariat has always been neglected by the national bourgeoisie and proletariat in much the same way that they neglected the peasantry. Social direction and political education are of the utmost importance and it is against this background that Fanon's thesis of the revolutionary lumpenproletariat should be viewed.

A weakness in Fanon's analysis is his failure to distinguish, as Colin Leys was later to do, between hard-core corrupted lumpenproletariat, e.g., pimps and prostitutes, and migrant or urbanized peasants who move between town and country.[50] It is these migrant workers who, presumably on account of their perception of the glaring inequality between the affluence of the city and rural poverty, are likely to possess the revolutionary fervors so graphically described by Fanon.

A similar distinction is made by Amilcar Cabral in a penetrating analysis of the social structure in Guiné-Bissau. Cabral puts forward the claim that "the importance of this urban experience (for the lumpen proletariat) lies in the fact that it allows comparison; this is the key stimulant required for the awakening of consciousness."[51] Cabral thinks that it is this lack of an "urban experience" that, in the context of Guiné-Bissau, makes it so difficult for the peasantry to join the revolutionary movement.

[49] Fanon, *Wretched of the Earth,* p. 129.

[50] Colin Leys, "The Politics of Economic Modernization in Theory and Practice: Interpreting the Kenya Experience," paper read at the Eighth World Congress of the International Political Science Association, Paris (31 August - 5 September, 1970), pp. 12-13.

[51] Amilcar Cabral, *Revolution in Guinea: Selected Texts,* translated and edited by Richard Handyside (New York: Monthly Review Press, 1961), pp. 62-63.

Another area of divergence is Fanon's implied rejection of the Marxist-Leninist notion of an international class solidarity. It is implied in the sense that it is not clear whether Fanon is ambivalent about it or that he totally rejects it. This is why there is some point in the observation of Peter Worsley that the tension between the revolt of class and the revolt of color is a characteristic feature of Black protest literature in the African Diaspora.[52] Fanon's ambivalence is based on his analysis of the racial factor in the colonial situation as reflected in the nationalistic attitude of the French Left on the colonial question.

Put differently, Fanon's ambivalence implies a rejection of part of the historical materialism of Marx in that Fanon is suggesting that socio-political and productive relations in the colonial situation should not be viewed as merely a reflection of the dominant bourgeois class interests, but also as a reflection of the racial aspirations of the dominant White race. The problem then becomes one of whether Fanon thinks class considerations should be subordinated to considerations of race or that he views the behaviour of the French Left as a transitory phenomenon or a form of false consciousness.

These areas of divergence should, however, be viewed as complementary to Marxism-Leninism, and as indicative of the personal experiences of Fanon and the historico-cultural situation of colonized peoples. Fanon accepts the basic Marxist assumption that the philosophic enterprise must be directed toward what Marx once described as "practical-critical activity."

On the Relationship Between Violence and Revolution in Marxism-Leninism and Fanon

What is the relationship between physical violence and revolution? Is violence a defining characteristic of revolution?

[52] Peter Worsley, "Frantz Fanon: Revolutionary Theories," *Studies on the Left*, Vol. 6, No. 3 (May/June, 1960), p. 32.

Popular opinion identifies or associates revolutions with violence. The mere mention of revolution raises in one's mind a spectre of destruction, brutality, and carnage, a reaction which, as John Dunn has pointed out, is partly fed by the pronouncements of revolutionaries.[53] An examination of a sample of the relevant social science literature will show that the notion of violence is often built into the meaning of revolution.[54] The very notion of a non violent revolution is, according to this view, a contradiction in terms. Is it?

What is the Marxist-Leninist formulation of this relationship and how much does Fanon have in common with it? Marxism-Leninism regards violence as an accompanying characteristic of revolution. Violence plays an essentially instrumental role in the revolutionary process. This means that it is plausible to argue that Marxism-Leninism need not regard the notion of a nonviolent revolution as an absurdity or a contradiction in terms. It is plausible because of the tension between the determinisms (historical and economic) of Marxism-Leninism and its insistence on praxis and the actors' will in hastening the proletarian revolution.

Marxism-Leninism views violence as an evil necessity called for by the violence of the bourgeois state apparatus. As Lenin puts it, "the replacement of the bourgeois by the proletarian state is impossible without a violent revolution."[55] Marx and Engels express similar views about the inevitability of a violent revolution in *The Communist Manifesto.* However,

[53] John Dunn, *Modern Revolutions: An Introduction to the Analysis of a Political Phenomena* (London: Cambridge, 1972), p. 12.

[54] Gurr, *Why Men Rebel;* Chalmers Johnson, *Revolution and the Social System* (Stanford, California: Hoover Institution, 1964); Harry Eckstein, "On the Etiology of Internal Wars," *History and Theory,* Vol. 4, No. 2 (1965).

[55] V. I. Lenin, *State and Revolution* (New York: International Publishers, 1932), p. 20.

in his discussion of England and the United States Marx sometimes gives the impression that a peaceful, nonviolent revolution was feasible in the two countries.[56] It is this ambivalence in Marx that has led to a division among his followers into "moderates," advocating the peaceful transformation of society and "extremists" whose position is that change must be through violent revolution.

How would Fanon characterize the relationship? Fanon's position is to some extent similar to that of Marxist-Leninists in that he regards physical violence as an accompanying characteristic of revolution, serving a partly instrumental role. Like Marxist-Leninists he also holds that violence is necessarily a defensive mechanism used by the oppressed. In other words, Fanon, like the Marxist-Leninist, looks upon physical violence as a structural necessity.

Fanon's distinction between true and false decolonization points to one connection which he sees between revolution and violence, one that is not obvious in Marxism-Leninism. This is Fanon's belief that a violent revolution is likely to be more "authentic" than a nonviolent one. It is his thesis that the future course of the revolution is, in an important sense, a function of whether it involves physical violence. This is also why he proposes in the context of Algeria that violent revolutions can be regenerative in that they can create "new" individuals and a "new" social consciousness.

Although this conception of a regenerative revolutionary violence does not receive as much emphasis in Marxism-Leninism as in Fanon, it is implied in Engels' reference to "the immense moral and spiritual impetus which has resulted from every victorious revolution."[57]

[56] M. G. Stekloff, *History of the First International* (New York: M. Lawrence, Ltd. 1928).

[57] Friedrich Engels, *Anti-Duhring*, quoted in Lenin, *State and Revolution*, p. 19.

Summary

Fanon's discussion of revolution is, broadly speaking, within the Marxist-Leninist tradition. But his main point of divergence from that tradition lies in his discussion of social classes in the revolutionary process. Fanon looks upon revolution as involving more than the violent or nonviolent overthrow of a political regime.

He views a revolution as a process of fundamental social change. This conception of revolution as a process serves a critical purpose for Fanon; it enables him to discriminate between true and false decolonization and the different mobilizational structures and regime types that can be deduced from either type of decolonization.

III

THE POLITICAL SOCIOLOGY OF POSTCOLONIAL AFRICA

Chapter 6

COMMITMENT AND THE MORAL BASIS OF POLITICAL ACTION

Morality and the Perspective of Methodological Individualism in Fanon

How does Fanon relate morality to political action or practice? A suggestive approach to answering this question is to focus on Fanon's discussion of the closely-related notions of *commitment* and *social responsibility*. These two notions, particularly commitment, must, however, be set in the wider context of Fanon's views about human nature and the rational basis of human action.

Put differently, what this means is that Fanon is concerned with what human beings make of themselves. To be concerned with what men make of themselves is necessarily to assume that men have a purpose in life. If this purpose is to be achieved, it is imperative to carry out a carefully reasoned analysis of man's social existence. It is this reasoned analysis that provides an orientation as well as the direction by means of which man's purpose can be achieved. This must be part of Fanon's meaning in observing that

> To educate man to be *actional*, preserving in all his relations his respect for the basic values that constitute a human world, is the prime task of him who, having taken thought, prepares to act.[1]

What this quotation brings out is Fanon's view, which has

[1] Fanon, *Black Skin, White Masks*, p. 222 (emphasis in original).

been elaborated elsewhere,[2] that philosophy should be used to organize and mobilize one's cognition of self and others. Philosophy is more than an intellectual endeavor; it is also a practical activity which can and should be used to direct one's personal life as well as one's relationship to others. But what is the basis for human action and conduct? In what does the rationality of human conduct consist?

Fanon provides some answers to this question and he does so from what is basically the perspective of methodological individualism. This perspective assumes that individuals are the basic unit of analysis. These individuals pursue their activities within a societal context that regulates and controls their behavior through the application of sanctions and the organization of social institutions to determine and designate those to decide and implement sanctions.[3]

While this perspective can reinforce the status quo, it also has implications for the rejection and replacement of the status quo because, by juxtaposing the individual within a societal context, the concern is with the effect of social structures and institutions on the individual — what opportunities are provided and what constraints are imposed by structures and institutions in the way of individuals realizing their interests. The assumption is, therefore, that individuals are capable of rationality, are self-interested, and will choose action strategies that will enhance their net well-being within the institutional networks provided by society. Failure to achieve this or a perception of the impossibility of doing so, given existing

[2] L. Adele Jinadu, "Philosophy and Ideology in Some Political Theorists of the Black Experience," *Journal of Business and Social Studies*, forthcoming.

[3] For the model of man and assumptions of methodological individualism see Vincent Ostrom, *Alternative Approaches to the Study of Public Organizational Arrangements* (Bloomington, Indiana: Workshop in Political Theory and Policy Analysis, 1974), pp. 7-8; James M. Buchanan and Gordon Tullock, *The Calculus of Consent: Logical Foundations of Constitutional Democracy* (Ann Arbor, Michigan: University of Michigan Press, 1965), pp. 11-14; Anthony Downs, *An Economic Theory of Democracy* (New York: Harper and Row, 1957).

social structures and institutions, is one reason for individuals seeking redress *outside* of the framework of those social structures by resorting to revolutionary activities.

Let us pursue this a little further with respect to Fanon, as a prelude to a more systematic examination of his concern with relating morality to political action. Fanon thinks that the rationality of human conduct and action is to be sought in two areas, although it is unclear whether he realizes that these two areas can be mutually exclusive or at least need to be reconciled.

First, he contends that the rationality of human action is to be sought in the nature and goals of collective human life. Man is, above all, a social animal with an incredible capacity for learning and self-improvement. Collective human life must be viewed, however, as primarily an attempt at regulating the interaction of individuals and groups. The tendency is for the individual to be ascribed a group identity, something that is also facilitated by the individual's need for reinforcement, especially in the face of scarcity, and the need to join with others to deal with the scarcity problem. There is necessarily a tension in this relationship, precisely because, once individuals acquire group membership and characteristics, they are viewed not as individuals but as group members. Fanon deals at great length with this issue in *Black Skin, White Masks:*

> It is through the effort to recapture the self and to scrutinize the self; it is through the lasting tension of their freedom that men will be able to create the ideal conditions of existence for a human world.
> Superiority? Inferiority?
> Why not the quite simple attempt to touch the other, to feel the other, to explain the other to myself?[4]

With respect to the colonial situation, for example, Fanon contends that it is inevitable to view the individual in group,

[4] Fanon, *Black Skin, White Masks,* p. 231.

i.e., racial terms. This is because of the polarization of collective life along racial lines. Challenges to, as well as the defense of, the nature and organization of collective life in such circumstances must also be viewed in group terms.

Fanon is, however, concerned to situate the analysis of the nature of collective life in the individual mind. He contends that each person is to judge for himself or herself what the nature of collective life is, what it should be, and what should be done or not done to change it. This, as will be argued later, is the thrust of his notion of commitment. Fanon realizes the importance of group attachment as a basis for human organization; but he is also acutely aware of the tendency of such attachments to derogate from the individual's freedom. This is why it is so important that one should not slavishly attach oneself to one's group:

> One duty alone: That of not renouncing my freedom through my choices.
> I have no wish to be the victim of the *Fraud* of a black world.[5]

The second area in which Fanon's concern with the rationality of human conduct and action manifests itself is in his discussion of psychoneuroses. The concern here is with the character and development of the individual. Fanon's reasoning proceeds on the assumption that human beings are creators and that the process of creation is essentially an introspective and reflective one:

> I should constantly remind myself that the real *leap* consists in introducing invention into existence. In the world through which I travel, I am endlessly creating myself.[6]

[5] Ibid., p. 229 (emphasis in original).
[6] Ibid.

What this means, as Fanon makes clear in an earlier passage, is that "society, unlike biochemical processes, cannot escape human influences. Man is what brings society into being."[7]

If Fanon views the rationality of man's social existence or collective life as involving creation and *recreation* through the decisions and actions of self-conscious human beings, he is also concerned that the historical process — which is what creation and recreation is all about — should contribute to and express what he considers should be man's self-worth. Fanon's position is based on the philosophical notion of respect for the person as such. This notion is further elaborated in Fanon's discussion of social responsibility to be examined later in this chapter.

The important point to note at this juncture is Fanon's concern that the interests and needs of the individual should not be subordinated to those of some larger, abstract or fictitious collective group. Social institutions and structures must be judged in terms of their impact on the individual.

Although human beings are creators, they are also corrupters and manipulators of their creations. The corruption and manipulation of social institutions and structures will be invariably justified or rationalized in terms of a higher social good or end. Yet social critics, indeed every human being, must look beyond the claim of some social good or end to the consequences and impact of various social structures and policy decisions on the individual. As Fanon states so well:

> The function of a social structure is to set up institutions to serve man's needs. A society that drives its members to desperate solutions is a nonviable society, a society to be replaced. It is the duty of the citizen to say this. No professional morality, no class solidarity, no desire to

[7] Ibid., p. 11.

> wash the family linen in private, can have a prior claim. No pseudo-national mystification can prevail against the requirement of reason.[8]

It is from this basic perspective of methodological individualism that Fanon condemns colonialism and the successor regimes to colonialism in postcolonial Africa. He has a passionate concern for humanity and the human condition. This concern makes him uneasy in a hypocritical world where lip service is paid to the ideals of freedom, social justice, and equality:

> Leave this Europe where they are never done talking of Man, yet murder men everywhere they find them.[9]

It is also this concern with humanity that is underlined by Fanon's bringing moral concerns and perspectives to bear on man's social existence. The vitality and strength of his position on this issue must also be set in the wider perspective of his critical spirit and of the following remarks at the end of *Black Skin, White Masks:*

> Was my freedom not given to me then in order to build the world of the *You?*
> At the conclusion of this study, I want the world to recognize, with me, the open door of every consciousness.
> My final prayer: O my body make of me always a man who questions.[10]

Morality and Political Action in Fanon

Fanon's writings attest to the strength of the moral impulses that led him to criticize and reject colonial society,

[8] Fanon, *Toward the African Revolution,* pp. 53-54.
[9] Fanon, *Wretched of the Earth,* p. 311.
[10] Fanon, *Black Skin, White Masks,* p. 232 (emphasis in original).

colonial rule, as well as postcolonial African societies and governments. His criticisms in this respect are essentially also moral criticisms. This is the didactic dimension of Fanon's political thought. In subsequent sections of this Chapter, focus will be on synthesizing fundamental moral concepts used by Fanon, concepts such as *commitment, collective responsibility,* and *ethical relativity,* with the aim of highlighting the individualistic underpinnings of Fanon's discussion of these concepts.

What this suggests is the view of Fanon as a humanist who is reacting against, and therefore also attempting to find solutions to, such evils as poverty, exploitation, and kindred sources of human suffering and man's inhumanity to man. Of him it is appropriate to observe that he has a passionate concern for, and commitment to humanity and the human condition as is reflected in his "quite simple attempt to touch the other, to explain the other to myself."[11]

This is to affirm that Fanon sees a close and strong connection between morality and politics. For him, political action, viewed as efforts to tackle and resolve problems and issues concerned with governing and scarcity management, is ultimately a moral activity. Put differently, political action is a moral activity precisely because it involves choosing among competing values for ameliorating and improving what Geoffrey Warnock has described as the human predicament.[12]

There is, therefore, no separating of politics and political action from morality for Fanon. His condemnation of ruling regimes in postcolonial Africa, so trenchantly expressed in *Wretched of the Earth,* is couched in moral terms. He castigates these regimes for their totalitarian tendencies and their

[11] Ibid., p. 231.

[12] G. J. Warnock, *The Object of Morality* (London: Methuen, 1971), Ch. 2; see also his *Contemporary Moral Philosophy* (London: Macmillan, 1967), Ch. 5. Also Bernard Williams, *Morality: An Introduction to Ethics* (New York: Harper, 1972), pp. 79-88.

"wrong" policy options, which is to suggest that the individual citizen's welfare is hardly the concern of the political class:

> It makes a display. It justles people and bullies them, thus intimating to the citizen that he is in continual danger. The single party is the modern form of the dictatorship of the bourgeoisie, unmasked, unpainted, unscrupulous, and cynical.[13]

Fanon's criticism of colonialism also points to the close connection that he sees between morality and politics. He rejects the argument that colonialism is progressive because such a debatable claim is irrelevant to a consideration of whether colonialism is ever morally justifiable, both intrinsically and particularly in terms of its consequences for the individual. As he puts it, "White civilization and European culture have forced an existential deviation on the Negro."[14]

Fanon's linking of morality and politics can be expressed in another way. Viewed in a very broad sense to include culture and ideology, for example, a shared morality is a *sine qua non* for societal cohesion or consensus-building. A shared morality can, of course, be a form of false consciousness; nevertheless, it can also create a mutuality of obligation that is so basic and vital to the creation and sustenance of viable social structures. It provides governors with a rationalization or justification for their positions of authority, and their exercise of authority on behalf of others.

A shared morality also places limits on what the governors can do. It arouses expectations on the part of the governed, provides them with a basis on which they can make demands, assess the performance of, and exercise some form of control over their governors. Any appeal against the governors or criticism of prevailing conditions within the societal boundary delimited by the shared morality must be made within the

[13] Fanon, *Wretched of the Earth*, p. 165.

[14] Fanon, *Black Skin, White Masks*, p. 231.

province of the shared morality. This is to say that conflict can be settled and conflicting or divergent interests reconciled through adversary procedures established by the shared morality.

Where there is virtually no shared morality, as expressed for instance in the absence of a mutuality of obligation as between governors and the governed, the resort is unavoidably to force by the underclass to express needs, wants, and opportunities which are neither provided nor satisfied by the society in question. The demand for such needs, wants, and opportunities necessarily involves a moral critique of the socioeconomic and political structures constituted by such a society. It is to offer an ethical or moral justification for its substitution, unavoidably by violent means.

This in effect turns on the possibility for effecting change from within or outside of procedural mechanisms available for reconciling or arbitrating demands in a society. Where there is some shared morality or mutuality of obligation, Fanon's thesis is that one can expect change from within, although there is bound to be resistance from those who want to perpetuate the status quo. Thus with respect to the United States he observes:

> The American Negro is cast in a different play. In the United States, the Negro battles and is battled. There are laws that, little by little, are invalidated under the Constitution. There are other laws that forbid certain forms of discrimination. And we can be sure that nothing is going to be given free.[15]

Fanon's critique of ruling classes as well as the socioeconomic and political order in colonial and postcolonial Africa is premised precisely on the absence of a shared morality or mutuality of obligation between governors and governed. This comes out clearly in his critique of the settler society in Algeria,

[15] Ibid., p. 221.

a critique which is highly pertinent and relevant to settler societies in Zimbabwe, Namibia, and South Africa. It is because a shared morality is absent in such societies that Fanon contends that "in decolonization there is therefore the need of a complete calling in question of the colonial situation."[16] As Fanon states:

> The test cases of civil liberty whereby both whites and blacks in America try to drive back racial discrimination have very little in common in their principles and objectives with the heroic fight of the Angolan people against the detestable Portuguese colonialism.[17]

Fanon's critique is, in other words, premised on his identification of needs and opportunities that are not and cannot be provided, given the nature of the societies in question. What those needs are and how Fanon comes to identify them is a problematical issue. It seems that what he has done is to set up negative criteria in that he criticizes colonial and postcolonial regimes and societies for their failings and shortcomings, their glaringly unjust modes of socioeconomic and political organizations and their failure to put "into practice a program with even a minimum humanist content."[18] The critical effort is thus essentially ethical in nature, concerned as it is not so much with putting forward alternatives, desirable as it is, as with analyzing what is morally wrong and suggesting the moral imperative for change.[19]

Commitment, Methodological Individualism, and the Rationality of Political Action in Fanon

According to Fanon there is necessarily an evaluative and prescriptive dimension to commitment. To say that one is

[16] Fanon, *Wretched of the Earth,* p. 37.
[17] Ibid., p. 216.
[18] Ibid., p. 163.
[19] Ibid., pp. 148-205.

committed to X is to say that one prefers X to Y and that one must act to bring X into existence. It seems then that Fanon's notion of commitment is premised on two factors. First, to be committed is to entertain certain beliefs about the nature of certain social phenomena. Secondly, to be committed is also to be dedicated to carrying out actions dictated by those beliefs.

While what one does is important, it must have reference to and be predicated on one's beliefs. In other words, one's actions do not necessarily imply commitment to X. For one's action to imply commitment it must be based on and be consistent with one's beliefs about what one is committed to. This is important because A and B may perform the same actions while holding different beliefs or being committed to different things.

Fanon's notion of commitment, as he himself makes clear, bears a close affinity to Sartre's notion of committed literature, or *literature engagée.*[20] According to Fanon, the "sole really contemporary task" of committed literature "is to persuade the group to progress to reflection and meditation. This book, it is hoped, will be a mirror with a progressive infrastructure, in which it will be possible to discern the Negro on the road to disalienation."[21]

Sartre's thesis on commitment is that "all the literary work is an appeal. To write is to appeal to the reader to bring into objective existence the discovery which I have undertaken by means of language."[22] Both Fanon and Sartre therefore emphasize that the aim of committed literature, as well as of the committed artist, is to change the world and make it a better place to live in. In this sense, commitment also implies and is inseparable from the notion of an obligation to mankind. This is why the effort of the committed artist is indistinguishable from social action. What marks out the committed from the uncommitted artist is, according to Sartre,

20 Fanon, *Black Skin, White Masks,* pp. 183-184.
21 Ibid., p. 184.
22 Cumming, *Philosophy of Sartre,* p. 376.

that the former "transfers his commitment from the level of the immediately spontaneous to the level of consciousness."[23]

There are, according to Sartre, two major arguments in support of commitment. First, he proposes that, since it rests on a determination to communicate one's ideas with others with a view to changing society, committed literature is a form of social action. Secondly, Sartre contends that there can be no committed literature without a public. Thus, in a bourgeois society or one ridden with contradictions, the committed writer necessarily invites the wrath of the bourgeoisie or the privileged by pointing to the socioeconomic and political basis of the contradictions.[24]

What then is the committed artist or writer committed to? According to Sartre:

> Whether he is an essayist, a pamphleteer, a satirist, or a novelist, whether he speaks only of individual passions or whether he attacks the social order, the writer, a free man addressing free men, has only a single subject — freedom.[25]

Fanon expresses a similar view of commitment as commitment to freedom when he asserts that "no attempt must be made to encase man, for it is his destiny to be free,"[26] an assertion consistent with his earlier claim that in writing *Black Skin, White Masks,* it is his "hope to persuade my brother, whether black or white, to tear off with all his strength the shameful livery put together by centuries of incomprehension."[27] The task of the committed writer is to work for the preservation of human dignity and the promotion of a community of free individuals.

23 Jean-Paul Sartre, *What Is Literature?* translated by Bernard Frechtman (London: Methuen, 1950).

24 Ibid.

25 Cumming, *Philosophy of Sartre,* p. 377.

26 Fanon, *Black Skin, White Masks,* p. 230.

27 Ibid., p. 12.

In talking about commitment, Fanon takes the perspective of methodological individualism in viewing the individual as an autonomous moral agent. Indeed the whole thrust of his thesis about commitment is to suggest that commitment is indispensable to the freedom of the individual. This is because to commit oneself is to make a moral decision. It is of the nature of moral decisions that one has to make up one's mind about them oneself. Commitment, like other ethical or moral choices, must issue from a subjective decision, in the sense that each person is his or her own best judge on such matters.

This view of the subjective ethical basis of commitment, as issuing from an autonomous moral agent, whose view of the social world is thereby transformed by the decision in favor of commitment, is brought out clearly in Fanon's letter of resignation from the French civil service in 1956. The kernel of his argument is contained in the following quotation:

> The worker in the commonwealth must cooperate in the social scheme of things. But he must be convinced of the excellence of the society in which he lives. There comes a time when silence becomes dishonesty.
>
> The ruling intentions of personal existence are not in accord with the permanent assaults on the most commonplace values. For many months my conscience has been the seat of unpardonable debates. And their determination is not to despair of man, in other words of myself.
>
> The decision I have reached is that I cannot continue to bear a responsibility at no matter what cost, on the false pretext that there is nothing else to be done.[28]

This theme of an autonomous moral agent is reiterated again and again in the concluding chapter of *Black Skin,*

[28] Fanon, *Toward the African Revolution*, p. 54.

White Masks. Thus, Fanon talks "of not renouncing my freedom through my choices."[29] He also asserts that:

> The body of history does not determine a single one of my actions. I am my own foundation. And it is by going beyond the historical, instrumental hypothesis that I will initiate the cycle of my freedom.[30]

The individualistic basis of Fanon's notion of commitment as a personal experience must therefore also be viewed as deriving from or grounded in his notion of freedom as necessity. That this is so is clear from Fanon's concern with "not renouncing my freedom through my choices." But it is also explicitly made clear in his discussion of Hegel's notion of *consciousness.* It is argued in Chapter 4 that, drawing on the Hegelian distinction between Master and Bondsman or Slave, Fanon contends that the individual (in this case the colonized subject) is really not free or human unless he or she acts consciously and rationally. Acting consciously and rationally in this respect involves making a moral decision in the form of a commitment to identify and engage in political action to remove the impediments to one's realizing oneself as a human being:

> Thus human reality in-itself-for-itself can be achieved only through conflict and through the risk that conflict implies. This risk means that I go beyond life toward a supreme good that is the transformation of subjective certainty of my own worth into a universally valid objective truth.[31]

[29] Fanon, *Black Skin, White Masks,* p. 229.

[30] Ibid., p. 231.

[31] Ibid., p. 218; also ibid., p. 231: "It is through the effort to recapture the self and to scrutinize the self, it is through the lasting tension of their freedom that men will be able to create the ideal conditions of existence for a human world."

The Problem of Commitment in Fanon

How plausible is Sartre and Fanon's notion of commitment? What problems does Fanon's discussion of commitment raise? What objections can be made against it? Let us first raise some questions about its plausibility.

First, Sartre's assertion that "to write is to appeal to the reader," raises the question of audience, namely to whom is the appeal directed. One writes for an audience or public. But the choice of both an audience and a public is problematic. This possibility is illustrated by Sartre's own experiences. A critic of bourgeois society, Sartre nonetheless finds his message unappealing to the French Communist Party. It is this dilemma that leads him to talk of a "virtual public" by which he means an imaginary public of the future.

Fanon is also faced with a similar problem. Martin Staniland has suggested that Fanon's message is directed primarily at the French Left and Liberals. There are also the psychoanalytic interpretations of Memmi and Gendzier to the effect that Fanon is attempting through the literary medium to resolve his own personal or family conflicts. There are, however, those who, like Zolberg, look upon Fanon as the "prophet" of "the wretched of the earth."[32]

Secondly, there is the problem relating to how one is to determine or measure the impact of the appeal. Committed or incendiary literature is by definition an attempt to incite people to political action, either against or in support of the political status quo. But to say that it causes the tinderbox of revolutionary discontent or conservatism to explode, or that it ignites it, is not to say that it necessarily brings "into existence the discovery I have undertaken by means of language."[33]

[32] Staniland, "Fanon and African Political Class," p. 12; Memmi, in *The New York Times Book Review* (March 14, 1971), p. 5; Gendzier, *Frantz Fanon*, pp. 11-12; Zolberg, "Frantz Fanon: A Gospel for the Damned," *Encounter* 27, (November, 1966), pp. 56-63.

[33] Cumming, *Philosophy of Sartre*, p. 376.

The problem is that, since to send out an appeal is to convey a message, people are likely to react differently to the content of the message. Words, the stuff out of which a message is composed, are generally ambiguous and therefore usually have a multiplicity of meanings. Once a writer has sent out his message, he has little, if any, control, over how it is going to be interpreted or received. This is why it is sometimes unfair to ascribe to writers the excesses of their followers. This is also why it makes sense to talk of the "bastardization" or corruption of the ideas of a writer.

These two problematic aspects of Fanon's notion of commitment must be set in the context of a more profound problem in social discourse. This is the need to reconcile analytical abstractions with positivistic or empirical observations. The criticisms which have been raised so far with respect to the notion of commitment assume that statements of commitment are based on empirical observations or that they constitute empirical generalizations. However, it is doubtful that such criticisms can be sustained if one regards Fanon's notion of commitment as an analytical abstraction that provides one with action orientation.

A third problem raised by Fanon's notion of commitment is the apparent inconsistency between his acceptance of commitment and his rejection of appeals to human reason as a strategy for social and political change. If the powers-that-be and the privileged understand only the language of force and are unmoved by appeals to their humanity, then committed literature is, in a sense, irrelevant and superfluous. This seems to be the point of Fanon's assertion that

> I do not carry innocence to the point of believing that appeals to reason or respect for human dignity can alter reality. For the Negro who works on a sugar plantation in Le Robert, there is only one solution: to fight. He will embark on this struggle, and he will pursue it, not as the result of a Marxist or idealistic analysis but quite simply

> because he cannot conceive of life otherwise than in the form of a battle against exploitation, misery and hunger.[34]

If this is indeed the case there is no need for committed literature since it is bound to fail *ab initio.* This apparent inconsistency and the anti-intellectualist element in the quotation must be viewed, however, in terms of what Fanon regards as the poverty of liberal thought and writing. Put differently, the apparent inconsistency and anti-intellectualism can be explained away in the light of Fanon's belief that moral exhortation must be matched by political action. Once the committed writer has analyzed the ills of society, he is also morally bound to take concrete action, dictated by political circumstances, to remove those ills. This is Fanon's way of deriving an *ought* from an *is.* As he puts it, "to educate man to be *actional...* is the prime task of him who, having taken thought, prepares to act."[35]

Fourthly, there is the problem of the "correct" or "right" ideological expression of commitment. This touches on the justification of commitment and the possibility of intersubjectively validated political ethics. For Sartre and Fanon there are two dimensions to commitment. First, one assumes a responsibility towards other persons. This is an identification of oneself with others. Secondly, the acquisition of responsibility must find expression in the way one acts, which is to say that one must take practical or moral actions that have political implications to make good one's profession of responsibility.

Now the problem is partly this: if commitment is grounded in an individual's choice, then not all individuals will make the same commitment. There arises, therefore, the need to decide which is the correct or right commitment. Yet to talk of a right commitment or a preferable one is to deny one's role as an

[34] Fanon, *Black Skin, White Masks,* p. 224.
[35] Ibid., p. 222 (emphasis in original).

autonomous moral agent since the validation of what is right or preferable is, in this context, extraneous to the individual.

It is at this juncture that Fanon's individualism falls short of anarchism or some other form of social or moral atomism. This is due partly to the notion of action built into Fanon's notion of commitment. If linked to action, commitment becomes advocacy or propaganda to influence and convince others of the "rightness" or "correctness" of the position of the committed writer. Fanon's qualified moral atomism is also partly due to his explicit rejection of some form of commitment manifested in his critique of the Négritude school and the position taken by some of its adherents over the Algerian issue.[36] In a sense, therefore, to argue, as Fanon does, that one ought to be committed is to beg the question of what it is to be committed, of how commitment is to be manifested.

The tension in Fanon's position on this issue is a common one in social and political theory: how does one reconcile, within the same analytic or conceptual framework, the subjective or interpretive view of the individual as actor with his need to belong and carry on meaningful discourse with others?

If there is an apparent shift in Fanon's emphasis from the individualistic perspective, it is due to his belief in the imperative of a shared morality or mutuality of obligation as a basis for man's social existence.[37] With respect to commitment one can then discriminate among types of commitment by posing the question, "What is one committed to or an ideologue of?"

The answer to this question will point to the clear distinction between the bourgeois or reactionary committed artist, who puts his knowledge at the disposal of the forces of oppression, and the revolutionary writer like Fanon or Cabral who, though objectively *petit-bourgeois,* puts his knowledge at

[36] Fanon, *Wretched of the Earth,* p. 235.

[37] Cf. Fanon, *Toward the African Revolution,* p. 54: "The worker in the Commonwealth must cooperate in the social scheme of things."

the disposal of the oppressed and whose basic goal is freedom. The test therefore ultimately turns on the consequences of various types of commitment for the freedom of the individual. In other words, although social order is necessary, its viability or rather its justification must rest on its not subordinating the needs and interests of the individual to those of some fictitious larger collectivity.

There is much more that is significant and highly pertinent to contemporary Africa in Fanon's notion of commitment. Although this issue is treated in another section of this chapter, it is apposite to observe here that an important merit of Fanon's discussion of commitment is its rejection of dogmatism. It is all at one with his critical mind. Being committed means being prepared to reject and remove whatever is anathema and inimical to the well-being and welfare of the individual. To be committed is to observe acutely, critically, imaginatively, and comprehensively. It is to distrust and be concerned with placing limitations on those who exercise political power.

Collective Responsibility as Political Virtue

Fanon's notion of commitment is reinforced by, or rather finds justification in his notion of collective responsibility. A connection between both notions resides in Fanon's attempt to link an individual's choice of commitment to a larger purpose, namely concern with other individuals. But that concern is nevertheless fundamentally a self-interested one; it is self-directed in that it rests ultimately on what one shares with others.

What this means for Fanon is, therefore, that political virtue demands that one condemns social evils and injustice wherever they may exist. One may not be directly or personally affected by acts of oppression and intimidation; yet one is also affected because one is a human being. In other words, political virtue implies a recognition of the common bond that links men as men together. The task of the individual is therefore to engage in social action that involves viewing himself not as an atom apart from others but in terms of what he shares in common with other individuals, of what is universal among human beings.

This is Fanon's notion of human dignity or respect for persons as such. This notion views man as subject. It is the spirit of the Kantian categorical imperative that we treat man as an end and never as a means:

> I cannot dissociate myself from the future that is proposed for my brother. Every one of my acts commits me as a man. Every one of my silences, every one of my cowardices reveals me as a man.[38]

Fanon borrows this notion from Karl Jaspers' equivalent notion of metaphysical guilt.[39] According to Jaspers this notion is analytically different from criminal guilt, political guilt and moral guilt.[40] As Jaspers puts it, metaphysical guilt arises in that:

> there exists among men, because they are men, a solidarity through which each shares responsibility for every injustice and every wrong committed in the world.[41]

It is unclear, however, from reading the relevant pages where Fanon cites Jasper's *Question of German Guilt* whether his (Fanon's) focus is on moral or metaphysical guilt. Jaspers has argued that "the moral guilt exists for all those who give room to conscience and repentance."[42]

Although the passage Fanon quotes is a statement of the

[38] Fanon, *Black Skin, White Masks,* p. 89.

[39] Ibid., p. 89, fn. 9.

[40] Karl Jaspers, *The Question of German Guilt,* translated by T. B. Ashton (New York: Capricorn Books, 1947), pp. 31-33.

[41] Quoted in Fanon, *Black Skin, White Masks,* p. 89, fn. 9.

[42] Jaspers, *Question of German Guilt,* pp. 63-64.

notion of metaphysical guilt, it seems to me that Jaspers' notion of moral guilt is more relevant to Fanon's concern with establishing the common bond of humanity. Thus, when Fanon asserts that "the passivity that is to be seen in troubled periods of history is to be regarded as a default on that obligation,"[43] he is echoing Jaspers' notion of moral guilt, of the thesis that,

> Blindness for the misfortune of others, lack of imagination of the heart, inner indifference toward the witnessed evil — that is moral guilt.[44]

Fanon's confusion is perhaps due to the close connection between the two notions in Jaspers. One's moral responsibility to other men derives from that "solidarity among men as human beings that makes each coresponsible for every wrong and every injustice" committed in one's presence or with one's knowledge or connivance.[45] In the words of Jaspers, "if human beings were able to free themselves from metaphysical guilt, they would be angels, and all other three concepts of guilt would become immaterial."[46]

Collective Responsibility and the Problem of Conscience

A basic problem raised by Fanon's discussion of collective responsibility is the question why one should assume a moral responsibility for or express a moral concern about wrongs being inflicted on others. To justify such a position on the grounds of a common bond that links men together is to beg the question whether such a bond in fact exists. Thus, by

43 Fanon, *Black Skin, White Masks,* p. 89, fn. 9.
44 Jaspers, *Question of German Guilt,* p. 70.
45 Ibid., p. 32.
46 Ibid., p. 33.

assuming that there can be no doubt that such a responsibility exists, Fanon is assuming what has to be argued.

Jaspers, however, links his discussion and justification of moral guilt to the notion of conscience, although he also accepts that there are "conscienceless" men like Hitler who may feel no sense of moral responsibility or common bondage with other men:

> There is a line at which even the possibility of moral judgement ceases. It can be drawn where we feel the other not even trying for a moral self-analysis ... where he seems not to hear at all. Hitler and his accomplices ... are beyond moral guilt for as long as they do not feel it.[47]

But how tenable is this implicit reference to an inner voice? How do we establish that Hitler "seems not to hear" this voice? It may well be the case that his conscience or inner voice has convinced him that there is no common bond linking him to other men. The problem with the notion of an inner voice or conscience — Jaspers' "moral self-analysis" — is that it is not an infallible guide to moral and social action.

If I am wavering between two moral options, it is not clear how I am to consult my conscience for direction or guidance. The point is that one's conscience is not like a map to which one can turn for directions. It is no use explaining away what one regards as Hitler's aberrations by saying that he has no conscience. How would one disprove him if he said that his conscience ordered him to exterminate Jews?

As was pointed out earlier in this chapter, although he emphasizes the moral autonomy of the individual, Fanon rejects the sort of moral atomism that will justify the position of the Nazi follower. This is because for Fanon the notion of a moral agent also implies that one can criticize the grounds upon which the moral agent's beliefs or actions are based. If moral autonomy or atomism is not to become incoherent, then

[47] Ibid., p. 63.

it must be open to rational discourse; otherwise the shared morality which should provide societal cohesion will be impossible of attainment.

This perspective to methodological individualism is, therefore, concerned with justifying a mode of inquiry or discourse in which one can engage in a dialogue or dialectic in the Platonic sense with others. Hopefully such a dialectic should enable one to derive a better understanding of what is common to human beings.

Commitment and the correlative notion of collective responsibility thus enables Fanon to require one to address other individuals while in turn both notions create an obligation on one's part to observe and listen to the plight and contention of others. All this should be done and proceed on the assumption that a commonly shared understanding lays the foundations for collective life and collective action to grapple with the human predicament.

Collective vs. Individual Responsibility

If the notion of collective responsibility is tenable, is it reducible into statements of individual responsibility and, by implication, individual culpability? Ordinarily, we speak about collective responsibility with respect to such associational groups as sports teams, social clubs, business organizations, and countries. Thus, it makes sense to say that Texaco Oil Company is responsible for pollution and health hazards resulting from oil spillage in Bendel and Rivers States in Nigeria. As a corporate body, Texaco Oil Company can be held culpable and made to pay costs for such an oil spillage.

Need one agree with Fanon and the methodological individualist that the ascription of collective responsibility (and culpability) to Texaco Oil Company is reducible to an ascription of responsibility (and culpability) to every one of its members or staff? It all depends on the sense in which one is using "responsibility" and "culpability." It also depends on the authority structure of the group in question. Jaspers' argument is that

> the political guilt does mean the liability of all citizens for the consequences of deeds done by their state, but not the criminal and moral guilt of every single citizen for crimes committed in the name of the state.[48]

Fanon's accusation that "European civilization and its best representatives are responsible for colonial racism"[49] is a claim about collective responsibility which, following Jaspers, is equivalent to a claim about the political liability of every European. But in what sense is this a plausible view to hold. It can be sustained to the extent to which citizens acquiesce to indignities perpetrated by their government and its agents. But is the citizen who refuses to accept the legitimacy, moral or otherwise, of the regime in whose territory he lives liable to this charge?

Fanon himself talks of Algerian settlers who not only denounced colonial rule in Algeria but also provided moral, financial, and logistical support to the Algerian freedom fighters. If the notion of culpability is to retain its sense it must discriminate among levels of worthiness and admit of mitigating circumstances.

It is in this sense that a blanket ascription of culpability, of "political" guilt becomes problematic. What Jaspers and Fanon seem to be saying is that since one lives under a government, thereby enjoying benefits it makes possible, one is *ipso facto* part and parcel of that government and must share the "political" blame for iniquitous policies it pursues. However, my taking advantage of opportunities afforded by a government, or even my voting for it, in no way commits me to supporting specific policies it pursues nor does it make me culpable in a "political" sense for those policies.

[48] Ibid., pp. 32-33.
[49] Fanon, *Black Skin, White Masks,* p. 90.

Fanon's position is, however, understandable in one crucial sense that is related to his notion of commitment or freedom as necessity. Political virtue demands that one should not be a passive citizen or shirk one's responsibility by failing to condemn what are patently atrocious policies being pursued domestically or externally by one's government. By keeping quiet or pretending not to be aware of the atrocities being perpetrated one is as guilty as the worst executor of those policies. It is to renounce one's freedom:

> I find myself suddenly in the world and I recognize that I have one right alone. That of demanding human behavior from the other.
> One duty alone: That of not renouncing my freedom through my choices.[50]

Ethical Relativism and the Possibility of Ethical Universalism

According to one interpretation ethical relativism holds that ethical standards and precepts are relative and culture-bound. They are neither universal nor absolute.[51] To what extent does Fanon subscribe to ethical relativism? His discussion of colonialism and racism offers interesting insight into his thinking on the role of morality and culture as props that support and sustain the social injustices of colonial rule.

There is indeed a strong element of ethical relativism in Fanon. This is due partly to the perspective of methodological individualism that he adopts. When applied to the culture sphere, Fanon's ethical relativism becomes a form of cultural relativism that holds that both the morality and culture of the colonizing country are not universal but rather a mask under which it imposes its rule on alien peoples.

[50] Ibid., p. 229.
[51] Clyde Kluckhohn, "Ethical Relativity: Sic et Non," *The Journal of Philosophy*, Vol. 52, No. 23 (November 10, 1956), p. 663.

In *Wretched of the Earth* Fanon devotes the chapter "On National Culture" to a disquisition on the social environment within which culture, politics and morality must be situated. The result is a sociology of morality which, while emphasizing the autonomy of every culture, justifies resistance to colonial rule on the ground that it is essential to resurrecting the authenticity of the culture of colonized peoples and to building postcolonial African nations on a cultural foundation.[52] It follows, therefore, that Fanon looks upon culture as providing a necessary, if not sufficient background against which the morality and the socio-economic and political institutions of a people should be viewed.

Fanon's belief in certain universal norms raises doubts about the consistency of his belief in ethical relativism. Here again we find the tension between the particular and the universal in Fanon. Just as he rejects unqualified moral atomism, he also rejects unqualified ethical or cultural relativism.

It has been argued in this chapter that Fanon is a humanist whose credo is summed up in his invocation: "For Europe, for ourselves, and for humanity, comrades ... we must work out new concepts, and try to set afoot a new man."[53] What he is advocating is, in effect, the establishment of supracultural norms to guide man's behavior toward his fellow man. This is the thrust of his discussion of commitment and social responsibility. Were he to opt for a radical moral atomism, the type of rational discourse implied in the notions of commitment and collective responsibility would be foreclosed.

Fanon's inconsistency or rather the tension between ethical relativism and universalism does not lie in his humanism only. His criticism of colonialism and racism implies his acceptance

[52] L. Adele Jinadu, "Some African Theories of Culture and Modernization: Fanon, Cabral and Some Others" *African Studies Review*, Vol. 20, No. 1 (April, 1978).

[53] Fanon, *Wretched of the Earth*, p. 316; also Fanon, *Black Skin, White Masks*, p. 231.

of certain supracultural norms and standards. To criticize is to set up criteria of evaluation. Yet from the ethical relativist point of view, one cannot validly criticize one culture from the standpoint of another culture.

How is Fanon's position to be defended from this charge of inconsistency? Two lines of defence come to mind. First, it can be argued that in criticizing colonialism Fanon is not setting up supracultural criteria of evaluation and is basically pointing to the gap between the theory and practice of colonialism, condemning the colonizer from the standpoint of the latter's morality and culture. On this view colonialism and colonial rule constitute departures from the ethical values and standards of the colonizing countries. This is what Fanon means when, at the end of *Wretched of the Earth,* he pleads thus: "Leave thus Europe where they are never done talking of Man, yet murder men everywhere they find them...."

Secondly, Fanon can be defended on the ground that from the fact that each culture or society has its own ethical standards and norms, it does not follow that any attempts to provide supracultural norms and standards of ethical justification and evaluation must fail. For example, we can read Fanon as holding that there are certain necessary conditions that any positive code of ethics must satisfy, if it is to be viable. This view is quite consistent with the view that what is held ethically satisfactory must vary from one culture to another. For one thing, it suggests a test of consistency or congruence between a code of ethics and what its practitioners do. Unless this is usually the case the ethics or culture in question will simply not hold. Moreover, there is a test of humane treatment of the person as such which represents a universal morality. For another thing, it can be held that Fanon's claim is that it is necessary for any code of ethics to specify reward for, say, honesty, virtue, etc., but that the nature of the reward may vary from one culture to another.

My own position is the following. There is an uneasy combination of ethical relativism and ethical universalism in

Fanon. To the extent that there is this tension in his writings, he is inconsistent. This is nevertheless understandable. The need to affirm the authenticity of the values and culture of the colonized in the face of the deliberate attempt of the colonizer to deny them, leads Fanon to emphasize the particularity of those values. This is but the first step in liberating colonizer and colonized from the shackles of ignorance and hate with which colonial rule has bound them.

Fanon's humanist or universalist concern and preoccupation involves rising above parochialism. It involves making a conscious and determined effort to establish love and justice as universal values, "basic values that constitute a human world."[54] The important point to emphasize is that the affirmation of the authenticity of the cultural heritage of the colonized is, according to Fanon, not an end in itself. It is a means to establishing harmony, brotherhood, and love in the world. It is essential to the construction of that "monument" at the top of which Fanon hopes to see "a white man and a black man hand in hand."[55]

Commitment and the Intellectual Vocation

Fanon's notions of commitment and collective responsibility reflect a basic concern with the role of the intellectual or intelligentsia in society.[56] What is his conceptualization of that role and of what importance is it in the African context? His conception of the role of the intellectual in society is that of an ideas man and social engineer. But it also views the intellectual as a social critic or "conscience" of society. For him the notion of a socially unconcerned intellectual is a contradiction in terms. Put differently, Fanon's thesis is that not

[54] Fanon, *Black Skin, White Masks*, p. 222.

[55] Ibid.

[56] Intellectual or intelligentsia is used here in the sense of those who have acquired western education up to and above the first degree or professional level.

only must the intellectual be involved in public life but he or she must also be concerned about the uses to which power is put; or, what is the same thing, the intellectual must be concerned lest those in office exploit his or her knowledge for purposes that derogate from man's basic humanity.

It is probably a fair assessment to say that a substantial number of African intellectuals are committed to the view which holds that scholarship must be divorced from advocacy or involvement in the public policy formulation process.[57] Taken to its extreme, this means that intellectuals should steer clear of politics and government, even to the extent of refusing to serve in advisory capacities.

It is doubtful whether there are African intellectuals who subscribe to this extreme version. There is little doubt, however, that many subscribe to its weak version and insist that if an intellectual feels compelled to enter the political arena, he or she should do so as an individual and not in his or her capacity as an intellectual.

The problem is that the alleged divorce between politics and scholarship or science is difficult to sustain in real life. A stronger objection, however, is that the tradition of intellectual detachment from politics is a luxury that Africa can ill-afford. One reason for this is that, as a result of the scarcity or paucity of man-power resources at top policy-making levels, intellectuals have to be co-opted now and again for national, that is political service.

A second reason relates to the high incidence of oppression that has characterized African politics, thereby making the thesis about intellectual detachment from political issues suspect and irresponsible. As Fanon makes clear, the duty of the intellectual in this respect is not only to understand and explain the functionings of society but also to work for its

[57] For a statement of this view see Maurice Cowling, *The Nature and Limits of Political Science* (Cambridge: Cambridge University Press, 1963), pp. 1-3, 6-7.

substitution, particularly if social structures are inimical to man's welfare.

The acting out of the role of the committed intellectual is problematic in another sense. The problem here concerns the conflict of social roles. It is part of the meaning of being a person that one necessarily occupies different roles — father, pastor, guardian, brother, friend, etc. Conflict is likely to arise because duties and obligations attaching to any of these roles can be incompatible with one's role as an intellectual. R. S. Downie points to the structure of role playing and the dilemma it poses for the individual when he argues that "there are various ways in which a role can be enacted, and a person can bring to his actions a quality which may either mitigate or exacerbate its evil effects. Indeed the actual structure of a role may be altered if it is enacted with a characteristic quality."[58]

Put concretely, such dilemmas may revolve around conflicts of roles similar to the following examples. There is intellectual A who has old parents, an unemployed wife, children, and other dependents to provide and cater for in an extended family system. He is living under what is patently in his opinion an oppressive regime. What should he do? Should he put his role as provider for his family above his role as a committed intellectual, the more so since the latter role, if played out by him, may lead to his incarceration or execution?

Intellectual B is living under a regime which is neither oppressive nor progressive. He has been invited to serve the regime in a cabinet or quasi-cabinet position. Should he accept the offer, hoping to influence the regime? Or should he reject the offer? This is of course the perennial problem of whether it is better to attempt to effect change from within or from without the system.

These are typical problems that African intellectuals must resolve. It is not easy to say how they are to be resolved in advance, even though one may accept Fanon's notion of

[58] R. S. Downie, "Social Roles and Moral Responsibility," *Philosophy*, Vol. 39, No. 147 (January, 1964), p. 36.

commitment. It is doubtful whether any useful purpose can be served by so doing, since it is the intellectual who must make the decision himself after considering the specific situations he or she is faced with. Fanon himself is acutely aware of the difficulty of coming to a decision in such situations of role conflict: "For many months my conscience has been the seat of unpardonable debates."[59]

There is another dimension to Fanon's model of the African intellectual as an ideas man and activist or social critic. This concerns Fanon's belief that an urgent task of the African intellectual is to help reform and recreate African societies out of the morass of colonial rule. By engaging in a dialectic of criticism and social action, African intellectuals can mould public opinion and influence the direction and implementation of public policies by charting out progressive options in policy matters.

What this also means is that if African intellectuals ought to advocate progressive policies, it also follows, according to Fanon, that they ought to assume a progressive stance in the study of their societies. Scholarship must be decolonized, research priorities must reflect and grapple with the underlying contradictions and cultural heritage of African societies.

Scholarship is universal in one sense. But in another sense it has an important subjective element. This is the point of Fanon's discussion of ethical and cultural relativism. The intellectual vocation must be placed within the cultural framework provided by one's society. This is to say that the search for solutions to African problems must be conducted with a view to relating these solutions to that cultural framework. It is thus within this limited framework provided by one's culture that one pursues scholarship.

Fanon's criticism of the African intellectual as a general social category reflects his disappointment at the way African intellectuals have been acting out their role as intellectuals. This criticism should be placed in the wider context of his

[59] Fanon, *Toward the African Revolution*, p. 54.

general indictment of the African middle class for failing to break out of the dependency complex generated by colonialism:

> A permanent wish for identification with the bourgeois representatives of the mother country is to be found among the native intellectuals...[60]

This is why he also condemns the African middle class for its failure "to put at the people's disposal the intellectual and technical capital that it has snatched when going through the colonial universities."[61]

Fanon does not, however, condemn *all* African intellectuals. In denouncing the excess and chicaneries of postcolonial regimes in Africa, Fanon finds some comfort in the dissident African intellectual. This comes out in his distinction between "illegal" and "legal" elements of the middle class, the former sub-category being made up of

> intellectual elements [who] have carried out a prolonged analysis of the true nature of colonialism and of the international situation [and who have begun] to criticize their party's lack of ideology and the poverty of its tactics and strategy.[62]

It seems that, according to Fanon, the intellectual role in Africa is that of political education, concerned with bridging the elite-mass gap and with moulding, like Plato's philosopher-king, existential society in the image of the knowledge acquired in the course of the contemplative vocation characteristic of the intellectual career as such. Fanon's denial that "there is no such things as a demiurge..."[63] notwithstanding, his

[60] Fanon, *Wretched of the Earth,* p. 178.
[61] Ibid., p. 150.
[62] Ibid., p. 124.
[63] Ibid., p. 197; for Fanon's discussion of the need for and role of the political educator, see also ibid., pp. 144, 146-147, and 200.

conception of the intellectual role is indeed that of a demiurge, grounded in and responsive to the needs and wishes of the people, so that the totalitarian option or arbitrary rule is foreclosed.

Summary

The argument developed in this chapter is that Fanon's discussion of the connection between morality and politics is based on the perspective of methodological individualism. Although he emphasizes the need to look upon the individual as an autonomous moral agent, Fanon rejects atomistic individualism. He does so because of his belief in the rationality of human action and the imperative of a shared morality for social order.

Thus, he views the rationality of human action as consisting in the individual's engaging in reflection and in the dialectic with others. The aim is to discover what is common to and universal among human beings. This process of reflection and dialectic presumes an obligation on the part of the individual to be concerned with the plight and contention of others. In this way, a shared morality can then lay the moral and logical foundations of collective life and collective action.

Fanon's discussion of commitment has great relevance to the role of the intellectual in contemporary African societies. But his notion of the intellectual role is not an elitist or ivory-tower one. The intellectual role is for Fanon necessarily an activist one in the sense of being grounded in social involvement and social criticism. It is quintessentially a public service role.

Fanon's notion is more relevant now than ever before. More often than not, African intellectuals who have gone into public service and immersed themselves in the policy-making process have apparently allowed themselves to be mesmerized by the trappings and appurtenance of power. Placing their lust for personal aggrandizement and advancement over concern for the plight of the common man, they invariably become apologists of regimes that have lost all moral claims to power. But as Fanon puts it:

> There comes a time when silence becomes dishonesty. The ruling intentions of personal existence are not in accord with the permanent assault on the most commonplace values.... The decision I have reached is that I cannot continue to bear a responsibility at no matter what cost, on the false pretext that there is nothing else to be done.[64]

We find encapsulated in this quotation Fanon's model of the intellectual role in society as well as his notions of commitment and collective responsibility. The picture that emerges is the refreshing and reassuring one of a humanist and intellectual who, in bringing morality to bear on politics, is prepared to commit himself to moral and political action so that man *qua* man should live as he ought to live.

The situation in Africa is, however, pointing to an acceptance and working out of the implications of Fanon's position. As the recent political history of Ghana and Nigeria has shown, the African intellectual is now playing the role of a dissident and radicalized intellectual.

It seems, therefore, that a small but articulate segment of the African intellectual has accepted and is demonstrating how the thesis about the critical role of the African intellectual in exposing and transcending basic contradictions in African societies can be worked out. One problem that remains is that of proving and sustaining organizational structures to link this radicalization to that of the proletariat and peasantry.

64 Fanon, *Toward the African Revolution,* p. 54.

Chapter 7

FANON'S THEORY OF AFRICAN POLITICS AND UNDERDEVELOPMENT

The Theory in Outline

Fanon's political ideas provide a useful theoretical framework for an understanding of the dynamics of political processes in Africa. Fanon is, in this respect, as much a political philosopher as a political sociologist. He has raised pertinent questions about the nature and structure of African politics. His answers are perceptive and thought-provoking.

Fanon's discussion of African politics, particularly in *Wretched of the Earth,* should be placed in the wider context of underdevelopment theory in general.[1] To do this is to underscore two related aspects of his political ideas. First, it means that his attempt to come to grips with and "stretch" Marxism spills over into his analysis of African politics. Secondly, it also means that he is concerned with situating and therefore explaining African politics in the wider context of the multifarious ramifications (e.g., sociocultural, economic, and political ones), of the historical processes generated and set in motion by the development of international finance capitalism as a global phenomenon.

[1] The literature on underdevelopment theory is now vast. For a short critical review of the underdevelopment literature see Colin Leys, *Underdevelopment in Kenya: The Political Economy of Neo-Colonialism, 1964-1971* (London: Heinemann, 1975), pp. 1-27 and the sources cited therein, particularly on p. 8, fn. 13. For an interesting theoretical application of underdevelopment theory to Africa in general, see Claude Ake, *Revolutionary Pressures in Africa* (London: Zed Press, 1978).

What then, in outline, is Fanon's theory of African politics and underdevelopment? Put differently, what explanatory strategy does Fanon utilize in his analysis of African politics and underdevelopment? The concern then is not with whether Fanon offers us a theory of African politics and underdevelopment in the natural science sense of the term "theory." Rather, the question to pose is one about strategy, namely, how does his analysis advance our knowledge of African politics and underdevelopment?

Fanon's strategy proceeds on the explicit assumption that African politics is inherently characterized by contradictions. The theoretical task then becomes one of stipulating variables that are relevant to the explanation of the sources and nature of these contradictions. One overarching or "compound" variable, which subsumes other variables, and which is explicit in Fanon's analysis can be described as the colonial inheritance — a variable that refers to Africa's enforced incorporation into metropolitan and world capitalist systems as an unequal partner.

This incorporation, according to Fanon, has had cultural, economic, social, political, and psychological dimensions and ramifications. More significantly, since it was based on the rapacious expropriation of surplus value from Africa, this incorporation was not only perverse but has also meant the development of weak material structures characterized by monocultural and "externally-oriented" economies in Africa. At the level of the political superstructure, this incorporation also meant authoritarian rule, which facilitated the monopolization of political power and economic activities by the metropolitan bourgeoisie and the successor national bourgeoisie.

What other explanatory variables are subsumed under the colonial inheritance variable? One variable pertains to class political behaviour. Fanon's emphasis on this variable is concerned not necessarily with class conflict but with how class political behaviour is leading towards political crises and underdevelopment. However, Fanon's preoccupation with the national bourgeoisie, particularly the failure of the national bourgeoisie to act out its historic role, points to the potential for violent class conflict, and the strong implication that the necessary structural changes would be brought about by revolutionary violence.

Fanon's theory of African politics and underdevelopment also emphasizes the relevance of another variable, the urban-rural dichotomy, to our understanding of the pattern of political processes in Africa. Fanon's emphasis on this variable is an extension of his focus on the analysis of class political behaviour. The political center — characteristically the haven of the bourgeoisie and the proletariat — is developed at the expense of the periphery. This neglect of the periphery, according to Fanon, is bound to give rise to rural radicalism, as it has indeed done in Nigeria, Zaire, and Sierra Leone.

This is Fanon's theory of African politics and underdevelopment in outline. It now remains to offer a more detailed and extended discussion of that theory. But before that is done, it is necessary to indicate Fanon's contribution to the study of African politics.

The Historiographer of African Politics

The nature of that contribution is best illustrated by placing it in the context of two dominant orthodoxies or paradigms in the study of African politics in the early 1960s. One such orthodoxy, drawing on structural-functional analysis, emphasized political institutional transfer. Apter's work on Ghana, for example, examines the process of institutional transfer of British parliamentary practices in that country.[2] Emphasis was placed on the functional roles of charisma, of

[2] D. E. Apter, *The Gold Coast In Transition* (Princeton, New Jersey: Princeton University Press, 1962). But see D. E. Apter, "Political Studies and the Search for a Framework," in C. Allen and R. W. Johnson, eds., *African Perspectives* (London: Cambridge University Press, 1970), pp. 213-223.

the charismatic leader in establishing western parliamentary and political institutions in a traditional polity.

The other orthodoxy was based on the assumption of pluralist politics and the need to build consensus if the goal of national integration was to be attained.[3] The emphasis of this orthodoxy was on the creation of consensus and on forging a nation out of the ethnic mosaic of each country.

Two criticisms of these orthodoxies have been made. First, as Sklar has argued, "at the very least, it can be said that functionalist thought in political science is not normally associated with social criticism and poses little threat of exposure to those who control the institutions of national power."[4] Secondly, the pluralist orthodoxy tended to overlook the conflictual nature of African politics and instead relied excessively on the self-serving rhetoric of political parties and their leaders.

If Fanon's focus on class political behaviour and class formation as the primary determinants of political processes in Africa is contrasted with the prevailing orthodoxies in the 1960s, the radical nature of his analysis stands out clearly. This is why Fanon was able in *Wretched of the Earth*, published in 1961, to probe beneath and expose the class interest that is hidden under the rhetoric of the political leadership in Africa.

The *Wretched of the Earth* is, moreover, a study in African underdevelopment. It views development or modernization as something more than the replication of Western institutions in Africa. Fanon's analysis of colonial rule as well as his focus on class political behaviour brings out the perverse and derivative nature of the developmental process in Africa. For example, the focus on class political behaviour links the national

[3] J. S. Coleman and C. G. Rosberg, *Political Parties and National Integration in Tropical Africa* (Berkeley and Los Angeles, California: University of California Press, 1964).

[4] Richard L. Sklar, "Political Science and National Integration — A Radical Approach," *The Journal of Modern African Studies*, Vol. 5, No. 1 (May, 1967), p. 5.

bourgeoisie to the capitalist global environment and thereby depicts clearly the dependency complex fostered and nurtured by this relationship. His analysis of colonial rule pointed to its unprogressive nature and the weak material base inherited despite about a century of colonial rule.

Fanon's position was not simply that development was not taking place in Africa or that only a privileged few were benefiting from the transfer of political power to Africans. It is part of the iconoclastic thrust of Fanon's analysis that it explicitly rejected the Western model of development that provided the implicit ideological assumptions of many Western social scientists working in and writing about Africa in the early 1960s.

Fanon's position is that there must be an African redefinition of development, suitable to African needs. To say this is to say in effect that if there was to be development in Africa, there would have to be a prior dissociation by African countries from an international sociocultural, political, and economic order that, being the creation of colonialism and imperialism, fosters and exacerbates political, economic, and cultural underdevelopment. As he states:

> So, comrades, let us not pay tribute to Europe by creating states, institutions, and societies which draw their inspirations from her.... If we wish to live up to our people's expectations, we must seek the response elsewhere than in Europe.[5]

In short, what sets Fanon's theoretical perspective apart from the prevailing orthodoxies in the 1960s is its emphasis on both the contradictions generated by Africa's incorporation into a global capitalist world system and the subsequent development and transfer of political powers to an indigenous ruling class. In a sense, much of the application of underdevelopment theory to the analysis of political processes in

[5] Fanon, *Wretched of the Earth*, p. 315.

contemporary Africa derives in part from Fanon's *Wretched of the Earth.* Put differently, Fanon has pioneered a reinterpretation of the developmental process in Africa and of the relevant variables that should provide the theoretical or organizing framework for studying that process.

Fanon also pioneered a historiographical revision of the sources and roots of African nationalism. It used to be the orthodoxy in the early 1950s and 1960s that African independence was achieved primarily because of the diffusion of Western liberal ideas and their impact on Western-educated African nationalists. On this view African nationalism is a creation of the West.[6]

Fanon offers two rebuttals to this orthodoxy. First, he asserts that the process of decolonization and devolution of political power in Africa involved a deal between the departing colonial regime and its successor regimes. Fanon's notion of false decolonization expresses this position. As he states:

> We have see that inside the nationalist parties, the will to break colonialism is linked with another quite different will: that of coming to a friendly agreement with it.[7]

Secondly, Fanon attempts to demonstrate that African masses, though unschooled in Rousseau, Locke or Marx, can be a politically active force. What more, there is a tradition of

[6] Rupert Emerson, *From Empire to Nation* (Cambridge, Massachusetts: Harvard University Press, 1960), pp. 22-36; Margery Perham, *The Colonial Reckoning* (New York: Knopf, 1962), Chapters 2-3; Elspeth Huxley, "What Future For Africa?" *Encounter* (June, 1961), p. 10; Edward Shils, "Further Observations on Mrs. Huxley," *Encounter,* (October, 1961), p. 46. For critiques of this orthodoxy, although from different perspectives, see Thomas Hodgkin, "The Relevance of 'Western' Ideas for the New States," in J. R. Pennock, ed., *Self-Government in Modernizing Nations* (Englewood Cliffs, New Jersey: Prentice-Hall, 1961), and A. D. Smith, *Theories of Nationalism* (London: Duckworth, 1971).

[7] Fanon, *Wretched of the Earth,* p. 124.

resistance to external rule that antedates the era of modern nationalism:

> But it may happen that the country people, in spite of the hold that the nationalist parties have over them, play a decisive part either in the process of the maturing of the national consciousness... or, less frequently, by substituting themselves purely and simply for the sterility of these parties.... The memory of the anticolonial period is very much alive in the villages, where women still croon in their children's ears songs to which the warriors marched when they went out to fight the conquerers...[8]

The weakness of the elitist explanation of African nationalism is, therefore, its narrow historical framework. It gives the impression that African nationalism is a post Second World War development. Fanon was not the first to direct our attention to uprisings against colonial rule by local peoples.[9] His contribution however is in pointing to the need for a theoretical framework which will contrast and relate or link these local revolts or uprisings — "incipient nationalisms" — to the wider movement for national independence. Eric Stokes has observed in this respect that:

> Whatever its emotive origins in the writings of the Fanon school, the newer interpretation has been pioneered for modern historical scholarship by work on those regions, notably East and Central Africa and the Congo, where the roots of the modern-educated elite and modern-style politics are shallowest.[10]

[8] Ibid., p. 114.

[9] See E. E. Evans-Pritchard, "Some Collective Expressions of Obscenity in Africa," *Journal of the Royal Anthropological Institute,* Vol. 59 (1929), pp. 311-331; George Shepperson, "The Politics of African Church Separatist Movements in British Central Africa," *Africa,* Vol. 24 (July, 1954), pp. 233-247; Kenneth Dike, *Trade and Politics in the Niger Delta* (London: Oxford University Press, 1954).

[10] Eric Stokes, "Traditional Resistance Movements and Afro-Asian Nationalism: The Context of the 1857 Mutiny Rebellion in India," *Past and Present,* Vol. 48 (August, 1970), p. 100. For this "newer" interpretation of African nationalism, see Martin Kilson, *Political Change in a West African*

One also gets the impression from Fanon that the expansion of the colonial center generally resulted in a betrayal of the tradition of resistance to colonial rule. According to him, this was principally due to the cooptation of important segments of both the traditional elite and the western-educated elite into the colonial system. The betrayal rested in the reluctance of both elites to utilize extraconstitutional means to challenge colonial rule.[11]

Fanon's Theory of the Party in Africa

The betrayal of trust thesis also provides the basis for Fanon's strident condemnation of the development of the one-party state in Africa. Fanon was again prescient in this respect: he saw much earlier than other analysts the connection between the one-party doctrine and the drift towards authoritarian rule.[12] The argument of the one-party state protagonists had been that the developmental imperative necessitated the monopolization of political power by the dominant single party if different ethnic groups were to be mobilized for the urgent task of consolidating political independence and securing economic development.[13] As

State: A Study of the Modernization Process in Sierra Leone (Cambridge, Massachusetts: Harvard University Press, 1966); Terrence Ranger, "Connexions Between 'Primary Resistance' Movements and Modern Nationalism in East and Central Africa," *Journal of African History,* Vol. 9, Nos. 3 and 4 (1968); John Lonsdale, "Some Origins of Nationalism in East Africa," *Journal of African History,* Vol. 9, No. 3 (1968); Georges Balandier, "Messianism and Nationalism in Black Africa," in Pierre L. Van de Berghe, *Africa: Social Problems of Change and Conflict* (San Francisco, California: Chandler, 1965).

[11] Fanon, *Wretched of the Earth,* p. 114.

[12] Ibid., pp. 164-166, 169-171, 174, 181-185. For other critiques of the one-party state, see W. Arthur Lewis, *Politics in West Africa* (London: Oxford University Press, 1965), pp. 55-63; S. E. Finer, "The One-Party Regimes in Africa: Reconsiderations," *Government and Opposition,* Vol. 2, No. 4 (July-October, 1964); Martin L. Kilson, "Authoritarian and Single Party Tendencies in African Politics," *World Politics,* Vol. 15, No. 2 (1963).

[13] For summaries of the one-party state doctrine, see Finer, "The One-Party Regime in Africa"; Aristide Zolberg, *Creating Political Order:*

Fanon himself observes, "Very often simple souls, who moreover belong to the newly born bourgeoisie, never stop repeating that in an underdeveloped country, the direction of affairs by a strong authority, in other words a dictatorship, is a necessity."[14]

Fanon did not regard the development of the one-party state as simply a betrayal of trust. He linked this thesis to his basic argument that the African one-party state was not and could not be, given the nature of the colonial inheritance in much of black Africa, the expression of the national interest which it purportedly claimed to be serving. Rather, it was the expression of the class interest of the national bourgeoisie, the inheritors of the state apparatus and its wherewithal at independence; for him "the single party is the modern form of the dictatorshp of the bourgeoisie..."[15] Or, as he puts it again:

> The people who for years on end have seen this leader and heard him speak, who from a distance in a kind of dream have followed his contests with the colonial power, spontaneously put their trust in this patriot. Before independence, the leader generally embodies the aspirations of the people for independence, political liberty and national dignity. But as soon as independence is declared, far from embodying in concrete form the needs of the people in what touches bread, land and the restoration of the country to the sacred hands of the people, the leader will reveal his inner purpose: to become the general president of that company of profiteers impatient for their returns which constitute the national bourgeoisie.[16]

The Party States of West Africa (Chicago, Illinois: Rand McNally, 1966), Chapter 1-2; Ruth Schachter (Morgenthau), "Single Party Systems in West Africa," *American Poltical Science Review,* Vol. 55 (June, 1961); Charles F. Andrain, "Democracy and Socialism: Ideologies of African Leaders," in David E. Apter, ed. *Ideology and Discontent* (New York: The Free Press, 1964), pp. 156-171.

[14] Fanon, *Wretched of the Earth,* p. 181.

[15] Ibid., p. 165.

[16] Ibid., p. 166.

Underlying this quotation is a view of what the relationshp between political leadership and followership should be. It is argued in Chapter 6 that Fanon looks upon government as a trust. On this view, government depends for its justification on a shared morality between those who rule and those who are being ruled. The existence of this shared morality also implies a mutuality of obligation as between governors and the governed. The political party as one organizing device for structuring social and authority relations must reflect and be shaped by the twin notions of a shared morality and a mutuality of obligation. This is indeed Fanon's manner of linking morality and politics.

It was precisely because there was no shared morality and, therefore, no mutuality of obligation between colonizer and colonized that Fanon's analysis of the colonial situation necessarily involved an overt prescription for the destruction of colonial structures. By the same token, his strictures against the African one-party state carried with it a strong emphasis on the need for, or rather the inevitability of radical transformation of postcolonial African societies.

Civic disorder then becomes the handmaiden of a radically restructured African polity because such a transformation can not be brought about by the ruling class or elite. It requires revolutionary praxis, activated and pursued by a coalition of disenchanted elements of the national middle class, the peasantry, and the lumpenproletariat to effect the transformation.[17]

From the perspective of underdevelopment theory two points must be emphasized in Fanon's condemnation of the one-party state. First, Fanon views the direction which the African postcolonial state was pursuing and the problems that it has given rise to as being directly intertwined with the nature of the colonial state and its inheritance. His notion of false

[17] What this implies in organizational terms is treated at length in Chapter 5.

decolonization is a useful analytical category in this respect. Secondly, Fanon goes beyond a concern with the contradictions arising from capitalist penetration of, and hegemony in the African postcolonial state to a concern with the internal sources of other contradictions: "the people find out that the iniquitous fact of exploitation can wear a black face, or an Arab one."[18] This is why he regarded the one-party state and such doctrinal programs as African Socialism as a ruse to mystify, so that colonial-type domination could continue unfettered under the guise of statism or indigenization.

It could be objected that Fanon's blanket condemnation of the single-party state as such failed to discriminate between those which were democratic or tending towards democracy and those which were not. For example, pointing to the structural differences between African "mass" and African "patron" parties, Ruth Schachter Morgenthau concluded that "in the present phase of West African party history, there is more evidence that the single party systems based on mass parties are moving towards democracy."[19]

It might, however, be argued in Fanon's favor that there was little distinction to be made between the African mass party and the patron party at the time Fanon was writing in 1960/1961. If there were the kinds of structural distinctions that Morgenthau made, it might, nevertheless, be pointed out that what such systems had in common, regardless of whether they were of the "mass" or "patron" party type, was a tendency towards the erosion of civil liberties and the emergence of a narrowly-based elite who had acquired political and economic power in virtue of their inheritance of the state apparatus.

Fanon's strictures were not limited to the one-party state. His basic concern was with the lack of accountability and

[18] Fanon, *Wretched of the Earth,* p. 145.

[19] Schachter (Morgenthau), "Single Party Systems in West Africa," p. 304. For a critique of Morgenthau's typology, see Zolberg, *Creating Political Order,* p. 10.

responsiveness to the grassroots by ruling parties in both single and multiparty systems in Africa. He detected a tendency, based on his knowledge of Ghana and the Ivory Coast,[20] for ruling parties to monopolize politics and clamp down on dissidents or members of opposition parties and groups:

> The embryo opposition parties are liquidated by beatings and stonings. The opposition candidates see their houses set on fire. The police increase their provocations.... All the opposition parties, which moreover are usually progressive and would therefore tend to work for the greater influence of the masses in the conduct of public matters and who desire that the proud, money-making bourgeoisie should be brought to heel, have been by dint of baton charges and prisons condemned first to silence and then to a clandestine existence.[21]

Was Fanon opposed to the one-party state as such? Or was he merely opposed to the perversion of the one-party state in Ghana and the Ivory Coast? If one proceeds from the assumption that Fanon is basically committed to democracy, the question then becomes whether a one-party state could be democratic. Viewed in this way, the question also touches on the meaning of democracy and its structural or institutional forms.

Although democracy is a contested concept, it is sometimes equated with tolerance of parliamentary opposition or dissent in the discussion of party systems in developing countries.[22] This view, based on the assumption that politics is pluralistic and pragmatic, a matter of reconciliation and argument, begs

[20] Cf. Caute, *Fanon,* p. 74: "his strictures were largely based on personal observations of society in Ghana and the Ivory Coast."

[21] Fanon, *Wretched of the Earth,* p. 182.

[22] D. E. Apter, "The Role of Political Opposition in New Nations," in I. L. Markovitz, ed., *African Politics and Society* (New York: The Free Press, 1970), pp. 226-241; D. E. Apter, "Political Religion in the New Nations," in D. E. Apter, ed., *Some Conceptual Approaches to the Study of Modernization* (Englewood Cliffs, New Jersey: Prentice-Hall, 1968).

the question of how opposition or dissent is to be expressed or organized.

Protagonists of the African one-party state tend to reject this pluralistic view of politics, preferring instead a collectivist view.[23] Their argument is also that, theoretically, there could be, and that there is in reality tolerance of dissent and opposition within the dominant single party. It is also argued that, on the wider societal level, particularly when it comes to defining and establishing party relationships with nonparty groups, there is necessarily a limit to how monopolistic the dominant single party can get.

Where then does Fanon stand? The answer to this question is not an easy one to offer. There seems to be an apparent similarity between him and such protagonists of the African one-party state as Touré and Nyerere, in that he shares their collectivist presuppositions. In this respect, there is some validity to Emmanuel Hansen's claim that "Fanon assumes that in his ideal society there will be a single-party system."[24]

Yet there is an important sense in which the issue of one-party or a multiparty system was epiphenomenal, as far as Fanon was concerned. Gendzier has observed quite rightly that in Fanon's view "whether there ought to be a single-party or a multiparty system was a secondary question."[25] What needs to be emphasized, however, is not the negative one that it mattered little to Fanon whether the party system was a single-party or multiparty one because in the postcolonial African state both party systems were under the control of the national bourgeoisie.

The answer to what party system Fanon preferred is that he was not particularly concerned about what form the party

[23] Madeira Keita, "Le Parti Unique en Afrique," *Présence Africaine,* No. 30 (February-March, 1960); Julius Nyerere, *Democracy and the Party System* (Dar-es-Salaam, 1963); Sekou Touré, *La Guinée et l'Emancipation Africain,* quoted in Andrain, "Democracy and Socialism," p. 159.

[24] Emmanuel Hansen, *Frantz Fanon: Social and Political Thought* (Columbus, Ohio: Ohio State University Press, 1977), p. 184.

[25] Gendzier, *Frantz Fanon,* p. 221.

system assumed. His overriding concern, the basic requirement he expected any party organization to conform with, was that any such organization must be open, should encourage participation by the mass membership and must not be taken over by political opportunists and careerists:

> The living party, which ought to make possible the free exchange of ideas which have been elaborated according to the real needs of the mass of the people, has been transformed into a trade union of individual interests.[26]

When Fanon, therefore, talks of *the party,* he is not talking of the single party. He is referring to what *any* party ideally should be. What matters most to him is the development of the social and political consciousness of the African masses. Whatever the form of the party organization, its task must be to facilitate the progressive attainment of this collective emancipation:

> In an underdeveloped country, the party ought to be organized in such a fashion that it is not simply content with having contacts with the masses. The party should be the direct expression of the masses. The party is not an administration responsible for transmitting government orders; it is the energetic spokesman and incorruptible defender of the masses.[27]

The type of party Fanon envisages, then, are mass parties that have socialist orientation, and there is no reason to assume that it is Fanon's contention that there must be only one socialist party in each African country.

Fanon's discussion of the role of the party in Africa points to the problematic nature of the relationship between party and class. The problem here is not simply that of elaborating the thesis that the political party, like the state, is an instrument

[26] Fanon, *Wretched of the Earth,* p. 170.
[27] Ibid., pp. 187-188.

of class rule. The problem rather is that, given the inherently oligarchical tendencies in any organization, how can we ensure that the socialist party "represents" those classes whose interest it is supposed to serve?

The problem is particularly relevant to Fanon's position since he places a great emphasis on the importance of the political educator as a revolutionary catalyst whose role is to organize and provide organizational direction for the party. The strategic question then becomes one of how to prevent the concentration of power in the hands of the leadership, or how to establish a congruence between party and class.

Fanon's answer to this problem is the vague one about the need to separate the party from "the administration" or government.[28] Yet the separation of the party from the administration would not necessarily prevent the bureaucratization of the party; nor would it necessarily ensure party accountability. The experience of Nkrumah's Convention People Party (C.P.P.) in Ghana is a case in point.

The C.P.P. under Nkrumah was taken over and dominated by political entrepreneurs who sought to maximize resources and rewards from the political marketplace for their own use. To use Fanon's terminology, the C.P.P. became in effect "a means of private advancement"[29] for these political entrepreneurs. To ascribe this development to the fusion of party and administration (whatever that may mean) is to overlook the intense ideological debate within the C.P.P. between 1960 and 1966 over the direction which the party should pursue.

What seems to matter, therefore, is not the separation of party from government but the attitude of party functionaries to government. What is also of importance is how the party organization is structured so as to prevent political entrepreneurs from taking advantage of their access to political power. If this is a plausible position to assume, then it is

[28] For cogent criticism of Fanon's formulation of this problem, see Hansen, *Frantz Fanon*, pp. 190-192.

[29] Fanon, *Wretched of the Earth*, p. 171.

consistent with Fanon's claim that the nature of the decolonization process has important ramifications for the kinds of structures, including party structures, that would ultimately emerge in the postcolonial state in Africa.

With respect to Ghana, Fitch and Oppenheimer have argued that Nkrumah's attempt to create a socialist party in Ghana was compromised *ab initio* by his opting for a gradual, reformist and constitutional path to decolonization.[30] This is because the strategy enabled the class of political entrepreneurs to consolidate its power base within the C.P.P.

A plausible interpretation of Fanon's enigmatic thesis about the separation of the party from the government can, however, be attempted. To do this one must view the thesis as reflecting a concern about the need to ensure the accountability of the party-in-government to its rank and file outside of government.

Writing towards the end of the nineteenth century in reaction to the emergent labour and socialist movements in Europe, Ostrogorski expressed the fear that caucus control might compromise the independence of elected MPs. Ostrogorski feared that such a development would turn the parliamentary parties into slaves of their extraparliamentary organizations.[31] This is a position which Fanon apparently rejects in observing that "we must above all rid ourselves of the very Western, very bourgeois and therefore contemptuous attitude that masses are incapable of governing themselves."[32]

Part of the problem revolves around what it is to democratize a party. One interpretation of Fanon's thesis about the

[30] Robert Fitch and Mary Oppenheimer, *Ghana: The End of an Illusion* (New York: Monthly Review Press, 1966). See also Basil Davidson, *Black Star: A View of the Life and Times of Kwame Nkrumah* (London: Allen Lane, 1973), particularly Chapter 4; and S. G. Ikoku, *Le Ghana de Nkrumah* (Paris, France: Maspero, 1971).

[31] R. T. Mackenzie, *British Political Parties: The Distribution of Power Within the Conservative and Labour Parties* (New York: Praeger, 1963), pp. 8-10.

[32] Fanon, *Wretched of the Earth*, p. 188.

separation of the party from the government is that it expresses a concern about the possible emergence of a power base independent of the party where there is a fusion of the party and government. Fanon is not making the obviously absurd claim that party members should not hold government positions. Nor is it his contention that a party in power should not disburse patronage to its members.

Fanon's thesis should be viewed as expressing a concern that party functionaries do not take advantage of their appointive positions in government to deviate from the ideals of their party. Since power tends to corrupt, it is of supreme importance, therefore, that some form of accountability be maintained by separating the party from the government, which is to say that the government should be accountable to its rank and file:

> The party is not a tool in the hands of the government. Quite on the contrary, the party is a tool in the hands of the people; it is they who decide on the policy that the government carries out. The party is not, and ought never to be, the only political bureau where all the members of the government and the chief dignitaries of the regime may freely meet together.[33]

This does not, as was indicated earlier, remove the problem of how the emergence of oligarchic tendencies *within* the party was to be prevented — something which has nothing to do with the separation of party and government. The problem would still be an important one, even if the party was not in power. This particular problem would seem to be an ineluctable one and vague references to the need for party decentralization and the imperative of the party's reflecting the wishes of the masses do not constitute adequate solution. For one thing it is problematic what constitutes the "party." For example, is it a homogeneous or heterogeneous entity? For another thing, how

[33] Ibid., p. 185.

are the wishes of the masses to be determined? At best, the problem might be regarded as one of formulating what the acceptable limit of oligarchy should be and how the structure of command and leadership inherent in any organization could be constrained. Fanon is quite right in maintaining that a distinction should be made between the party and the state apparatus and for insisting that the structure of the party can be an important limitation on the prerogatives of the party in government vis-è-vis its mass organization outside.

Although Fanon is concerned with the need to separate the party from the government, he offers no discussion of the relationship between the governing party and the state bureaucracy. Colin Leys has pointed to the ambiguity in Fanon's reference to a "bourgeoisie of the civil service."[34] My concern here, however, is with the tension, now endemic in African politics, evident in the relationship between ministers or cabinet office-holders and the senior or higher civil service. Part of the problem in this respect concerns the notion of the impartiality or neutrality of the civil service and whether it should serve an interest "higher" or different from that of the particular regime in power. The problem is further exacerbated by a number of factors.

First, there is the fact that the higher civil service was indeed politicized under colonial rule, in that it served the interest of colonial administration. Secondly, there is the tendency of the inheritance elite to view the civil service as providing a source of reward and opportunities for its political supporters. Thirdly, there is the alleged professionalization of the higher civil service which is supposed to make it difficult to remove senior civil servants who are antagonistic to the programs or policies of the party in power.

Fanon would have ridiculed the notion of an apolitical civil service as a myth. Yet one wonders what his prescription for

[34] Leys, *Underdevelopment in Kenya*, p. 193, fn. 34.

the separation of party and government implies for the relationship between the party and the higher civil service.

Fanon seems to have given inadequate thought to a concern such as Nyerere's with how to constrain the higher civil service and ensure that it does not engage in antiparty activities or usurp the policy-making mandate of the executive. Fanon's mistake, perhaps, is similar to that made by Marx. Assuming that the state bureaucracy is epiphenomenal, Marx had not assigned it an important role in his analysis of the dynamics of class conflict. He simply assumed that the state was an instrument of class domination. Yet, as has become increasingly clear, not only may the state bureaucracy develop its own corporate or class interest, it may also assume an existence independent, and even subversive of the ruling class.

Class and Politics in Fanon

I have suggested earlier in this chapter that Fanon's analysis of African politics in terms of class political behaviour marked a radical and pioneering effort, if placed in the context of prevailing orthodoxies in the study of African politics in the early 1960s. Fanon's analysis, however, raises two problems.

One problem concerns the applicability of a class model of political conflict to Africa. It might be objected that ethnic, regional, religious or some other primordial attachment was more important than class divisions in explaining political processes in Africa. It might also be contended that the class conflict model was inapplicable to Africa because the data on which to differentiate classes are hard and, perhaps, impossible to obtain in Africa.[35] A second problem arises out of Fanon's implicit assumption, in discussing the historical processes set in motion by the colonization of Africa, that

[35] Cf., P. C. Lloyd, ed., *The New Elites of Tropical Africa* (London: Oxford University Press, 1966), pp. 46-62; V. L. Allen, "The Meaning of the Working Class in Africa," *The Journal of Modern African Studies*, Vol. 10, No. 2 (July, 1972).

precolonial African societies were basically classless. A corollary of this implicit assumption is Fanon's explicit attribution of the emergence of class division in Africa to the factor of colonial rule. The problem, then, is one of determining whether precolonial Africa was basically classless and also whether it was the case that colonial rule gave rise to class division.

How applicable is a class conflict model to Africa? There are two aspects to this problem. There is the conceptual problem of determining whether "class" has the same meaning in Africa as in industrial Europe. The other aspect of the problem is whether class, as an analytical category, is preferable to ethnicity for appraising African politics.

Let us consider the conceptual problem. It arises because most African economies are nonindustrial (or industrially undeveloped) and are characterized by the juxtaposition of precapitalist and capitalist modes of production. What this means, however, is not that there are no classes in Africa or that class analysis is inapplicable; rather it means that such an analysis must proceed with caution. The relevance of class analysis lies in the objective situation in African societies and the contradictions arising from it. To say that class contradictions have not matured in Africa owing to its embryonic industrial structure is not to deny the existence of classes in the Marxian sense.[36]

Fanon defines classes in terms of their relationship to the means of production. But he also defines them in terms of their access to the sources of political power. This is reflected in his discussion of the relationship between the center and the periphery. Thus, he identifies the national bourgeoisie and the proletariat in terms of their cosmopolitan character and the peasantry in terms of its suspicion of the "townspeople." In this dichotomy, the center represents the seat of political power.

Fanon's focus on access to the source of political power in

[36] Cf. Ake, *Revolutionary Pressures in Africa*, pp. 61-69.

defining class is also reflected in his discussion of the national bourgeoisie. According to him, the privileged position of the national bourgeoisie rests less on its control of the economic infrastructure or the means of production than on its acquisition of political power:

> The national middle class discovers its historic mission: that of intermediary. Seen through its eyes, its mission has nothing to do with transforming the nation; it consists prosaically of being the transmission line between the nation and a capitalism rampant though camouflaged, which today puts on the mask of neocolonialism.[37]

In a sense, therefore, Fanon's emphasis on access to the source of political power and the emergence of a comprador bourgeoisie marks a partial modification, in the African context, of the Marxian identification of class with modes and relations of production. It seems that Fanon is pessimistic about the possibility for independent industrialization in Africa, since this comprador bourgeoisie is unprepared "to repudiate its own nature,"[38] and is only interested in perpetuating the economic system inherited from the colonizer:

> The precariousness of its resources and the paucity of its managerial class force it back for years into an artisan economy. From its point of view, which is inevitably a very limited one, a national economy is an economy based on what may be called local products.[39]

Let us now consider the question whether class is a better analytical category than other alternative ones for appraising African politics. The problem then revolves around whether horizontal divisions possess more explanatory potential than vertical ones. This, however, is a pseudo-problem in that both

[37] Fanon, *Wretched of the Earth*, p. 152.
[38] Ibid., p. 150.
[39] Ibid., p. 151.

approaches are not mutually exclusive. An emphasis, such as Fanon's, on horizontal divisions is not incompatible with one on vertical divisions. Richard Sklar's classic study of Nigerian political parties is a case in point.[40]

Fanon himself admits the salience of ethnicity, religion, nationalism, and language as factors to consider in analyzing African politics. But he looks upon them as factors that should be considered primarily in the context of intra-elite conflict and power struggle among the national bourgeoisie. This comes out in his discussion of the relationship between party politics and ethnicity:

> This party which of its own will proclaims that it is a national party, and which claims to speak in the name of the totality of the people, secretly, sometimes even openly, organizes an ethnic dictatorship. We no longer see the rise of a bourgeois dictatorship, but a tribal dictatorship.[41]

Let us now consider another set of problems, that are raised by Fanon's implicit assumption about the classless nature of precolonial African societies. This assumption is shared by a number of African political thinkers;[42] but it has been rejected by others.[43] While it may be the case that there was some

[40] Richard L. Sklar, *Nigerian Political Parties* (Princeton, New Jersey: Princeton University Press, 1963). See also his, "Political Science and National Integration: A Radical Approach," *The Journal of Modern African Studies*, Vol. 5, No. 1 (May, 1967), p. 6.

[41] Fanon, *Wretched of the Earth*, p. 183.

[42] See Kenneth Grundy, "The 'Class Struggle' in Africa: An Examination of Conflicting Theories," *The Journal of Modern African Studies*, Vol. 2, No. 3 (November, 1964), pp. 379-393.

[43] Kwame Nkrumah, *Class Struggle in Africa* (New York: International Publishers, 1970). For an earlier support of the classlessness thesis by Nkumah, see his *Consciencism*, rev. ed. (New York: Monthly Press, 1970), pp. 68-69; Samir Amin, "The Class Struggle in Africa," *Révolution* (Paris, France, September 9, 1964).

degree of classlessness in precolonial societies,[44] Fanon's claim is, however, debatable.

In this respect the claim must be qualified because of the wide divergence of precolonial African political systems. In addition, ethnographic data tend to suggest the existence of different levels of social stratification in precolonial Africa. Peter Lloyd's study of the social structure in the Yoruba kingdom is a case in point.[45]

If Fanon's implicit assumption about the classlessness of precolonial Africa is tendentious, what about his explicit attribution of the emergence of class formation in Africa to colonialism? There can be little doubt that colonial rule induced profound structural changes in Africa and that it led to the creation of a duality of political and particularly economic structures in Africa.

The economic transformation effected by colonial rule was even more significant than the impact of colonial rule on political structures. The expansion of the market system into the periphery under colonial rule created new economic actors as competitors with, and in many cases to replace, the traditional political elite, namely kings, chiefs, and noblemen. But because the market system created by colonial rule was essentially a monopolistic one protected by mercantilist policies, it precluded the participation of African entrepreneurs and therefore stunted the development of an indigenous bourgeoisie that owned and controlled the means of production: "Under the colonial system, a middle class which accumulates capital is an impossible phenomenon."[46] At best, as Fanon points out, the role of the African entrepreneur in

[44] Cf. Robin Cohen, "Class in Africa: Analytical Problems and Perspectives," in Ralph Miliband and John Saville, eds., *The Socialist Register, 1972* (London: Merlin Press, 1972), p. 231.

[45] Peter C. Lloyd, *Africa in Social Change* (London: Penguin, 1967), pp. 42-43. See also Szyman Chodak, "Social Classes in Sub-Saharan Africa," *African Bulletin*, No. 4 (Warsaw, 1966), p. 20.

[46] Fanon, *Wretched of the Earth*, p. 150.

this type of monopoly capitalism was that of an "intermediary," a "transmission line," a "business agent."[47]

The attribution of a "causal" power to the colonial factor insofar as the emergence of class division in Africa is concerned raises the question whether, had there been no colonization or colonial rule, such a division would not have occurred. Though a hypothetical question, it is one that must be answered if one is to understand the nature of emergent class conflict in places like Ethiopia and Liberia which were never under colonial rule.[48] What then is the connection between colonial rule and class conflict in Africa? Put differently, is colonial rule a necessary and sufficient condition for the emergence of classes and class conflict in Africa?

The case of Ethiopia and Liberia seems to imply that classes and class conflict could emerge without colonial rule;[49] and that, therefore, colonial rule is neither a necessary nor sufficient condition for the emergence of classes in Africa. It must be pointed out, however, that Fanon's thesis is not that it is colonial rule as such that gave rise to classes in Africa, but that the development is to be sought in Africa's incorporation into and involvement in a particular world economic system, whose logic inevitably leads to class differentiation and the emergence in Africa of a comprador bourgeoisie. Although they were nominally independent, Ethiopia and Liberia, like the rest of Africa, were peripheral appendages of this global capitalist economic system.

It now remains to point out one further respect in which Fanon's conceptualization of the relationship between class and politics needs to be modified. There is need to relate the

[47] Ibid., pp. 150-154.

[48] Ethiopia was of course occupied by Mussolini's Italy in 1936, but the short period of Italian occupation cannot be equated with colonial rule; rather it was a case of foreign military occupation.

[49] Donald N. Levine, "Class Consciousness and Class Solidarity in the New Ethiopian Elites," in Peter C. Lloyd, ed., *New Elites of Tropical Africa* (London: Oxford University Press, 1966), pp. 312-325; Merran Fraenkel, *Tribe and Class in Liberia* (London: Oxford University Press, 1964).

development of classes to the natural resource endowment of African countries, since it is such a resource endowment that partly determines the place of each African country in the periphery of world capitalism and what industrial infrastructure is developed by the colonial power. It should therefore be expected that the more endowed an African country is with natural resources, the more highly developed will be its infrastructure and therefore its middle class.[50]

The Dialectics of Class Political Behavior

Fanon's analysis of class political behaviour in *Wretched of the Earth* points to one inescapable conclusion: African politics is inherently unstable, is characterized by violence and is marked by an absence of commitment to the public interest. The element of instability is reflected in the fragility of political institutions and Fanon's anticipation of the proliferation of one-party regimes, including military regimes in African politics:

> It is in these conditions that the regime becomes harsher. In the absence of a parliament it is the army that becomes the arbiter: but sooner or later it will realize its power and will hold over the government's head the threat of a manifesto.[51]

There is an element of pessimism in Fanon's analysis of the course of politics in Africa. He offers a prognosis of political deterioration and decay. He also seems to be hopeful that the contradictions generated by the dynamics of political conflict will create a revolutionary situation. Just as the colonial regime placed so much emphasis on violence because it was illegitimate, so also did the successor regime in postcolonial

[50] Cf. Ake, *Revolutionary Pressures in Africa,* pp. 63-64.
[51] Fanon, *Wretched of the Earth,* p. 174.

Africa. However, the more repressive the regime becomes, the more politicized disgruntled elements become:

> The revolutionary minority finds itself alone, confronted with leaders who are terrified and worried by the idea that they could be swept away by a maelstrom whose nature, force or direction they cannot even imagine.[52]

This paradox of pessimism tempered by optimism pervades Fanon's analysis in *Wretched of the Earth.* It now remains to examine his identification of the basic contradictions or pathologies exhibited by various classes in Africa. To do this is to assess the force of his attribution of the latent element of political instability in Africa to the working out of these contradictions.

Let us start with the national bourgeoisie. Among the pathologies of this class are its parasitic dependence on the West; its contemptuous disregard of rural areas; its lack of a sense of direction and national purpose. But above all this class exhibits an inability to act out an enterprising and entrepreneurial role similar to that of the bourgeoisie in the West: "...here the dynamic, pioneer aspect, the characteristic of the inventor and of the discoverer of new worlds which are found in all national bourgeoisies are lamentably absent."[53]

Not only are members of the bourgeoisie unenterprising and lacking in managerial and entrepreneurial ability, they are also wasteful, corrupt and given to conspicuous consumption: "scandals are numerous, ministers grow rich, their wives doll themselves up."[54] Fanon also condemns the narrow nationalism of the ruling elements of the bourgeoisie, evident in their strategy of diverting responsibility for the mismanagement of the national economy to non-national Africans and

[52] Ibid., p. 124; see also ibid., pp. 125-126.
[53] Ibid., p. 153.
[54] Ibid., p. 172.

other aliens who are engaged in competitive trade with nationals.[55]

Nigeria typically provides confirmation of Fanon's identification of the pathologies of the African bourgeoisie. The corruption of the Nigerian bourgeoisie, particularly of political office holders and public functionaries, has been amply documented by various commissions of inquiry. The findings of these public commissions have generally pointed to the abuse of public trust by public officials.[56]

Fanon's analysis is open to a number of criticisms. First, he tends to use "bourgeoisie" and "middle class" synonymously. It seems that he identifies the middle class as the class which by virtue of its training and intermediary role between the colonizer and colonized, steps into the void left by the departure of the colonizer. But if this is the case, which class has stepped into the position hitherto held by the middle class? Yet, Fanon also seems to contend that there is really no bourgeoisie but only a middle class.[57] A second criticism pertains to the issue of class consciousness. Objectively, there may be an African bourgeoisie or middle class. It remains problematic, however, whether the various strata of this class subjectively perceive their collective interest and act as a class. The problem is further complicated by the fact that Fanon lumps together under the category, middle class or national bourgeoisie groups with differing relationships to the means of production: intellectuals, professionals, the landed aristocracy, industrialists, financiers, businessmen, and civil servants.

Thirdly, Fanon does not explore the possibility of a clash of interests between the middle class and Western bourgeois and neocolonial interests. He tends to ignore how much room for maneuver the ruling elements of the middle class have at their

[55] Ibid., pp. 156-158.

[56] See, for example, *Report of the Coker Commission of Inquiry into the Affairs of Certain Statutory Corporations in Western Nigeria, 1962,* 4 Vols. (Lagos, Nigeria: Federal Ministry of Information, 1962).

[57] Fanon, *Wretched of the Earth,* p. 175.

disposal by virtue of their political power and control of the state apparatus. This room for maneuver is further enlarged by competition among Western bourgeois interests in the various African countries, as Richard Sklar's study of Zambia has illustrated.[58] Economic nationalism, in the form of indigenization policies as in Kenya, Nigeria, and Tanzania, may serve to consolidate the privilege of the middle class, but it also serves a diversionary purpose in so far as it is directed against Western investors.

This distinction between political power and economic power brings out the reciprocal nature of the dependence relationship. This reciprocal relationship is, however, asymmetrical in that the exercise of the economic power of the Western bourgoisie can ultimately undermine the political power of the middle class in peripheral African countries.[59]

Fourthly, Fanon's claim that "the bourgeois phase in the history of underdeveloped countries is a completely useless phase,"[60] is one of the many dark or enigmatic passages in *Wretched of the Earth.* It is unclear what Fanon means by it. Woodis and Nzongola have contended that the bourgeois phase of the African revolution is not a useless one in that it is dialectically necessary for the transition to socialism.[61] It seems to me that this contention fails to take into account Fanon's argument that contradictions in the postcolonial African state are creating a revolutionary situation.

Although Fanon's meaning is unclear, it makes some sense if it is placed in the context of his skepticism concerning the validity of a two-phased strategy for achieving the socialist

[58] R. L. Sklar, *Corporate Power in an African State: The Political Impact of Multinational Mining Companies in Zambia* (Berkeley and Los Angeles: University of California Press, 1975).

[59] Cf. Ake, *Revolutionary Pressures in Africa,* pp. 27-28; Jack Woodis, *New Theories of Revolution,* p. 96.

[60] Fanon, *Wretched of the Earth,* p. 176.

[61] Woodis, *New Theories of Revolution,* p. 97; Georges Nzongola (Ntalaja-Nzongola), "The Bourgeoisie and Revolution in the Congo," *The Journal of Modern African Studies,* Vol. 8, No. 4 (December, 1970), p. 529.

revolution in Africa. The issue then becomes, as discussed in Chapter 5, the empirical and ideological one as to whether a bourgeois nationalist revolution can and ought to be simultaneously a socialist one. In other words, Fanon's contention that a bourgeois nationalist revolution must be simultaneously a socialist one does not entail the proposition that the bourgeois phase is not a dialectically necessary one for the transition to socialism.

What does Fanon say about the political behavior of the African proletariat? The most glaring pathological behavioral characteristic of the African proletariat, according to Fanon, is its lack of revolutionary consciousness. Fanon contends that the involvement of the African proletariat with the neocolonial economic system and the advantages it was deriving from it have led to its *embourgeoisement.*[62]

Fanon, however, concedes that the African proletariat does not lack political or trade union consciousness:

> During the colonial phase, the nationalist trade-union organizations constitute an impressive striking power. In the towns, the trade unionists can bring to a stand-still, or at any rate slow down at any given moment, the colonialist economy. Since the European settlement is often confined to the towns, the psychological effects of demonstrations on that settlement are considerable: there is no electricity, no gas, the dust bins are left unemptied, and goods rot on the quays.
>
> These little islands of the mother country which the towns constitute in the colonial structure are deeply conscious of trade-union action; the fortress of colonialism which the capital represents staggers under their blows.[63]

This trade-union consciousness is carried over into the postcolonial era during which it assumes more potentially

[62] Fanon, *Wretched of the Earth,* pp. 108-109.
[63] Ibid., pp. 121-122.

explosive dimensions because of the revolution of rising expectations that have set in since the attainment of independence:

> The trade union leaders, steeped in working class political action, automatically go from there to the preparation of a *coup d'état*.... The national middle class taking up the old traditions of colonialism, makes a show of its military and police forces, while the unions organize mass meetings and mobilize tens of thousands of members.[64]

The problem with this manifestation of trade union consciousness is that it is not linked with the need to organize the peasantry and lumpenproletariat for revolutionary action; so much so that " 'the interior' — the mass of country dwellers — knows nothing of this conflict."[65] However, when they find it convenient for their own purposes, trade union leaders "in a kind of Machiavellian fashion all make use of the peasant masses."[66] But because of the cultural distance between town and country and "since at no time have they taken care to establish working links between themselves and the mass of the peasants... the trade unions will give proof of their inefficiency and find out for themselves the anachronistic nature of their programs."[67]

In view of such criticisms as those by Woodis and Ledda,[68] it must be emphasized that Fanon is not condemning trade union consciousness as such. As Lenin's *Left Wing Communism — An Infantile Disorder*[69] makes clear, partial

[64] Ibid., p. 123.
[65] Ibid., p. 122.
[66] Ibid., p. 123.
[67] Ibid.
[68] Woodis, *New Theories of Revolution*; Ledda, "Social Classes and Political Struggle," *International Socialist Journal*, No. 22 (August, 1967).
[69] V. L. Lenin, *Left-Wing Communism: An Infantile Disorder*, rev. translation (New York: International Publishers, 1939).

reforms can be accommodated and channelled to revolutionary ends. But what Fanon, like Lenin, is emphasizing is that the ideological stance from which trade union consciousness and, therefore, socioeconomic and political reforms are pursued is of crucial importance.

Fanon's counterposing of the trade union consciousness of the African proletariat with revolutionary consciousness is his way of emphasizing that this particular brand of trade union consciousness proceeds from an ideological perspective which does not seek more than partial and incremental reforms. It does not look beyond them to a sustained effort to pose a radical challenge to, and therefore seek to bring about fundamental changes in the status quo. This is why Fanon, linking the development of the trade union movement to the process of false decolonization in much of Africa, characterizes the program of most African trade unions as being "above all a political program and a nationalist program."[70]

Where Fanon seems to part company with some Marxists is whether in the contemporary African context and, given the structure of political and economic relations, there is some basis for expecting that the trade union consciousness of the African proletariat would in due course be translated into revolutionary consciousness. Fanon is vulnerable in foreclosing this possibility. But his vulnerability does not arise from the fact that empirical evidence has invalidated his position. It arises from the fact that, as Sir Karl Popper has argued, it is logically impossible for us to "anticipate today what we shall only know tomorrow."[71]

What does the empirical evidence suggest? A recent study by Richard Sandbrook concludes that:

> Frantz Fanon's sketch of the role of organized labour in an economically dependent former colony is largely

[70] Fanon. *Wretched of the Earth*, p. 121.

[71] Sir Karl Popper, *The Poverty of Historicism* (London: Routledge and Kegan Paul. 1961)

> correct in its application to Kenya. Top union leaders, drawn from the more privileged occupations, receiving relatively high rewards, and apprehensive of the sanctions wielded by the ruling elite, have generally seen their role as obtaining a larger piece of the pie for the workers within the capitalist political economy.[72]

Recent studies have suggested that as the underlying contradictions of neocolonial economies in Africa mature and become manifest, trade union consciousness has assumed radically militant dimensions which aim at destroying and transforming existing socioeconomic and political structures.[73]

Yet, as most of these studies also agree, "economism has been the prevalent orientation (of trade unions) in all African countries."[74] The reason for this is partly that the ideological perspective from which this trade union consciousness springs is limited to piecemeal reforms. It is also partly due to what Fanon correctly diagnoses as the failure of African trade unions to establish links with and organize the peasantry for revolutionary or transformatory political action.

In Nigeria during the 1964 general strike, political action by the trade unions was limited to the urban areas and there was little effort to mobilize and organize the peasantry. During the "Agbekoya" peasant riots of 1969 in Western Nigeria, there was little attempt by the trade unions to get involved in the challenge posed to the military government by the peasantry. In Ghana, part of the failure of the spate of industrial unrest triggered by the trade unions, students and professionals in 1976 was due to its being urban-centered. As

[72] Richard Sandbrook, *Proletarians and African Capitalism: The Kenya Case, 1960-1972* (London: Cambridge University Press, 1975), p. 191.

[73] See Richard Sandbrook and Robin Cohen, *The Development of an African Working Class: Studies in Class Formation and Action* (London: Longman, 1975), Part. III, pp. 195-316.

[74] Ibid., p. 200.

the conclusion to a collection of case studies of African trade unions puts it:

> At this stage it cannot be firmly asserted that workers will assume a permanent and leading radical role in their societies. Such manifestations that could superficially point in this direction have all indicated that a counter-ideology to that of the ruling classes remains at the level of a loosely-held populist sentiment. *Moreover, workers have generally failed to make their own struggles relevant to the vast masses outside the urban areas, and have failed to sustain a radical political alternative once the dust has settled on their immediate sources of grievances.*"[75] (emphasis mine).

Let us now examine one criticism of Fanon's version of the labour aristocracy thesis.[76] Fanon has made the empirical claim that the urban worker is privileged and pampered, if compared to the peasantry: "The embryonic proletariat of the town is in a comparatively privileged position."[77] It is important to emphasize that Fanon is contrasting the urban worker to the peasantry and lumpenproletariat.

Fanon's position does not entail a denial of the fact that, if demographic and ecological data of living conditions in African towns are considered, it will be found that the urban worker does not enjoy affluence or that his living conditions are grossly worse off than those of the middle class.[78] That Fanon realizes this state of affairs is clear from his description

[75] Ibid., p. 316.

[76] The explicit formulation of the thesis, described by Sandbrook on page 18 of the study cited in footnote 72, as a quasi-Fanonist formulation, can be found in G. Arrighi and J. Saul, *Essays on the Political Economy of Africa* (New York: Monthly Review Press, 1973), pp. 44-102, 105-151. For the controversy the thesis has generated, see Sandbrook and Cohen, *Development of an African Working Class*, Part III.

[77] Fanon, *Wretched of the Earth*, p. 108.

[78] Ledda, "Social Classes and Political Struggle," pp. 572-573; Woodis, *New Theories of Revolution*, pp. 108-113; Sandbrook and Cohen, *Development of an African Working Class*, pp. 3-4.

of the Manichaeism or structural violence, characteristic of the large cities under colonial rule.[79] His reference to trade union consciousness also attests to his realization of the relative deprivation of the typical urban work.

Fanon is not arguing that in an absolute sense all is a bed of roses for the urban worker; rather his contention is that to the extent to which the urban area is developed at the expense of the countryside, the urban worker stands to gain more in an economic and social sense than the peasant. It is not enough, therefore, to argue that the African worker is economically and socially depressed. It has to be shown also that the urban worker is worse off than the peasant.

The tendency to misinterpret Fanon on this issue is related to another misinterpretation of his thesis about the privileged position of the African proletariat. Fanon's enigmatic reference to the proletariat as "the 'bourgeois' fraction of the colonized people"[80] may have contributed to this misinterpretation. Yet this is no ground for assuming that Fanon is contending that there is necessarily an identity of interest between the proletariat and the middle class. To say that both classes have an interest in perpetuating the colonial or neocolonial system is not to say that they do so for the same reasons; nor is it to argue that they are not in a dialectical relationship.

Fanon's thesis that the African proletariat is in a privileged position has also been countered by reference to other demographic data. Thus, it has been argued that whatever income disparity there is between the urban worker and the peasant is offset by inflationary pressures in urban areas as well as the social and economic obligations which derive from mores attaching to the extended family system.[81]

[79] Fanon, *Wretched of the Earth*, pp. 39-40.

[80] Ibid., p. 109.

[81] Woodis, *New Theories of Revolution*, p. 108; Cohen, "Class in Africa," pp. 239-240; Sandbrook and Cohen, *Development of an African Working Class*, p. 204.

Although there may be some reason to see a weakening of the extended family system in the development of the nuclear family, the reference to the socioeconomic obligations of the urban worker is true. But it is also true that the middle class bears the same responsibility. Does it then mean that the middle class is not in an exploiting situation vis-à-vis the other classes, in much the same sense that the proletariat, as a social category as opposed to individual urban workers, stands vis-à-vis the peasantry and lumpenproletariat? Moreover, inflationary pressures do extend to the rural areas as the Agbekoya riots in Western Nigeria in 1969 have shown.

In a sense, the existence of these responsibilities cannot be used to argue for the revolutionary proclivities of the proletariat. What it explains is the fact of relative deprivation. It cannot explain class political behaviour. To do that, some other intervening variable like political organization must be utilized. For example, it can plausibly be argued that, in spite of his relative deprivation vis-á-vis the lawyer or medical doctor, the urban worker, on account of his economic and social obligations to his extended family, will be less willing to resort to radical, revolutionary action for fear of being laid off.

Fanon's discussion of trade union consciousness is problematic in another respect. It is arguable that, in discussing trade union involvement in national politics, particularly at the center, Fanon should have distinguished between trade union leadership and its followership. It is unclear from his analysis whether he is criticizing trade union leaders or the trade union membership generally. His emphasis on revolutionary organization (what he calls, again vaguely, "political education") suggests that he should have focused more on trade union leadership. By so doing, Fanon's analysis would have provided a framework for partly explaining why in some African countries, like Nkrumah's Ghana, the trade union movement has virtually become branches of the ruling party. In such cases, it is not unlikely that trade union leaders see in trade unionism a means for cooptation and upward mobility.

This has happened to some extent in Nigeria where a number of trade union leaders have ended up in management positions, and where the history of the trade union movement has been characterized by internecine rivalry among the trade union leadership for recognition and favours from various regimes.

Fanon was also concerned with the pathological behaviour of the peasantry and the lumpenproletariat, even though he assigned revolutionary potentials to both classes. It was pointed out in Chapter 5 that Fanon not only made explicit reference to the paradoxical nature of African peasants societies, but also recognized that the lumpenproletariat could be reactionary.

With respect to the African peasantry, Fanon saw it as symbolizing resistance and opposition to the diffusion of Western influence in the countryside. The peasantry therefore reflects both cultural authenticity and political radicalism in its resistance to Western influence. Fanon's point, like Debray's, is that the peasantry is not inherently conservative or anarchistic.

What Fanon attempts to do is to explain, as Debray also does with respect to the Cuban revolution, peasant involvement in the Algerian revolution in terms of the intervention of "external" agencies or groups which mobilized them for revolutionary action. The role of these external agencies is, according to Fanon, and as I have already suggested, to provide the peasantry with direction and orientation, an ideology or cognitive map of the world as well as an organizational medium for action.

Fanon's discussion of peasant conservatism in the context of sub-Saharan Africa contains an implicit theory of the articulation of socioeconomic and political power in rural Africa and its relationship to the central political authority. Contrary to the position of Jack Woodis,[82] Fanon neither

[82] Woodis, *New Theories of Revolution*, p. 55.

paints a picture of a socially undifferentiated rural Africa nor does he overlook the existence of peasant landlordism.

Fanon repeatedly refers to the feudal structure of rural Africa: "ringed around by marabouts, witch doctors, and customary chieftains, the majority of country dwellers are still living in the feudal manner."[83] Within this feudal structure, although the applicability of Marxian class categories might be inappropriate, Fanon identifies an exploiting group as well as an exploited one.

The sources of control by the exploiting group ("marabouts, witch doctors, customary chieftains") derive basically from their status in the traditional social hierarchy, and the spiritual or religious aura surrounding these status roles. The development of the market economy partly contributed to and reinforced the emergence of an exploiting group ("the national landed proprietors")[84] whose position derives from its control of economic resources, particularly land.

Fanon is not clear on the composition of the exploited group in rural Africa. It seems, however, that he would include peasant labourers, and landless peasants in the category. This list can also be extended to include migrant or urbanized peasant labourers who seasonally move between town and country.

Although Fanon makes reference to the "spontaneity" or radicalism of the peasantry, his discussion of the mode of articulation of power in traditional (i.e., rural) African societies gives the impression that such societies are "closed"[85] societies: "The bulk of the country people for their part continue to live within a rigid framework."[86] If what Fanon means by "rigid

[83] Fanon, *Wretched of the Earth*, pp. 109-110.

[84] Ibid., pp. 154-155.

[85] For an application of the concept of closed society to African societies, see Robin Horton, "African Traditional Thought and Western Science, Part. II: The 'Closed' and 'Open' Predicaments," *Africa*, Vol. 37 (1967), pp. 155-187; M. G. Marwick, "How Real Is the Charmed Circle in African and Western Thought?" *Africa*, Vol. 43, No. 1 (1973), pp. 59-70.

[86] Fanon, *Wretched of the Earth*, p. 111.

framework" is an unquestioning attitude towards the authority of traditional rulers, for example, or lack of an awareness of alternatives to traditional structures of control, such a thesis must be qualified by an argument such as that advanced by J. H. M. Beattie, that "it is plain from the more thorough ethnography of the past half century or so that the authority of such rulers is generally restricted by a wide range of social institutions."[87]

How does Fanon relate the structure of socioeconomic and political power at the periphery to the center? Under colonial rule, the need to encapsulate or incorporate the periphery into the central political framework necessarily posed a challenge to and partly succeeded in altering traditional socioeconomic and political structures.[88] Yet Fanon does not consider at great length the fact that center penetration of the periphery under colonial rule, particularly in its political dimensions, was problematic. This is because the role of traditional chiefs as agents of colonial rule, to take one example, was viewed with ambivalence by their subjects. Although the agent's role was defined by and supported by the coercive powers of the center, that role was nevertheless circumscribed by the normative structure of traditional political organizations. This is particularly true with traditional rulers who were also acutely aware of their traditional responsibilities to their subjects.

This ambivalent attitude of subjects to the role of their

[87] J. H. M. Beattie, "Checks on the Abuse of Political Power in Some African States: A Preliminary Framework for Analysis," *Sociologus*, Vol. 9, No. 2 (1959), p. 97. See also Peter C. Lloyd, "The Political Structure of African Kingdoms: An Exploratory Model," in Michael Banton, ed., *Political Systems and the Distribution of Power* (London: Tavistock Publications, 1965), especially pp. 99-106.

[88] Fanon, *Wretched of the Earth*, pp. 94-136; but see ibid., p. 111 for a contrary position which reflects what Hannah Arendt once described as Fanon's "rhetorical excesses": "The native peasantry lives against a background of tradition where the traditional structure of society has remained intact." This statement should, however, be interpreted as reflecting Fanon's view that the colonial center was only partially successful in incorporating traditional political structures.

traditional rulers was manifested in the high incidence of tax revolts in rural Africa. As Fanon himself implies, this ambivalent attitude was also exploited by the nationalist parties who cast the traditional rulers in the role of agents of foreign rule:

> The colonial system encourages chieftaincies.... Thus the nationalist parties show no pity at all toward the caids and the customary chiefs. Their destruction is the preliminary to the unification of the people.[89]

Fanon also offers some discussion of the relationship between traditional political structures and central political ones in postcolonial Africa. The relationship, according to him, is an antagonistic one. It is not clear from reading him whether he attributes the source of the antagonism to the contempt of the inheritance elite for the traditional rulers,[90] or to the latter's (traditional rulers') determination to preserve its authority from being eroded by the emergent central political authority.[91]

Fanon gives the impression that the resistance of traditional authority to the center in postcolonial Africa is unprogressive.[92] In this respect, he reflects the tendency of some national political leaders in Africa to view insistence, such as that of the Ashanti and Baganda, on the autonomy of their traditional political institutions as a threat to national unity. As I have argued elsewhere, we need to view the

[89] Ibid., p. 94.

[90] Ibid., p. 113: "The traditional chiefs are ignored, sometimes even persecuted.... The old men surrounded by respect in all traditional societies and usually invested with unquestionable moral authority, are publicly held to ridicule."

[91] Ibid., p. 110 where Fanon observes of the traditional chiefs that "they know very well that the ideas which are likely to be introduced by these influences coming from the towns call in question the very nature of unchanging, everlasting feudalism."

[92] Ibid., p. 110.

insistence as constituting an attempt to check and restrain the abuse of power by the political center.[93]

It is not, however, always the case that there is an antagonism between traditional authority and the nationalist leaders. As Syl Whitaker has shown, traditional authority in Northern Nigeria served a "modernizing" role[94] and was not necessarily antagonistic towards the rising Northern middle class or educated elite.

What Fanon perhaps fails to understand is that traditional political authority underwent various changes under colonial rule and that such changes must be viewed in the context of the nature of the traditional political authority in question, the impact of colonial administration and the nature of the emergent nationalist party.[95]

Summary

Fanon's framework of analysis in explaining African politics emphasizes class political bahavior in its historical and cultural context. The framework is neither a neat one nor one that is methodologically and empirically unassailable. Yet, as I have argued in this chapter, there is also much that is provocative and insightful in Fanon's attempt to explain the pathologies and contradictions of African politics in terms of class and the historical processes that influence and constrain class political behavior. Blind Fanonism is as bad as rabid

[93] L. Adele Jinadu, *Structure and Choice in African Politics* (Bloomington, Indiana: African Studies Program, Indiana University, Tenth Annual Hans Wolff Lecture, 1978), pp. 25-26.

[94] C. S. Whitaker, Jr., *The Politics of Tradition: Continuity and Change in Northern Nigeria, 1946-1966* (Princeton, New Jersey: Princeton University Press, 1970), pp. 317-467.

[95] Peter C. Lloyd, "Traditional Rulers," in J. S. Coleman and C. G. Rosberg, Jr., eds., *Political Parties and National Integration*, p. 384.

anti-Fanonism. Or, as Thomas Hodgkin puts it, "critical Fanonism is much to be preferred to dogmatic Fanonism."[96]

What needs to be emphasized above all is the basic relevance of a perspective such as Fanon's to an understanding of the sources and implications of counter-revolutionary and reactionary trends in Africa. Perhaps the picture it offers is a partial one; nevertheless it offers some insight.

The moral dimension that informs the perspective is no less important because Fanon's strong advocacy of the need to restructure African societies is premised on a value or normative preference for the freedom of the individual, an assumption which also underlines his contention that government is a trust which must not be abused. In the next chapter I examine what policy options can be deduced from this ideological perspective.

[96] Thomas Hodgkin, review of Fitch and Oppenheimer, *Ghana: End of an Illusion* in *Journal of Modern African Studies,* Vol. 4, No. 3(1966), p. 383.

Chapter 8

SOME POLICY IMPLICATIONS

Introduction

Fanon was concerned with a policy-oriented political philosophy. His concern springs from his notion of commitment as a practical, problem-solving activity.[1] It is of course to be expected that any political philosophy is explicitly concerned with, in fact motivated by, policy matters. This is reflected in his declaration that:

> I believe that the fact of the juxtaposition of the white and black races has created a massive psychoexistential complex. I hope by analyzing it to destroy it.[2]

Fanon believed that there is necessarily an important connection between ideas and events. They shape, influence, and constrain each other. In a sense, man provides the link between ideas and events; he does this by designing policies that are goal-oriented. To be concerned with policy is therefore to be concerned with the wider societal context in which policy is to be formulated and implemented:

> But society, unlike biochemical processes cannot escape human influences. Man is what brings society into being. The prognosis is in the hands of those who are willing to get rid of the worm-eaten roots of the structure.[3]

[1] See Chapter 5.
[2] Fanon, *Black Skin, White Masks*, p. 12.
[3] Ibid., p. 11.

Policy formulation is, on this view, not an isolated activity. If policy is set in a wider social context, then it should be possible to reason out the consequences of a particular policy and compare it with what might reasonably be expected from the adoption and pursuit of a different policy. Fanon therefore regards policy formulation as necessarily experimental in nature. It is experimental in the sense that where there is reason, based on our experiential observation, to believe that policy is not working as well as it should or that its social vision is limited, then it should be rejected.

The social context within which policy is formulated and executed is important for Fanon in another respect. The adoption of the wrong policy options or failure of policy to work as well as it should may point to a more fundamental problem inherent in the structure of economic and political power in society. If that is the case, then even the best conceived policy is inevitably bound to be distorted in its execution.

It is not only the execution of policy that is likely to be distorted by the structure of socioeconomic and political power. The very formulation of policy as well as the problem to which policy addresses itself can be a function of the structure of power relations in society. Policies designed to effect radical transformation of society must therefore be concerned with the destruction and transformation of existing structures of power relations. This view of the relationship between policy and the structure of power relations is expressed in Fanon's letter of resignation to the Resident Minister in Algiers:

> Although the objective conditions under which psychiatry is practiced in Algeria constituted a challenge to common sense, it appeared to me that an effort should be made to attenuate the viciousness of a system of which the doctrinal foundations are a daily defiance of an authentically human outlook.[4]

[4] Fanon, *Toward the African Revolution*, p. 52.

If structures have an important effect on the formulation and execution of policy, then we must have some evaluative criteria for distinguishing and discriminating among them. The determination of these evaluative criteria is problematic, although Fanon's ultimate criterion is on the impact of structures on the individual: "The social structure existing in Algeria was hostile to any attempt to put the individual back where he belonged."[5] By the same token, there must be some evaluative criteria to guide policy choices. In this respect, Fanon again vaguely refers to "the principle that man is the most precious of all possessions."[6]

Fanon then was concerned with policy issues and the problems posed for policy formulation and execution in the economic and social welfare spheres by the structure of socioeconomic and political power within and outside of Africa. According to one view, "the trouble here is that he did not tackle the problems of constructing a socialist economy and society in any detail."[7] What meaning is to be attached to "in any detail" in this context is unclear. But it is, however, clear that Fanon's political writings contain in broad outlines his views on the nature of policy formulation and the type of policy programs that he wanted to see implemented.

It must be borne in mind that *Wretched of the Earth* was written under the pressures of a war of national liberation and the awareness of impending death. The impression that "he did not tackle the problems of constructing a socialist economy and society in any detail" is perhaps due to the general polemical and didactic thrust of the book. Yet, there can be little doubt that a number of policy recommendations can be implied from his normative assumptions and his analysis of the pathologies of African politics and underdevelopment. I now

[5] Ibid., p. 53.
[6] Fanon, *Wretched of the Earth*, p. 99.
[7] David Caute, *Fanon* (London: Fontana/Collins, 1970), p. 77.

turn to an examination of some of these policy recommendations.

The Design of Socioeconomic Policies

Fanon's discussion of the design of policies and strategies to cope with problems of African underdevelopment proceeds on the assumption that there is an imperative need to restructure the world economic system. As he puts it, "What counts today, the question which is looming on the horizon, is the need for a redistribution of wealth. Humanity must reply to this question, or be shaken to pieces by it."[8] Unless this is done, the situation in much of Africa will be such that "the apotheosis of independence is transformed into the curse of independence, and the colonial power through its immense resources of coercion condemns the young nation to regression."[9]

Economic policy must then have as one of its basic purposes the creation of new international economic structures to replace current structures that are characterized by situations of unequal exchange between Western countries and African countries. What these new structures would entail was not satisfactorily explored by Fanon. For example, what form should the "redistribution of wealth" take?

Fanon's answer seems to be reflected in his notion of reparation or compensation for the economic exploitation of Africa by the West. The moral and legal issues raised by the notion of reparation are complex. Should the present generation be held accountable for the "sins" of earlier generations? How is the extent of injury to be determined? How much surplus was extracted by the colonial powers and their commercial surrogates? Was the surplus extracted by the state or by individual entrepreneurs? If injury was suffered by

[8] Fanon, *Wretched of the Earth*, p. 98.
[9] Ibid., p. 97.

individuals, then why should the reparations be made to a collectivity, like the nation-state?[10]

Fanon is unconcerned about these fundamental problems. He merely assumes, as he does in his discussion of collective responsibility, that the case for reparations is self-evident:

> We are not blinded by the moral reparation of national independence, nor are we fed by it. The wealth of the imperial countries is our wealth too .... For in a very concrete way Europe has stuffed herself inordinately with the gold and raw materials of the colonial countries: Latin America, China, and Africa.[11]

For him a basic form that reparation should take is aid, and perhaps capital investment:

> This help should be the ratification of a double realization: the realization by the colonized peoples that *it is their due*, and the realization by the capitalist powers that in fact *they must pay*.[12]
>
> Then the monopolies will realize that their true interests lie in giving aid to the underdeveloped countries — unstinted aid with not too many conditions.[13]

Fanon does not therefore rule out foreign aid and the encouragement of foreign capital investment as implements of economic policy. Realizing that the objective situation is such

[10] For aspects of the controversy, see Boris I. Bittker, *The Case For Black Reparations* (New York: Random House, 1978); D. K. Fieldhouse, *The Colonial Empires: A Comparative Survey from the Eighteenth Century* (London: Weidenfeld and Nicolson, 1966), pp. 380-394; Walter Rodney, *How Europe Underdeveloped Africa* (Washington, D.C.: Howard University Press, 1974); Douglas Rimmer, "The Economics of Colonialism in Africa," *Journal of African History*, Vol. 19, No. 2 (1978), pp. 265-273.

[11] Fanon, *Wretched of the Earth*, p. 102.

[12] Ibid., p. 103 (Emphasis in original); also ibid., "The plans for nuclearizing the world must stop, and large scale investments and technical aid must be given to underdeveloped regions."

[13] Ibid., p. 105.

as to make African countries dependent on external sources of economic assistance, Fanon is, however, concerned that nationals exercise a large measure of control over their national economy. Whether this is possible then depends partly on the domestic economic policy of the national government and also partly on its ideological orientation.

Fanon's answer to the problem of the "redistribution of wealth" seems principally to be economic aid and private investment from the West. It seems, however, that he is also concerned with the terms of trade that sustain the relationship of unequal exchange between the West and Africa. This concern is implied in the following passages:

> But another danger threatens it as well. Insofar as the Third World is in fact abandoned and condemned to regression or at least to stagnation by the selfishness and wickedness of Western nations, the underdeveloped peoples will decide to continue their evolution inside a collective autarky. Thus the Western industries will quickly be deprived of their overseas markets.[14]

> The Third World does not mean to organize a great crusade of hunger against the whole of Europe. What it expects from those who for centuries have kept it in slavery is that they will help it to rehabilitate mankind.... But it is clear that we are not so naïve as to think that this will come about with the cooperation and the goodwill of the European governments.[15]

Fanon therefore seems to be arguing that an instrument of economic policy for African countries should be to join other primary commodity or raw material producing countries, so that they would be in a strong position to demand improved terms of trade with the West and other industrialized nations. This cartelization is a form of violence, a continuation of the

[14] Ibid., pp. 104-105.
[15] Ibid., p. 106.

struggle for political independence and it depends on the economic strength of these African countries:

> So we see that the young nations of the Third World are wrong in trying to make up to the capitalist countries. We are strong in our own right, and the justice of our point of view.[16]

The strategy implied in Fanon's position has been articulated by developing countries at various times since the early 1960s. For example there is the challenge that has been posed to the General Agreement on Tariffs and Trade (GATT) by developing countries. This challenge culminated in 1964 in the formation of the United Nations Conference on Trade and Development (UNCTAD) whose aim is to seek improvement in the inequities arising out of the terms of trade for primary commodities. The economic leverage of the UNCTAD members has also been reinforced by their numerical strength in the United Nations General Assembly.

Other examples are the Organization of Petroleum Exporting Countries, The International Tin Agreement, and the International Bauxite Association. In a sense, developing countries are now demanding, individually and collectively, and in the spirit of Fanon, a greater share of the benefits from foreign trade and investment. Their bargaining strength is further enhanced by the growing competition for such scarce resources as petroleum by the industrialized countries.

It is, of course, questionable to what extent cartelization has resulted in a restructuring of the global economic system. The gap between the rich and poor countries has not narrowed, which is to say that there has been little "redistribution of wealth." Moreover, the price-fixing monopoly of the West over technological goods and services, as well as the dependence of developing countries on these goods and

[16] Ibid., p. 105.
[17] Ibid., p. 177.

services, has enabled the industrialized countries to recoup the increased prices they have had to pay for some primary commodities by charging higher prices for their technological goods and services. Moreover, the success of cartelization as a strategy depends on the elasticity of demand of, or the ready availability of substitutes for the various commodities and raw materials.

The issue of the "redistribution of wealth" is further compounded by two factors. The first factor relates to the rivalry and ideological schism within the various primary producing cartels. This situation poses problems of coordination, unity, and compliance with cartel decisions. The second factor is the concentration of the benefits from improved terms of trade in a few hands in primary producing countries.

It seems, therefore, that Fanon's advocacy of an economic war against the industrialized countries is of limited value. How much weight or importance he attaches to it is not clear. Nor is it clear whether he views it as being more than a symbolic gesture of protest. However, the foreign trade components of his strategy for national economic development must be viewed in the context of its domestic aspects.

An underlying theme in Fanon's discussion of national economic development is the need for social control of the national economy. But since he realizes the tendency for power to be concentrated in few hands, Fanon does not necessarily equate social control with state centralization. Such a centralization would go against his emphasis on self-reliance, local autonomy and the decentralization of power. What his prescription for social control of the national economy implies, however, is "the necessity for a planned economy."

A basic problem to confront in designing domestic economic policies directed toward social control of the economy is that posed by the nature and direction of the economy inherited from colonial rule:

> Perhaps it is necessary to begin everything all over again: to change the nature of the country's exports and not

> simply their destination, to reexamine the soil and mineral resources.[18]

But, "in order to do all this other things are needed over and above human output — capital of all kinds, technicians, engineers, skilled mechanics and so on."[19]

How is the change to be brought about? Fanon's answer is partly that the intermediary sector of the national economy be indigenized. Given the problems of generating capital from internal sources, Fanon seems to prefer a strategy based on "trade and small business enterprises" to one designed "to set on foot an embryonic industrial revolution."[20] As he states:

> Nationalizing the intermediary sector means organizing wholesale and retail cooperatives on a democratic basis; it also means decentralizing these cooperatives by getting the mass of the people interested in the ordering of public affairs.[21]

It seems, therefore, that Fanon is skeptical of the possibility for independent industrialization in Africa. It is not clear whether Fanon would like to see the development of an indigenous entrepreneurial class in the intermediary sector; nor is it clear whether his position is that the intermediary sector should be made up predominantly of parastatals. The problem is not clarified by Fanon's claim that "it is clear that such a nationalization should not take on a rigidly state-controlled aspect."[22]

The problem arises because it is unclear what Fanon means by "a rigidly state controlled" intermediary sector. Fanon's concern is probably the avoidance of a state-protected capitalism which, by establishing "a dictatorship of civil

[18] Ibid., p. 100.
[19] Ibid.
[20] Ibid., p. 179.
[21] Ibid., p. 180.
[22] Ibid.

servants ...," would result in inefficiency, graft and corruption.[23] But it is unclear whether this also implies an open market system in which, with the role of the state limited to providing security and the formulation of fiscal and monetary policies, the state does not engage directly in productive enterprises. It seems, however, that Fanon's concern that "nationalization should not take on a rigidly state-controlled aspect," does not rule out a public sector.

Another indication of Fanon's meaning is provided by his discussion of the rural sector and the need to avoid its being swamped by the central authority. Fanon makes constant and repeated references to decentralization as a principle of political and socioeconomic organization. What he is opposed to is government acting as a big brother. He is therefore concerned that local communities make vital decisions affecting their economic life autonomously. The role of the state should be to coordinate the economic activities of the various communities and integrate them into a national economic planning strategy:

> The people must understand what is at stake. Public business ought to be the business of the public. So the necessity of creating a large number of well-informed nuclei at the bottom crops up again. Too often, we are content to establish national organizations at the top and always in the capital.[24]

The creation of "well-informed nuclei at the bottom" implies the creation of extension services and rural cooperatives. The emphasis should be on communal projects. The learning or citizenship training aspect of these forms of economic organization is no less important than their economic aspect for the process of national development.

What Fanon's theory of participation or mobilization

[23] Ibid.
[24] Ibid., p. 194.

implies for economic organization and policy is illustrated by Algeria's experiment in *autogestion* (or self-management) and Tanzania's experiment in rural socialism.[25] Gendzier has pointed out that "one source, a contemporary of Fanon's, maintains that the organization of councils for self-managed communities was a distinctly Fanonian innovation."[26] Another source has informed this author that President Julius Nyerere's speech-writer at the time the Arusha Declaration was proclaimed in Tanzania was an avid reader of Fanon.

Algeria's experiment in self-management represents a programmatic attempt to institutionalize and create structures that will ensure a high degree of decentralization and populist democracy in the organization of economic activities. It is viewed as an antidote to creeping state capitalism. It's adoption in Algeria is closely linked to the experience of revolutionary action, the almost total collapse of the Algerian economy with the rushed and hasty departure of French settlers in the summer of 1962; and the initiatives of the Union Travailleurs Algeriens (UGTA) with regard to the expropriation of factories and commercial enterprises left by the settlers in Grand Alger and Oran.

The circumstances that led to *autogestion* in Algeria therefore vindicate Fanon's observation that "as soon as the capitalists know ... that their government is getting ready to decolonize, they hasten to withdraw all their capital from the colony in question. The spectacular flight of capital is one of

[25] For Algeria's *autogestion*, see Ian Clagg, *Workers' Self-Management in Algeria* (London: Penguin, 1971); J. R. Nellis, "Socialist Management in Algeria," *The Journal of Modern African Studies*, Vol. 15, No. 4 (1977), pp. 529-554. For Tanzania's *ujamaa* socialism, see C. Ake, "Tanzania: The Progress of a Decade," *The African Review*, Vol. 2, No. 1 (June, 1972), pp. 56-64; L. Cliffe, "The Policy of Ujamaa Vijijini and Class Struggle in Tanzania," *Rural Africana*, Vol. 13, (1971); D. Feldman, "The Economics of Ideology: Some Problems of Achieving Rural Socialism in Tanzania," in C. Leys, ed., *Politics and Change in Developing Countries* (London: Cambridge University Press, 1969).

[26] Gendzier, *Fanon*, p. 258.

the most constant phenomena of decolonization."[27] The indigenization of the economy is also a preliminary step in restructuring productive relations.

The theoretical justification of *autogestion* as a programmatic implementation of socialism in Algeria was first set forth in the Tripoli Program (1962) and later in the *Charte et Code de la Gestion Socialiste des Enterprises* (1971). Both doctrinal documents emphasize, as Fanon does, that *comites des gestion* (worker's management committees) should offer individuals unique opportunities for controlling and getting involved in matters that concern and affect them. As a form of socioeconomic and political organization, these committees are designed to function as experiments in participatory democracy; they can thus be viewed in the spirit of Fanon's insistence that "there must be decentralization in the extreme."[28]

In the case of Tanzania, the Arusha Declaration represented an attempt to formulate and implement concrete programs to reflect the socialist path the country has chosen. Its emphasis was on a developmental strategy rooted in self-reliance and with a strong focus on rural development. The Declaration thus addresses itself to a basic concern of Fanon: the general exodus of enterprising young men from the rural to the urban areas, the general experience of poverty in the rural areas and the ever-widening socioeconomic gap between town and country. As Fanon puts it, "the moment for a fresh national crisis is not far off. To avoid it we think that a quite different policy should be followed: that the interior, the back country ought to be the most privileged part of the country .... The capital must be deconsecrated."[29]

The strategy pursued in Tanzania has been the creation of *ujamaa* villages with the aim of transforming the rural areas and rural cultivators. Such a transformation should be brought

[27] Fanon, *Wretched of the Earth*, p. 103.
[28] Ibid., pp. 197-198.
[29] Ibid., p. 186.

about by the creation of modern collective agricultural areas that are, in effect, cells or socioeconomic communities. But these cells or communities are also political artifacts or structures in that they are expected to provide outlets, as part of the ruling party's organizational network, for increased political communication between town and country.

The theoretical thrust animating the form and structure of economic organization in Algeria and Tanzania proceed from the same source. But the nature of the colonial inheritance, particularly the material bases of economic relations and production, has called for differing tactical and programmatic emphasis in both countries. The colonial economy in Algeria, unlike that in Tanzania, was heavily tilted in favor of the modern sector, with emphasis on an incipient capital intensive industrial sector for the extraction of petroleum and mineral resources.

In short, heavy emphasis is placed on industrialization in Algeria whereas in Tanzania there has been a deliberate policy, that is due perhaps to the virtual absence of a modern industrial sector, against industrialization. From the perspective of Fanon, however, the large expansion of the public enterprise sector in both countries might be worrisome in that it could lead to increasing state capitalism and bureaucratization. The operation of the parastatals in Tanzania has, in this respect, come under attack by the left wing of the political spectrum in Tanzania.

It must be admitted that the operation of *autogestion* in Algeria and of *ujamaa* socialism in Tanzania has not been immune from the tendency of any form of political and socioeconomic organization or structure to deviate from the expectations of those who have designed it. Thus, in both countries one can point to deviations which Fanon's emphasis on decentralization was intended to avoid: increasing centralization at the center, the diminishing role and degeneration of the party, the emergence of class formation that is due in part to access to power at the center and the resurgence of individualism, particularly by workers and peasants who, opposed to central control, have come to view the experiment in decentralization in both countries with strong distrust.

The basic problem is one that Fanon did not resolve and that is inherently an ineluctable one: how to reconcile the need for central control (Fanon's "social control") with the autonomy of the periphery and the prevention of central impingement. Yet this is not to disparage the commitment to decentralization in Algeria and Tanzania. This is because such a commitment does constrain behavior, and therefore makes a difference, in an important sense. It offers a corrective as well as a point of departure for confronting contradictions that must inevitably arise out of the process of governing or constituting a political system.

The Design of a Constitutional Order

Fanon was concerned about the condition under which a political system is constituted. The legitimacy of any political system cannot therefore be separated from the nature of its origins: what gave rise to it? Who were involved in its creation and in what capacity? What and whose needs is the system designed to serve? It was stated earlier on in this chapter that Fanon views policy formulation as an experiment. If this is the case, then it also follows that there must be a way of relating an experiment to its results or consequences.

What does all of this have to do with the constitution of a political order? It is that if there is reason to believe that a political system is not functioning well, then a new experiment might plausibly be designed to replace the old one. This implies that we can identify what was wrong with the old experiment or why it did not conform to our expectations. This is why Fanon views the design of a constitutional order as a deliberative and reasoned exercise in political choice.

The problem of constituting a political order in Africa has assumed increasing importance in recent years, particularly with the appearance in 1976 of *la charte nationale* in Algeria, the adoption of new constitutions in Nigeria and Ghana in 1978-1979, and the on-going controversy over the nature of the constitutional settlement in Zimbabwe.

What experimental guidelines for the design of a constitutional order emerge from Fanon's political writings? The answer to this question is provided by Fanon's analysis of the pathologies of African politics. As I have indicated earlier, the pathologies are to be explained in terms of both the incorporation of Africa into a world capitalist system and the nature of the colonial inheritance. The design problem then becomes one of seeking alternatives to the constitutional order inherited or established at independence:

> Come, then, comrades; it would be as well to decide at once to change our ways. We must shake off the heavy darkness in which we were plunged, and leave it behind.[30]

The culture concept is relevant to Fanon's concern with the design of a constitutional order. Indeed Fanon regards political systems as cultural artifacts: "We believe that the conscious and organized undertaking by a colonized people to re-establish the sovereignty of that nation constitutes the most complete and obvious cultural manifestation that exists."[31] Fanon therefore argues that, in solving the problem of constitutional design, Africans should have recourse to their culture and ask whether the desired solution is to be found in traditional political structures:

> the underdeveloped countries ought to do their utmost to find their own particular values and methods and a style which shall be peculiar to them.[32]

[30] Ibid., p. 311.
[31] Ibid., p. 245.
[32] Ibid., p. 99.

Fanon is also concerned that the exercise of power should be limited. This is why he placed so much premium on decentralization. To design a constitution is, according to Fanon, to limit and constrain the exercise of power. This is why colonial rule is necessarily authoritarian rule; and to the extent to which successor regimes in Africa have assumed wide, unlimited power, they also are authoritarian.

The strategic or design problem posed by Fanon's reference to culture is that of determining what aspects of it should be reflected in the constitution. Or, put differently, what ideas about government in traditional African societies are of contemporary relevance and significance? Unfortunately, Fanon offers neither concrete examples of how culture can be reflected in the constitution nor indicators of which aspects of traditional political culture are most appropriate for contemporary needs.

Given his concern for decentralization and the imposition of checks on the exercise of power, one can conjecture that Fanon would have found much to recommend in those traditional systems such as the Bemba, Ashanti, Pondo, and Khoisa which some social anthropologists have characterized as federative monarchies.[33] The ideas of government underlying political organization and the structure of social relations in the federative monarchies can then be used to inform the design of constitutions in postcolonial Africa.

Why should culture inform the design of constitutions? Fanon's answer would be that there is a strong connection between culture and freedom or self-government. Where the political institutions of a people reflect an alien culture or value system, there may be some reason to doubt whether the people in question are free. Fanon's argument would be that self-affirmation and pride in their culture constituted part of the basic conditions of freedom for a people. To refuse to

[33] S. N. Eisenstadt, "Primitive Political Systems: A Preliminary Comparative Analysis," *American Anthropologist*, Vol. 61, No. 2 (1959), p. 211.

reflect that culture or aspects of it in their political institutions is to deny their freedom.

It is surprising that, in spite of his emphasis on decentralization, Fanon rejects federalism as a constitutional form of government. Federalism as a system of concurrent regimes in which the decentralization or nonconcentration of power is assured by a constitution and not by the center would seem to offer a solution to Fanon's concern about the encroachment of the center on the periphery. Why then did Fanon reject the federalist option?

Fanon's rejection of federalism seems to be based on his equating it with regionalism or ethnic chauvinism. Presumably the exigencies of national unity and development make it imperative that regionalism or ethnic loyalty be subordinated to the higher purpose of creating a nation-state. According to him:

> Even after the struggle for national freedom has succeeded, the same mistakes are made and such mistakes make for the maintenance of decentralizing and autonomist tendencies. Tribalism in the colonial phase gives way to regionalism in the national phase, and finds its expression as far as institutions are concerned in federalism.[34]

> The party which advocates unity will be drowned in the computations of the various splinter groups, while the tribal parties will oppose centralization and unity.[35]

It is also problematic that Fanon who argues that "there must be decentralization in the extreme," should condemn it in another context: "This tribalizing of the central authority, it is certain encourages regionalist ideas and separatism. All the decentralizing tendencies spring up again and triumph, and the nation falls to pieces, broken in bits."[36] Tribalization then

[34] Fanon, *Wretched of the Earth*, pp. 113-114.
[35] Ibid., p. 119.
[36] Ibid., p. 183.

becomes synonymous with decentralization. It may well be the case that Fanon is not against decentralization but only the form it assumes in the guise of tribalism or regionalism.

But why should Fanon equate tribalism with federalism? Obviously tribalism can be a problem in a nonfederal, i.e., unitary system of government. There is therefore no casual connection between federalism and tribalism, i.e., federalism is neither the cause nor effect of tribalism. Fanon's position is probably due to the equation of federalism with weak government and the duplication of human and other resources. Moreover, his rejection of federalism may be owing to what he perceives as the tendency of the federal system to emphasize what divides rather than unites the nation. In such a circumstance it is only too easy for antinational or separatist elements to exploit ethnic divisions for their own goals.

Fanon never really confronts the issue of how to organize the various ethnic groups in each African country under the umbrella of a national government. Here again, vague references to education for citizenship will not do. The point rather is that if Fanon's counsel for decentralization is to take a political form, then one inescapable criterion for decentralization will be the ethnic community. This is because decentralization implies territorial demarcation and the identification of the human population to occupy the territory so demarcated. Devolution of power under a unitary system is as likely as decentralization or deconcentration of power under federalism to involve limited autonomy of ethnic groups.

What does all this point to ? It is that Fanon was concerned with specifying certain conditions for constitutional order. First, he argued that any attempt to constitute a constitutional order must raise questions about the domestic and external structural conditions under which the exercise in constitutional choice is to be carried out. From his point of view the crisis of constitutional order in Africa is due precisely to the failure to deal with the structural questions. Decolonization was equated with the "transfer" of metropolitan constitutional norms and forms to Africa.

Secondly, since to constitute a political system is to structure social relations, Fanon was concerned with the constitutive rules of the political system. As I have already indicated, he contended that any such rules must reflect and be informed by indigenous values and ideas of government. His position in this respect is similar to that expressed by Cabral's dictum about the need to "return to the source." The constitutive rules must also be based on the assumption that government should be limited and constrained in the exercise of its power.

Fanon's perspective on the problem of constitutional order also carries with it a number of implications. First, the political system so constituted must be a highly participant, i.e., nonauthoritarian one. This is why he was strongly opposed to the African one-party state. Secondly, there must be equity in the allocation of resources between persons and also between the various sections (geographical zones) of the political system. Social justice thus becomes a crucial factor in the design of a constitutional order; hence, Fanon's opposition to both bourgeois capitalism and state capitalism.

Thirdly, there must be decentralization of power and decision-making processes. Not only would decentralization constitute a learning process, but it would also give citizens multiple access to those who exercise the prerogative of ruling.

Cultural Policy

Fanon sees in culture a potentially liberating force. The design of socioeconomic and political structures must be accompanied, indeed reinforced with the appropriate policy for the cultural transformation of Africa. The enjoyment and enrichment of culture, of course, depends on power structures within society. However, culture can play the dialectical role of exposing, confronting and transcending contradictions in society.

Put differently, Fanon's position is that, although culture is dependent on and reflects the material base and social reality, it can also affect consciousness and, in so doing, can facilitate or slow down the processes of social change. In any case, Fanon views culture as a superstructure around which socio-economic and political institutions should be organized.

Fanon's concern with culture points to the psychological or reorientational dimension of national development in Africa. On this view ideology is a cultural phenomenon, an agent of cultural management. What then must be the components of a cultural policy?

An approach to indicating what Fanon's answer would be is to consider his critique of négritude as a form of cultural nationalism. Fanón was not opposed to cultural nationalism as such. Indeed he would agree with Cabral's observation that "the study of the history of national liberation struggles shows that generally the struggles are preceded by an increase in expression of culture".[37] Fanon's quarrel with négritude was that it tended to become a form of mystification, elitist in orientation and direction; above all, it lacked a populist vision; it did not constitute a radical ideological program; rather, it became an ideology of collaboration with the West:

> It is around the peoples' struggle that African-Negro culture takes on substance, and not around songs, poems or folklore. Senghor, who is also a member of the Society of African Culture and who has worked with us on the question of African culture, is not afraid for his part either to give the order to his delegation to support French proposals on Algeria. Adherence to African-Negro culture and to the cultural unity of Africa is arrived at in the first place by upholding unconditionally the peoples' struggle for freedom....[38]

[37] Amilcar Cabral, *Return to the Source: Selected Speeches* (New York: Monthly Review Press, 1973), p. 43.

[38] Fanon, *Wretched of the Earth*, p. 235.

For Fanon, therefore, a cultural policy is more than simply indulging in annual or periodic ritual of cultural festivals of art and dance. It is more than a symbolic change in school curriculum. Such a policy must be animated by a social purpose. As he states:

> The problem is to get to know the place that these men mean to give their people, the kind of social relation that they decide to set up, and the conception they have of the future of humanity. It is this that counts; everything else is mystification, signifying nothing.[39]

A cultural policy must, then, take the concrete, programmatic form of political action, in other words, "to fight for nation culture means in the first place to fight for the liberation of the nation, that material keystone which makes the building of a culture possible."[40]

One area in which Fanon's discussion of culture has important application is in the area of language policy. It is argued in Chapter 3 that Fanon's thesis about the function of language as a subtle form of colonialism is relevant to an understanding of both the incipient class formation and the gap between the center and periphery in Africa. If one accepts Fanon's linguistic *Weltanschauung* hypothesis, then one may want to make a case for a language policy aimed at encouraging local languages and substituting them for foreign ones. If one does not accept Fanon's hypothesis, one may nevertheless want to encourage literacy in, and therefore wider use of, local languages in order to bridge the gap between the elite and the masses.

Somalia's experiment in a national written language is, in this respect, in the spirit of Fanon. In October, 1972, President Siad Barre announced that the Somali language had been chosen as the official language of the country. The decision

[39] Ibid., pp. 234-235.
[40] Ibid., p. 233.

was set in the wider context of the ideological and cultural goals of the Somali Revolution. But it was not a hasty decision, in that the previous two years had been spent in reasoning out what problems its adoption might create.

The mass literacy campaign at the end of March, 1973 was well-received and it enabled the masses to relate to the broad goals set by the government. It would have been a different case with English, Italian, or Arabic. As one official source puts it, the adoption of Somali as a national language was meant to

> eliminate illiteracy, to introduce compulsory general education for the new generations, to prepare numerous intellectual cadres from the ranks of the people, to form cadres of scientists from the ranks of the people, to educate the population in the socialist spirit, to strengthen the capacity of putting public interests above individual interests, to promote and strengthen feelings of patriotism and internationalism, to develop literature and art in every way, placing them in the service of the cause of socialist education.[41]

All this might be self-serving and hyperbolic. What is important, however, is the detailed study that was undertaken before the decision to adopt Somali as a national language was taken as well as the eventual development of a Somali script and Somali texts. It is also noteworthy that "the road was open to reconsider from scratch the questions of public education, from a standpoint that saw Somali as the language of the elementary and middle school grades, where foreign languages were to be supplementary; to become basic in the upper school age."[42]

The role of education as a catalyst for cultural transformation has also been emphasized in Tanzania. As if in reaction to Fanon's injunction that socioeconomic and political transformation be linked to cultural transformation, Tanzania

[41] Quoted in Luigi Pestalozza, *The Somialian Revolution* (France: Société d'Editions Afrique, Asie, Amérique latine, 1974), p. 206.

[42] Ibid., p. 204.

policymakers have mapped out a long-term strategy whose aim is the revamping of the structure and philosophy of the educational system inherited from the British.[43] Particular emphasis is placed on the education of farmers since they constitute a preponderant percentage of the population. The doctrinal pronouncement, *Education For Self Reliance* was conceived with a view to transforming the inherited educational curriculum and it also underscored the attempt to create a new culture pattern to counter elitist tendencies and the drift toward the urban centers.

Swahili has been adopted as a national language. Although the composition of plays and poems in Swalili is encouraged and there are annual school-theatre competitions, the cultural renaissance so generated does not yet match the Somali experiment. Yet the implementation of *ujamaa* socialism, with all the problems it has encountered and sacrifices it has entailed, has had an impact on the collective cultural consciousness of Tanzanians.

The important point to emphasize is that in both countries, as well as in Algeria, cultural policy is not pursued in isolation but is consciously linked to the social, economic, and political goals of the governments in these countries as part of an overall ideological view of national development and of the world. Or put differently, the goal of national development in each country is to effect a cultural transformation along socialist lines.

Pan-African Policy

Fanon's concern for Pan-African unity pervades much of his political writings. But what form should that unity assume? What practical steps should be taken to make it a reality? One obstacle to the attainment of Pan-African unity that Fanon identifies is the manifestation of micronationalism at the level

[43] D. Court, "The Social Function of Formal Schooling in Tanzania," *The African Review*, Vol. 3 (1973), pp. 577-593.

of the nation-state. Such a manifestation fails to take a wider view of developmental problems facing the continent:

> African unity, that vague formula, yet one to which the men and women of Africa were passionately attached, and whose operative value served to bring immense pressure to bear on colonialism, African unity takes off the mask, and crumbles into regionalism inside the hollow shell of nationality itself.[44]

Attachment to the notion of the sovereign nation-state in Africa, therefore, manifests itself in discriminatory practices against non-national Africans:

> The Dahomian and Voltaic peoples who control the greater part of the petty trade are, once independence is declared, the object of hostile manifestations on the part of the people of the Ivory Coast. From nationalism we have passed to ultra-nationalism, to chauvinism and finally to racism. These foreigners are called on to leave; their shops are burned, their street stalls are wrecked, and in fact the government of the Ivory Coast commands them to go.[45]

It seems plausible to infer from Fanon's condemnation of this manifestation of micronationalism that he would like to see a free movement of labor and capital between, for example, neighboring African countries.

Fanon was concerned to emphasize the interdependence of African countries, an interdependence which should be further strengthened in virtue of Africa's colonial experience. One area in which interdependence can be pursued and taken advantage of is in the area of economic cooperation. Fanon does not explicitly address himself to this issue. His concern for new international economic structures and his advocacy of the need for primary commodity producing countries to join

[44] Fanon, *Wretched of the Earth,* p. 159.
[45] Ibid., p. 158.

together in an economic war against the industrialized countries, however, point to the possibility that he would favor a customs union among African countries.

Although he did not consider what institutional forms Pan-African unity should take, there can be little doubt that he would have wanted to see the establishment of functional organs to reflect and pursue the developmental needs of African countries. Fanon was, of course, hostile to federal or quasi-federal arrangements; yet it is hard to envision in what form than federal or quasi-federal ones his desire for Pan-African unity can be achieved, particularly since he placed so much emphasis on decentralization. The continental equivalent to his call for the decentralization of domestic political power structures is to be found in the gradualist approach to Pan-African unity entertained by president Nyerere of Tanzania, among others.

Fanon was aware that the Sahara was more than a physical barrier separating North Africa from the rest of Africa. Colonial rule had weakened commercial, political and economic ties that linked Africa north and south of the Sahara in precolonial times. Moreover, deliberate attempts were made to create a gap, a misunderstanding between Arab and Black Africa.[46] Fanon therefore saw the need to establish more durable social, political, economic and cultural links not only between Africa north and south of the Sahara but also between North Africa and the African Diaspora. This was why he wanted to go to Cuba as the Ambassador of the Algerian Provisional Government.

Fanon would also like to see independent African countries give moral, financial, and logistical support to national liberation movements in Africa. This was why he placed the Algerian Revolution in a wider Pan-Africa perspective:

[46] Ibid., pp. 160-162.

> To put Africa in motion, to cooperate in its organization, in its regrouping behind revolutionary principles. To participate in the ordered movement of a continent — this was really the work I had chosen.[47]

This does not settle the question, however, of the determination of which national liberation movements to support in territories where there were more than one liberation movement, as in Angola.

Summary

I have indicated some of the policy implications that could be deduced from Fanon's political writings. Fanon himself was concerned with transforming the world, which is to say he was concerned about what policies and strategies would bring about the desired transformation.

But he also saw the close, even inseparable connection between policy in one area and policy in other areas. Economic, political, and cultural problems facing Africa cannot be treated in isolation from one another. What was also important for him was the context of policy as well as the ideological perspective from which it is pursued.

[47] Fanon, *Toward the African Revolution*, pp. 177-178.

IV

EPILOGUE

Chapter 9

FRANTZ: A REVIEW AND AN ASSESSMENT

Introduction

I have offered in the preceding chapters critical interpretations of Fanon's sociology of African politics. This is a problematic task. There are the obvious dangers referred to in Chapter 1 — those relating to the possibility of misunderstanding and the imposition of a forced coherence on Fanon's ideas. Yet there are "occupational hazards" built into the very notion of literary exegesis and criticism.

What now remains to be done is three-fold. First, there is the need to review the manner in which Fanon has been regarded and interpreted by other scholars. Secondly, one must point to what has been omitted or underemphasized by these scholars. To do this is to inquire whether there are more persuasive and valid criticisms of Fanon than those offered by these scholars. Thirdly, one must offer one's assessment of the current status and importance of the man and his ideas. To do this is, in a sense, to justify writing about the man.

Fanon and His Critics — The Charge of Incoherence

Fanon is controversial. This is understandable, the more so since he does not mince words in expressing his views and, in fact, does so with a trenchant moral outrage that some find uncomfortable. As a result he has received sharp criticisms from all segments of the political spectrum. Much of this criticism is, however, wilful distortion of his work, or else it reveals crass ignorance.

A general criticism is that Fanon is neither systematic nor coherent. This claim is sometimes linked to the claim that his style is tortuous or dull, or both. Another aspect of this general criticism is the claim that he is carried away by his emotional immersion into the issues he is discussing; so much so that he loses all objectivity. This general criticism is to be found in Connor Cruise O'Brien, Lewis Coser, and Fred Gottheil.[1] As Coser puts it:

> Frantz Fanon's *The Wretched of the Earth* ... is badly written, badly organized and chaotic. The author's reasoning is often shoddy and obviously defective ... This is not a work of analysis. Its incantatory prose appeals not to the intellect but to the passions.[2]

The problem with this general criticism is one that is all too common in political thought: this is that it is not always clear what it is to be a systematic or coherent writer or political thinker. In any case, it should matter less that the work of Fanon is neither systematic nor coherent than that it offers, even as O'Brien admits, penetrating insights and arises out of a passionate concern for humanity.

This general criticism is problematic in another respect. Were it Fanon's intention to be systematic, coherent, and objective, this criticism might to some extent be regarded as a valid one to make. Fanon was however a highly programmatic and didactic writer who explicitly disdained objectivity and sought instead to project the subjective aspects of the colonial experience from the perspective of the victim of the colonial order.

[1] Connor Cruise O'Brien, "The Neurosis of Colonialism," *The Nation*, Vol. 200 (June, 1965), p. 674; Lewis Coser, "The Myth of Peasant Revolt," *Dissent*, Vol. 13, No. 3 (May-June, 1966), p. 209; F. M. Gottheil, "Fanon and the Economics of Colonialism: A Review Article," *Quarterly Review of Economics and Business* (Autumn, 1967), p. 78.

[2] Coser, "Myth of Peasant Revolt," p. 298.

Fanon and His Critics: The Social Functions of Violence

The main target of pungent criticisms, however, have been, and will continue to be the political dimensions of Fanon's work: his thesis about the cathartic and social functions of violence: his conception of the colonial situation: his analysis of class political behavior in Africa; the alleged inadequacy of his political or programmatic prescriptions for a socialist state, and his alleged romanticism.

Let us start with criticisms levelled at his thesis about the social functions of violence. Elie Kedouri and Hannah Arendt are repulsed by Fanon's discussion of violence, the one regarding it as savage lyricism while the other characterizes it as rhetorically excessive.[3] Nghe, Klein, Rohdie, Caute, and Gendzier, while not necessarily condemning Fanon's discussion of violence as such, challenge his thesis about the cathartic function of violence.[4]

Much of this criticism is mistaken. That this is so is due to a conflation of two different issues that should be separated and kept apart for purposes of analysis. There is the question raised by Fanon's thesis about the cleansing functions of violence. What is involved here is a problem of interpretation. If one regards Fanon's claim as an analytically true proposition or a law-like hypothesis or generalization, then one case in history where violence is not cleansing is enough to discredit the thesis. But if one regards it as a contingent proposition, as I think one should, then one or more cases where violence is not cleansing will not necessarily constitute a refutation of the thesis.

[3] Kedouri, *Nationalism in Asia and Africa* (New York: The World Publishing Co., 1971), p. 139; Hannah Arendt, "Reflections on Violence," *The New York Review of Books* (February, 1969), pp. 19-32.

[4] N. Nghe, "Fanon et les Problèmes de l'Indépendance," *La Penseè* (January/February, 1963), p. 28; S. Rohdie, "Liberation and Violence in Algeria," *Studies on the Left,* Vol. 6, No. 6 (May-June, 1966), p. 86; N. Klein, "On Revolutionary Violence," *Studies on the Left*, Vol. 4, No. 3 (May-June, 1966), p. 82; D. Caute, *Frantz Fanon,* p. 95; Gendzier, *Fanon,* p. 198.

The second issue concerns Fanon's distinction between true and false decolonization and his thesis about the role of violence as a strategy for achieving true decolonization. Fanon, however, realizes that there is more to decolonization than the use of physical violence: he does not say that the use of violence will necessarily lead to the creation of responsible and committed individuals.

Another flaw in the discussion of violence in Fanon, particularly evident in the biographies by Caute and Geismar is that there is usually an overemphasis on Fanon's claim that decolonization is necessarily violent. Yet Fanon entertains serious doubts on this point. Related to this is the question, usually neglected by his critics, about the meanings Fanon attaches to the concept of violence, and the problems that are raised, especially on a conceptual level, by his use of the concept.

Fanon and His Critics: The Nature of the Colonial Situation

Fanon's conception of the colonial situation is another target of criticism. Connor Cruise O'Brien challenges Fanon's claim that violence is a creation of colonialism. According to O'Brien:

> as far as violence and power are concerned, colonialism introduced no new principles into Africa, merely the more effective application of existing principles.[5]

Kedouri characterizes Fanon's claim about the Manichaen structure of the colonial situation as "specious invective."[6]

Both criticisms are based on the debatable assumption that Fanon's thesis is that the phenomena of physical and structural violence are unique to the colonial situation. Fanon is indeed aware that violence can, and does exist in other than colonial

[5] O'Brien, "Neurosis of Colonialism," p. 674.
[6] Kedouri, *Nationalism in Asia and Africa.*

situations, as his discussion of the phenomena of the dance in precolonial societies shows.

The criticisms are, however, open to two objections. One is that they miss the dialectical purpose served by Fanon's characterization of the colonial situation as inherently violent. In other words, Fanon's characterization arises out of the need to counter the rationalization of colonial rule and colonial expansion as progressive and humanitarian enterprises. Fanon so defines the colonial situation that by its very nature it is characterized by violence.

To say this is neither to say that violence is a creation of colonialism nor to assert that the colonial situation is uniquely violent. In short, the observations of O'Brien and Kedouri[7] that there are other situations in which violence is a feature of social relations is not a refutation of Fanon's characterization of the colonial situation as a violent one. Secondly, their criticisms miss the force of Fanon's emphasis on the racial factor as the crucially important basis of socioeconomic and political organization in the colonial situation.

Fanon and His Critics: Class Analysis and Policy Recommendations

Fanon's analysis of class political behavior also comes in for criticism, particularly from orthodox Marxist-Leninist perspectives. He is criticized for denying the revolutionary consciousness of the African proletariat as a class-for-itself and for placing more emphasis on the peasantry and lumpen-proletariat as potential agents for revolutionary change in Africa.[8]

[7] Ibid.

[8] Nghe, "Fanon et les Problèmes de l'Indépendance"; J. Woodis, *New Theories of Revolution* (New York: International Publishers, 1972); R. Ledda, "Social Classes and Political Struggle," *International Socialist Journal*, No. 22 (August, 1967); Michel Pablo, "Les Damnés de La Terre," *Quatrième Internationale*, Vol. 15 (1962).

As I have argued in Chapters 5 and 6, much of this criticism is misleading and mistaken. It fails to give adequate consideration to the role of the political educator in Fanon's analysis of class political behavior in Africa.

Another criticism of Fanon's analysis of African politics is that it offers no concrete policy recommendations for the construction and organization of the socialist society that Fanon envisions.[9] This criticism is unfair on at least two grounds.

First, a political philosopher, though concerned with influencing and affecting the direction of events in society, is not necessarily a social engineer or architect of a new society. The two tasks are analytically different, although in another sense they are closely connected: in the real world of social existence the distinction is hard to sustain. It is, however, part of the tantalizing mystery of a Plato, Rousseau or Marx that there is some ambiguity surrounding what needs to be done to establish their envisioned societies.

Secondly, early death at the age of thirty-six made it impossible for Fanon to articulate in any great detail concrete policy recommendations for his envisioned society. *The Wretched of the Earth* was written in a hurry and with his awareness of impending death from leukemia.

Wretched of the Earth, as I have argued, however, contains in broad outlines policy recommendations and opinions that can be deduced or inferred from the book. This is because, although political thinkers as purveyors of ideas are not necessarily social engineers, their writings necessarily imply policy or programmatic recommendations. This may be in the negative sense that there will necessarily be certain policy options that are inconsistent with their political thought. Thus, as I have argued in Chapter 9, the very adoption of Fanonian orientations towards politics places a constraint on the range of options available to a policy-maker.

[9] Caute, *Fanon,* p. 83.

Fanon and His Critics: The Charge of Romanticism

A set of critical remarks focuses on Fanon's alleged romanticism or utopianism. The criticism is that Fanon's statement on a number of issues, ranging from his discussion of traditional African society to his elevation of the peasantry and vision of the future, betrays the romantic, utopian or mythical aspects of his political thought. A related criticism is that Fanon is masquerading as a prophet of a new social order.[10]

This criticism itself raises a number of questions. First, Zolberg, Klein, and Coser tend to equate myth with utopia and illusion. Henry Tudor has suggested that it is both vague and tendentious to use myth and illusion synonymously.[11] Little effort is in fact made by these critics to distinguish the mythical from the utopian. Moreover there is a failure to clarify what are regarded as the mythical or utopian elements in him.

Secondly, the unfortunate and perjorative equation of myth with political messianism in Fanon, as Zolberg does, or with idealism (or lack of realism) as Klein does, obscures the critical function which the vision of a new man and a new world serves for Fanon. This vision is his way of exposing the shortcomings of contemporary society. The vision is necessary because of the disjunction between social reality and what society, according to Fanon, ought to be like. To borrow phrases used by Anthony Wallace,[12] the vision is called for because the "mazeway" or "cultural gestalt" of members of a particular society is disturbed by their perception of reality.

Thirdly, it is debatable whether Fanon should be regarded as a prophet. Political thinkers are hardly prophets, except perhaps in a metaphorical sense. That the society of their

[10] Zolberg, "Frantz Fanon: A Gospel for the Damned," *Encounter* (November, 1966); Coser, "Myth of Peasant Revolt"; Klein, "On Revolutionary Violence"; W. B. Quandt, *Revolution and Political Leadership in Algeria, 1954-1968* (Cambridge, Massachusetts: M.I.T. Press, 1969).

[11] Henry Tudor, *Political Myth* (New York: Praeger, 1972).

[12] A. F. C. Wallace, "Revitalization Movements," *American Anthropologist*, Vol. 58, No. 2 (April, 1956).

so-called illusion or fantasy is yet to be created is neither here nor there. Thus, in comparing the Algeria of 1968 with what Fanon said it ought to be or hoped it would be, Quandt misses the point of Fanon's analysis. This is because, underlying Fanon's analysis, are implicit and explicit normative assumptions about man and society which are to be fulfilled only under *certain* conditions, and not under *any* conditions. This is the thrust of Graeme Duncan and Steven Lukes' defense of the classical theorists of democracy against some of their critics, the empirical theorists of democracy:

> their theories are a critique of reality in terms of a vision of human nature and possibilities, and for this reason cannot be refuted on the grounds that people do not satisfy the required standards and that "soi-distant" democracies nonetheless survive. Their ideals can logically contrast with the facts without being invalidated by empirical research, which does not in any *obvious* way call for their general revision.[13]

In short, merely to suggest that Fanon's vision of a new Algeria or Africa has not been borne out by events in Algeria and other African countries is not to invalidate Fanon's analysis and prescriptions.

I have argued, however, in Chapters 6, 7, and 8 that Fanon is, in a sense, pessimistic and disappointed about the course of political developments both within Algeria and the rest of Africa. In this respect, my thesis is that *Wretched of the Earth* is best looked upon as an essay in pessimism in which Fanon, the political sociologist, hits at the impossibility of creating and maintaining what Fanon, the political moralist, says ought to be the ideal. About the fragility and basic contradictions of political institutions and social relations in Africa, Fanon certainly entertained no romantic illusions or utopian thought.

[13] Graeme Duncan and Steven Lukes, "The New Democracy," *Political Studies*, Vol. 11, No. 2 (June, 1963), p. 165.

Thought and Action: Some Problems

I have attempted in the preceding sections to indicate, and then defend Fanon against some of the criticisms often levelled at him. It seems to me that there is another area of criticism, pertaining to his discussion of the relationship between thought and action, which has been ignored by his critics.

This aspect of Fanon's discussion of the relationship between thought and practice relates to the bridging of the gap between the urban political elite — or the center, in other words — and the rural masses, i.e., the periphery. Fanon seems to believe that one solution lies in renewed contact, no doubt involuntary initially and dictated by the logic of intra-elite contradictions, between the two groups. This is one implication of Fanon's description of the return of the "illegalist" elements of the urban political elite to the countryside.

The problem is, however, much more complex than Fanon makes it out to be. He talks of decentralization, of the need, "the necessity of creating a large number of well-informed nuclei at the bottom ... cells that supply content and life."[14] Yet, as Fanon himself knows too well, if the "cells" are to be meaningful, the nature of leadership selection at the "bottom" as well as its linkages to the center are crucial. This is all the more crucial if the political elite from the center is not to impose a solution or structure.

The problem is further compounded by the language and symbolism available to the political elite. How is socialism to be explained, for example? The experience of Algeria with the experiment in self-management and the on-going problems connected with rural development programs and policies in Tanzania illustrate difficulties connected with creating and sustaining elite-mass linkages.

It seems to me that while Fanon views the problem as a structural one, "creating ... nuclei at the bottom ...," there is

[14] Fanon, *Wretched of the Earth*, pp. 194-95.

also need to focus on psychological and cultural variables, something that Fanon focuses on in other respects and that impinge on elite-mass linkages. This is therefore not so much a criticism of Fanon as it is a recognition of the need to integrate these attitudinal (or psychological) and cultural variables into an overall framework of elite-mass linkage in his work.

Fanon's discussion of elite-mass linkage raises, in addition, epistemological questions. These are standard questions regarding the role of the Platonic philosopher-king or, in Fanon's case, the political educator. Fanon's faith in the ultimate bridging of the elite-mass gap rests on the political educator who is expected, like Plato's philosopher-king to recast or mold political society in the image of the political knowledge he acquired in the course of his contemplative career.

Now, the epistemological problem is two-fold. First, Fanon seems to have assumed as given or unproblematic the experiences on which the expertise or knowledge of the political educator is to be based. Yet it is meaningful to ask questions about the nature and basis of these experiences. An important question in this respect is concerned with why some experiences are more relevant or preferable than others. Secondly, it is problematic what is to constitute the education and training of the political educator. What criteria and standards must he satisfy? These are not easy questions to answer, although given the corpus of Fanon's writings there is some indication of what constitutes, from his own viewpoint, the wrong type of training and leadership orientation.

Fanon: An Assessment

What is the nature of Fanon's appeal? In what sense is his political thought important and suggestive? Fanon's appeal and relevance are due primarily to his impact on the historical situation of which he was a part. It is an impact that is difficult to measure; yet he has had some influence on the political attitude and behavior of a great many people. There is also a captivating force to his observations about African politics. There is in his work an incomparable insight into the nature of political developments in postcolonial Africa.

Fanon's importance and relevance rest on his articulation of at least five issues. These are: his discussion of theory; his concern with racism and colonialism; his class analysis of African politics; his conception of the link between culture, ideology, and modernization; and his idea of Pan-Africa. Let us take each of these issues in turn.

Theory: I have argued that Fanon looks upon critical theory as a practical, instrumental, i.e., policy-oriented and programmatic endeavor. A recurrent theme in his political work is that theory, as well as the vocation of the committed intellectual, is indispensable to the construction of viable political systems in Africa. It must be a theory, however, that is grounded in Africa's cultural heritage and one which is therefore adequate to Africa's needs.

Racism and Colonialism: Fanon's discussion of racism and colonialism makes two important contributions to the sociology of race and colonial relations. First, his notion of psychological violence is particularly illuminating in its focus on cultural alienation engendered by race contact within colonial settings. Secondly, he offers powerful rebuttal to the thesis that colonialism was progressive and humanitarian.

Class and African Politics: Fanon's contribution to the study of African politics is to have pioneered a movement for the historiographical revision of perspectives to the study of African politics. *Wretched of the Earth* provides one of the earliest attempts to apply class categories to the analysis of African politics. His achievement in this respect is in refusing to be mystified by political forms and the self-serving rhetoric of political leaders in the wake of the euphoria created by the achievement of independence.

Culture, Ideology, and Modernization: Fanon sees a close connection between culture, ideology, and modernization. Part of his appeal in this respect lies in the fact that his theoretical speculations on the modernization process point to some of the limitations of orthodox Marxism in Africa.

Fanon, as I have attempted to show, views modernization as a process that is concerned with the spread and use of political power within a political system. It is a process that is concerned with incorporating a periphery into a political center. The connection between this process and culture is that the incorporation process involves search for new values to regulate behavior and conduct. Ideology, on this view, represents the expression of this search for new values to sustain the incorporation process. Put differently, the modernization process and ideology are best regarded as cultural phenomena that are concerned with the management of culture and culture change.

Fanon's focus on ideology and modernization also raises interesting questions about the direction of and moral issues raised by modernization strategies in postcolonial Africa. Fanon's important contribution in this connection is that he provides theoretical inspiration to the application of dependency theories to the analyses of political processes in contemporary Africa.

The Idea of Pan-Africa: Fanon's contribution to the idea of Pan-Africa rests on his attempt to provide a link not only between Arab and Black Africa but also between Arab Africa and the African Diaspora in the Caribbean. Fanon also looks upon the Algerian Revolution in a wider Pan-African perspective: he views it as a phase in the continental, indeed the world-wide struggle against colonialism and neo-colonialism. As he states:

> To put Africa in motion, to cooperate in its organization, in its regrouping, behind revolutionary principles. To

> participate in the ordered movement of a continent — this was really the work I had chosen.[15]

It is also from this Pan-African perspective that he condemns manifestations of micronationalism in Africa, observing that "African unity takes off the mask, and crumbles into regionalism inside the hollow shell of nationality itself."[16]

[15] Fanon, *Toward the African Revolution*, pp. 177-178.
[16] Fanon, *Wretched of the Earth*, p. 159.

BIBLIOGRAPHY

A. *Works by Frantz Fanon*

Peau noir/Masques Blancs. Preface by François Jeanson. Paris: Editions du Seuil, 1952. Translated by Charles Markmann as *Black Skin, White Masks.* New York: Grove Press, 1967.

L'an de la Révolution Algérienne. Paris: F. Maspéro, 1959. Translated by Haakon Chevalier, with an introduction by Adolfo Gilly, as *Studies in a Dying Colonialism.* New York: Monthly Review Press, 1967.

Les Damnés de la Terre. Preface by J-P. Sartre. Paris: F. Maspéro, 1961. Translated by Constance Farrington as *The Wretched of the Earth.* New York: Grove Press, 1968.

Pour la Révolution Africaine. Paris: F. Maspéro, 1964. Translated by Haakon Chevalier as *For the African Revolution.* New York: Monthly Review Press, 1967.

B. *Select Bibliography on Fanon (Biographical and Critical)*

Abel, Lionel. "Seven Heroes of the New Left." *The New York Times Magazine* (May 3, 1968).

Abrash, Barbara. "Bio-Bibliography — Frantz Fanon." *African Library Journal.* Vol. 11, No. 3 (Autumn, 1971).

————. "Fanon: Political Philosopher as Mythmaker," in mimeo, 1973.

Achour, H. "Les Idées Politiques de Frantz Fanon." Mémoire, D.E.S., de Science Politique, Paris, 1965.

Adam, Hussein M. "Frantz Fanon and His Understanding." *Black World* Vol. 21, No. 1 (December, 1971).

————. "Black Thinkers and the Need to Confront Marx." *Pan-African Journal* Vol. 4, No. 1, (Winter, 1971).

Adams, Paul. "The Social Psychiatry of Frantz Fanon." *American Journal of Psychiatry,* Vol. 127, No. 6 (December, 1970).

Africanus, Polybius. "Frantz Fanon's Essays." *Liberation* Vol. 12, No. 5 (August, 1967).

Ali, B.H. "Some lessons of the Liberation Struggle in Algeria." *World Marxist Review* (January, 1965).

Alloula, Malek. "L'Oeuvre de Fanon Aujord'hui." *Algérie Actualité* (December 5-11, 1971).

Alsop, Joseph. "Passing of New Left's Hero: An Odd Facet in U.S. History." *Washington Post* (February 21, 1969).

Anspreger, Franz. Review of *Wretched of the Earth,* in *The Journal of Modern African Studies,* Vol. 1, No. 3, (1963).

Armah, Ayi Kwei. "Fanon: The Awakener." *The Negro Digest,* Vol. 18, No. 12, (October, 1969).

Beavoir, Simone de. *Force of Circumstance.* London: Andre Deutsch and Weidenfeld and Nicholson, 1965.

Beckett, Paul A. "Frantz Fanon and sub-Saharan Africa: Notes on the Contemporary Significance of His Thought." *Africa Today*, Vol. 19, No. 2, (Spring, 1972).
———. "Algeria vs. Fanon: The Theory of Revolutionary Decolonization and the Algerian Experience." *The Western Political Quarterly*, Vol. 26, No. 1, (March, 1973).
Bernard, Roger. "Frantz Fanon." *New Society* (January 4, 1968).
Bienen, Henry. *Violence and Social Change: A Review of Current Literature.* Chicago, 1968.
———. "State and Revolution: The Work of Amilcar Cabral." *The Journal of Modern African Studies*, Vol. 15, No. 4 (December, 1977).
Blackey, Robert. "Fanon and Cabral: A Contrast In Theories of Revolution for Africa." *The Journal of Modern African Studies* Vol. 12, No. 2 (June, 1974).
Bondy, François. "The Black Rousseau." *The New York Review of Books* (31 March, 1966).
Bouvier, Pierre. *Fanon.* Paris: Editions Universitaires, 1971.
Breitman, George. Review of *Wretched of the Earth*, in *The Militant*, No. 33 (September 20, 1965).
Brown, Phil. "Notes on Fanon," in *Radical Therapist.* Ballantine Books, 1971.
Caute, David. "Philosopher of Violence." *Observer* (London) (October 10, 1965).
———. *Frantz Fanon.* New York: Viking Press, 1970.
Césaire, Aimé, et al. "Homages è Frantz Fanon." *Présence Africaine*, XL, ler tr. (1962).
———. *"La Révolte de Frantz Fanon." Jeune Afrique* (December 13-19, 1961).
Cherif, Mohamed A. "Frantz Fanon et la Révolution Africaine." *Présence Africaine*, Vol. 30, No. 58, (1962).
———. "Frantz Fanon: La Science au Service de la Révolution." *Jeune Afrique*, No. 295 (4 September, 1966).
Coles, Robert. "Abused and Abusers." Review of *Black Skin, White Masks*, in *The New York Times Book Review* (April 30, 1967).
———. "What Colonialism Does," review of *Wretched of the Earth, The New Republic*, Vol. 153, No. 12 (September 18, 1965).
Copuya, Emile. "Time to Turn a Tide of Violence." *Saturday Review*, Vol. 48, No. 17 (April 24, 1965).
Coser, Lewis. "The Myth of Peasant Revolt." *Dissent*, Vol. 13, No. 3 (May-June, 1966).
Czarnecki, Jan. "Un Livre Révolutionnaire: *Les Damnés de la Terre.*" *Christianisme Sociale* (Paris, 1963).
Daniel, J. "Les vrais damnés de la terre sont-ils les Europeen?" *L'Express*, No. 64 bis (November 20, 1961).
———. "Les Damnés de la Terre." *L'Express*, (November 30, 1961).
Denn[illegible], Barbara. "On Revolution and Equilibrium." *Liberation*, Vol. 12, No. 2 (February, 1968).
Denis, M. "Frantz Fanon (1921-1961) el Pensamiento Anticolonialista Contemporano." *Revista de Ciencias Sociales* (Puerto Rico) (March, 1967).
Dieng, Amady Aly. "Les Damnés de la Terre et les Problèmes d'Afrique Noire." *Présence Africaine*, No. 62 (1967).
Domenach, Jean-Marie. "Sur une preface de Jean-Paul Sartre." *Espirit* (Paris) (March, 1962).
———. Review of *Wretched of the Earth*, in *Espirit* (Paris) (April, 1962).

———. "A propos des "Damnés de la Terre." *Espirit* (September, 1962).
Dubois, François. Review of *Toward the Afeican Revolution,* in *Tiers Monde,* (Paris), No. 19, tome V (1964).
Fabre, Geneviève and Naaman Kassous. "Frantz Fanon et la révolte noire." *Le Monde Diplomatique* (December, 1971).
Fanon, Mme Josie (Fratz). "A propos de Frantz Fanon, Sartre, le racisme et les Arabes." *El Moudjahid,* No. 614 (10 June, 1967).
Fontenot, Chester J. "Fanon and the Devourers." *Journal of Black Studies,* Vol. 9, No. 1 (1978).
Forsyth, Dennis. "Frantz Fanon: Black The Oretician," *The Black Scholar* (January 1970).
Foster, Frances. "The Black and White Masks of Frantz Fanon and Ralph Ellison." *Black Academy Review,* Vol. 1, No. 4 (1970).
Garrett, Jean. Review in *Young Socialist* (New York), November-December 1965.
Geismar, Peter. "Frantz Fanon: Evolution of a Revolutionary." *Monthly Review* (New York) (May, 1969).
———. *Fanon: The Revolutionary as Prophet.* New York: Grove Press, 1971.
Gendzier, Irene. "Frantz Fanon: In Search of Justice." *The Middle East Journal* (Autumn, 1966).
———. "Reflections on Fanon and the Jewish Question," *New Outlook,* 12 (January, 1969).
———. *Frantz Fanon: A Critical Study.* New York: Pantheon, 1973.
Gilly, Adolfo. "Frantz Fanon et la Révolution en Amérique Latine." *Partisans* (Paris), No. 21 (June-August, 1965).
Gleason, Ralph. "Introduction to Frantz Fanon." *Ramparts,* Vol. 4, No. 11 (March, 1966).
Goldman, Lawrence. "Fanon and Black Radicalism." *Monthly Review* (New York), Vol. 18, No. 6 (November, 1966).
Gordon, David C. "Frantz Fanon: Voice of the Algerian Revolution." *The Middle East Forum* (September, 1963).
Gottheil, F. M. "Fanon and the Economics of Colonialism: A Review Article," *Quarterly Review of Economics and Business,* Vol. 7, No. 3 (Autumn, 1967).
Gramont, Sanche de. "Frantz Fanon: The Prophet Scorned." *Horizon,* Vol. 14, No. 1 (Wintor, 1972).
Green, Philip. Review of Gendzier's *Frantz Fanon,* in *The New York Times Book Review* (February 25, 1973).
Greki, Anna. "Les Damnés de la Terre." *Jeune Afrique,* No. 63 (December 13-19, 1961).
Grohs, Gerhard K. "Frantz Fanon and the African Revolution." *The Journal of Modern African Studies,* Vol. 6, No. 4 (December, 1968).
Hamdani, Hassan. "La Pensée révolutionnaire de Frantz Fanon." *Révolution Africaine,* Nos. 71 and 72, 6 and 13 (June, 1964).
Hansen, Emmanuel. "Frantz Fanon: A Bibliographical Essay." *Pan-African Journal,* Vol. V, No. 4 (Winter, 1972).
———. "Frantz Fanon: Portrait of a Revolutionary Intellectual." *Transaction,* No. 46, Vol. 9 (October-December, 1974).
———. "Freedom and Revolution in the Thought of Frantz Fanon." *African Development,* Vol. II, No. 1 (1977); also in *Pan-African Journal,* Vol. X, No. 1 (1977), and in *Ufahamu* Vol. VII, No. 1 (1976).
———. Review Essay of R. Zahar's *Fratz Fanon's Colonialism and*

Alienation, in *Ghana Social Science Journal*, Vol. 4, No. 2 (November, 1977).

———. *Frantz Fanon: Social and Political Thought.* Columbus, Ohio: Ohio State University Press, 1977.

Hantoff, Nat. "Bursting into History." *New Yorker* (January 15, 1966).

Hermansi, Adbelbaki. "L'Idéologie Fanonienne." *Jeune Afrique*, No. 295 (4 September, 1966).

Hobsbawn, E. J. "Passionate Witness." Review of Gendzier, *Frantz Fanon*, in *New York Review of Books* (February 22, 1973).

Hoechstetter, Irene. "Fanon chez Sartre." *Jeune Afrique*, No. 162 (December 22, 1963).

———. "L'Homme de la décolonisation," *Reforme*, (December, 1966).

Ilunga-Kabongo, Andre. "Les Damnés de la Terre," in Joseph Okpaku, *New African Literature and the Arts*, Vol. 1. Thomas Y. Crowell, 1970.

Irele, F. Abiola. "Literature and Ideology in Martinique: René Maran, Aime Césaire and Frantz Fanon." *Research Review.* Institute of African Studies, University of Ghana, Vol. 5, No. 3, Trinity Term (1969).

Isaacs, Harold. "Portrait of a Revolutionary." *Commentary*, Vol. 40, No. 1 (July, 1965).

Jackson, Henry. "Political and Social ideas of Frantz Fanon. Relevance to Black America," *Pan-African Journal*, Vol. V, No. 4 (Winter, 1972).

Jinadu, L. Adele. "Fanon: The Revolutionary as Social Philosopher," Review of Caute, *Frantz Fanon* and Geismer, *Fanon* in *Review of Politics*, Vol. 34, No. 3 (July, 1972).

———. "Some Aspects of the Social and Political Philosophy of Frantz Fanon." *Pan-African Journal*, Vol. V, No. 4 (December, 1972).

———. "Frantz Fanon and the Historiography of African Politics." *Journal of Developing Areas*, Vol. 7, No. 2 (January, 1973).

———. Review of Gendzier, *Frantz Fanon. Journal of Developing Areas* Vol. 7, No. 2 (January, 1973).

———. "Language and Politics: On the Cultural Basis of Colonialism." *Cahiers d'Etudes Africaines*, 63-64, XVI (3-4).

———. "Some African Theorists of Culture and Modernization: Fanon, Cabral and Some Others." *African Studies Review*, Vol. 21, No. 1 (April, 1978).

Jones, John Henry. "On the Influençe of Fanon." *Freedomways*, Vol. 8, No. 3 (1968).

Kamenju, Grant. "Frantz Fanon." *Transition*, Vol. 26, (1966).

Kershaw, Richard. "Manifesto of Rebellion." *London Sunday Times* (10 October, 1965).

King, Slater. "The Wretched of the Earth are here, too." *Monthly Review* (New York), Vol. 18, No. 2 (1966).

Klein, Norman. "On Revolutionary Violence." *Studies on the Left*, Vol. 4, No. 3 (May-June, 1966).

Labica, G. "Un itineraire militant, la vie de Frantz Fanon." *El Moudjahid*, Vol. 105 (December 8, 1962).

Lacouture, Jean. "L'Oeuvre de Frantz Fanon." Paper Read at l'Ecole Nationale d'Administration, Paris, 1963, in mimeo.

———. "Frantz Fanon et Notre Temps." Paper read at l'Ecole Nationale d'Administration, Paris, 1963, in mimeo.

Lacovia, R. M. "Frantz Fanon: through European Mirrors." *Black Images*, Vol. 1, (1972).

Ledda, Romano. "Social Classes and Political Struggle." *International Socialist Journal*, No. 22 (August, 1967).

Lomax, J. A. "Martyr to Hope." *The Tribune* (London) (May, 1965).
London, Perry. "Multi-Faced Treatise on Colonial Revolution." *Los Angeles Times* (June 5, 1965).
Maiberger, Father Gonslav. "Frantz Fanon: Myth and Reality of the Negro," *Présence Africaine*. Vol. 18, No. 46 (1963).
Malabre, Alfred. "A Disturbing Diatribe from the Third World." *Wall Street Journal* (July 23, 1965).
Martin, Guy. "Fanon's Relevance to Contemporary African Political Thought." *Ufahamu*, 4 (Winter, 1974).
Martin, Tony. "Rescuing Fanon from the Critics." *African Studies Review*, Vol. 13, No. 3 (December, 1970).
———. Review of Caute, *Frantz Fanon* and Geismar, *Fanon*, in *The Journal of Modern African Studies*, Vol. 9, No. 2 (August, 1971).
Martin-Kane, Guy. "Fanon on Violence and the Revolutionary Process in Africa." *African Insight*, 2 (1974).
Martinet, G. "La Chartre du Jacobinisme Algérien." *France Observateur*, No. 603 (23 November, 1961).
Marton, Imre. "A propos des Thesis de Fanon, 1: Le Rôle de la Violence dans la lutte de Liberation Nationale." *Action* (Fort-de-France), No. 7 (1965).
———. "A propos de Theses de Fanon 2: Le Rôle des Classes Sociales après l'indépendance.".*Action* (Fort-de-France), Nos. 8 and 9 (1965).
Maschimo, Maurice. "Frantz Fanon: l'Itinéraire de la Générosité," *Partisans*, No. 8 (February 3, 1962).
Masilela, Ntongela. "Theory, Praxis and History: Frantz Fanon and Carlos Mariategui," *Ufahamu*, Vol. VIII, No. 2, 1978.
McDade, Jesse N. *Frantz Fanon and the Ethical Justification of Revolution*, unpublished Ph.D. dissertation, Boston University, 1970.
Magherbi, Abdelghani. "Frantz Fanon: Apôtre de la Non-Violence," *Algérie-Actualité*, December 5-11, 1911.
Memmi, Albert. "Frantz Fanon and the Notion of 'Deficiency.' in Albert Memmi," *Dominated Man*. Boston, Mass: Deacon, 1968.
———. Review of Caute, Frantz Fanon, and Geismar, *Fanon*, in *The New York Times Book Review* (14 March, 1971).
———. "La Vie Impossible de Frantz Fanon," *Espirit*, September 1971.
M'Hamsadji, Kaddour. "Sociologie de Frantz Fanon," *El Moudjahid*, (January 14, 1972).
Mili, Mohammed el. "Frantz Fanon et la Pensée Occidentale," *Al Thaqafa* (March 1971).
———. "Frantz Fanon et la Révolution Algérienne," *Al Thaqafa* (May 1971).
Mintz, Donald. "Find Something Different," *Washington Evening Star* (March 21, 1965).
Mohiddin, Ahmed. "Nyerere and Fanon on African Development and Leadership." *Pan-African Journal* Vol. VI, No. 2 (Summer, 1973).
Morgenthau, Ruth Schachter. "Frantz Fanon: Five Years Later," *Africa Report* (May 1966).
———. "The Foresight of Frantz Fanon," Center for International Affairs, Harvard University, March 1966.
el Moudjahid, "Frantz Fanon: Notre Frère," Vol. 3, No. 88 (December 21, 1961).
Museveni, Yoweri T. "Fanon's Theory of Violence: Its Verification in Liberated Mozambique." N. Shamuyarira, ed., *Essays On the Liberation of Southern Africa*. Dar-es-Salaam: Tanzania Publishing, 1971.

Mutiso, G-C. M. "Towards Pan-Africanism: Fanon, Kathue and the African Revolution," *Black World* (May, 1971).

Nghe, Nguyen. "Frantz Fanon et les Problèmes de l'Indépendance." *La Pensée,* No. 107 (January-February, 1963).

Nursey-Bray, Paul. "Marxism and Existentialism in the Thought of Frantz Fanon." *Political Studies,* Vol. 20, No. 2 (June, 1972).

Obiechina, Emmanuel. "Frantz Fanon: The Man and His Works." *Ufahamu* 3 (Fall, 1972).

O'Brien, Connor Cruise. "Neurosis of Colonialism." *The Nation,* Vol. 200, No. 25 (June 21, 1965).

Oladitan, Olalere. "Une lecture fanonienne du roman africain: vue ensemble d'une approche." *Présence Africaine,* No. 104, 4th Quarterly (1977).

Olorunsola, Victor, and Ramakris Vaitheswaran. "Reflections prompted by Frantz Fanon's *Wretched of the Earth:* A Review Essay." *Journal of Developing Areas,* Vol. 9, No. 1 (October, 1971).

Pablo, Michel. "Les Damnés de la Terre." *Quatrième Internationale,* Vol. 15, (1962).

Paris, Robert. "Sur un premier bilan du 'Fanonisme.'" *Partisans,* No. 8 (January-February. 1963).

Partisans. "A Frantz Fanon." No. 3 (February, 1962).

Perinbam, B. Marie. "Fanon and the Revolutionary Peasantry: The Algerian Case." *The Journal of Modern African Studies,* Vol. 11, No. 3 (September, 1973).

————. "Parrot or Phoenix? Frantz Fanon's View of the West Indian and Algeria Woman." *Journal of Ethnic Studies,* Vol. 1, No. 2, (1973).

————. "Violence, Morality and History in the Colonial Syndrome: Frantz Fanon's Perspectives." *Journal of Southern African Affairs,* Vol. III, No. 1 (January, 1978).

Posinsky, S. H. Review of *Wretched of the Earth,* in *Psychoanalytical Quarterly,* Vol. 35, No. 4 (1966).

Pouillon, Jean. "Décolonisation et Révolution." *Les Temps Modernes,* No. 191, 17e Annee (April, 1962).

Quellel, Charif. "Frantz Fanon and Colonized Man," *Africa Today,* Vol. 17, No. 1 (January-February, 1970).

Ranly, Ernest W. "Frantz Fanon and the Radical Left." *America,* Vol. 121, No. 14 (November, 1969).

Rohdie, Samuel. "Liberation and Violence in Algeria." *Studies on the Left,* Vol. 6, No. 3 (May-June, 1966).

Seigel, J. F. "On Frantz Fanon." *American Scholar,* Vol. 38, No. 1 (Winter, 1968).

Smith, Robert C. "Beyond Marx: Fanon and the Concept of Colonial Violence." *Black World,* Vol. 22, No. 7 (May, 1973).

Stambouli, F. "Frantz Fanon Face aux Problémes de la Décolonization et de la Construction Nationale." *Revue de l'Institut de Sociologie,* No. 2/3 (1967).

Staniland, Martin. "Frantz Fanon and the African Political Class." *African Affairs* (London), Vol. LXIII, No. 270 (January, 1969).

Sutton, Horace. "Fanon: The Revolutionary as Prophet." *Saturday Review,* (July 17, 1971).

Les Temps Modernes, Review of *Studies in a Dying Colonialism.* No. 167-168 (1960).

Thompson, Willie. "Frantz Fanon." *Marxism Today* (August, 1968).

Times Literary Supplement (London). Review of Caute, *Fanon* (29 January, 1970).

Tomatis, Y. "Frantz Fanon: Vie et Pensée," Mémoire, D.E.S., de Science Politique, Aix-en-Provence (1966).
Traoré, Bakary. "On 'les Damnés de la Terre.'" *Présence Africaine,* Vol. 17, No. 45, 1st Quarter (1963).
United Nations Centre Against Apartheid, (Department of Political and Security Affairs). *International Tribute to Frantz Fanon: Record of the Special Meeting of the United Nations Special Commitree against Apartheid, 3 November 1978,* N.Y.,: United Nations Centre Against Apartheid, 1979.
Wallerstein, Immanuel. "Frantz Fanon: Reason and Violence." *Journal of Sociology* (Berkeley), 15 (1970).
———. "Class and Class Conflict in Contemporary Africa." *Canadian Journal of African Studies,* Vol. 7, No. 3 (1973).
———. Review of *Studies in a Dying Colonialism. New World Quarterly.* Vol. 3, No. 3 (1967).
Woodis, Jack. *New Theories of Revolution: A Commentary on the View of Frantz Fanon, Regis Debray and Herbert Marcuse.* New York: International Publishers, 1972.
Worseley, Peter. "The Coming Inheritor." *The Manchester Guardian* (October 22, 1965).
———. "Frantz Fanon: Revolutionary Theories." *Studies on the Left,* Vol. 6, No. 3 (May-June, 1966).
———. "Frantz Fanon and the 'Lumpenproletariat' in Ralph Miliband and John Saville. *The Socialist Register, 1972.* The Merlin Press, 1972.
Wright, Frank. "Frantz Fanon: His Work in Historical Perspective." *Black Scholar* (6, July-August, 1975).
Yacine, Kateb. "Fanon, Amrouche et Ferraoun." *Jeune Afrique,* (November 5, 1962).
Zahar, Renate. *L'Oeuvre de Frantz Fanon.* Trans, from the German original by Roger Dangeville. François Maspero, 1970.
Zolberg, Aristide. "Frantz Fanon: A Gospel for the Damned," *Encounter* (November, 1966).
Zolberg, Aristide and Vera Zolberg. "The Americanization of Frantz Fanon." *The Public Interest,* No. 9 (1967).

C. Relevant Select Bibliography (other than those on Fanon)

Ajayi, Jacob F. "Colonialism: An Episode in African History," in L.H. Gunn and Peter Duignan, *Colonialism in Africa, 1870-1914.* Cambridge. 1969
Ake, Claude. *Revolutionary Pressures in Africa.* London: Zed Press, 1978.
Alleg, Henrig *The Question.* Trans by John Calder. George Braziller, 1958.
Allen, V.L. "The Meaning of the Working Class in Africa." *The Journal of Modern African Studies,* Vol. 10, No. 2 (July, 1972).
Andrain, Charles F. "Democracy and Socialism: Ideologies of African Leaders," in David E. Apter, *Ideology and Discontent.* The Free Press.
Andreski, Stanilav. *The African Predicament: A Study in the Pathology of Modernization.* Michael Joseph, 1968.
Apter, David E. *Some Conceptual Approaches to the Study of Modernization,* Prentice-Hall, 1968.
———. "The Role of Political Opposition in New Nations," in Irving L. Markovitz (ed.) *African Politics and Society.* The Free Press, 1970.
Arendt, Hannah. *On Revolution.* Viking Press, 1966.
———. *On Violence.* Harcourt Brace, 1969.

Arrighi, Giovanni and John Saul. "Nationalism and Revolution in sub-Saharan Africa," in Ralph Miliband and John Saville (ed.), *The Socialist Register,* 1969. The Merlin Press, 1969.
Avineri, Shlomo. *Karl Marx on Colonization and Modernization.* Doubleday, 1969.
Balandier, Georges. "Messianism and Nationalism in Black Africa," in Pierre L. Van den Berghe, *Africa: Social Problem of Change and Conflict.* Chandler, 1965.
————. *The Sociology of Black Africa: Social Dynamics in Central Africa.* Praeger, 1970.
Benedict, Ruth. *Patterns of Culture.* Houghton Mifflin, 1934.
Bernstein, Edward. *Evolutionary Socialism: A Criticism and Affirmation.* Schoken, 1961.
Bienen, H. "Waht Does Political Development Mean in Africa?" *World Politics,* Vol. 20, No. 1, 1967.
Blackey, Robert and C.T. Paynton. *Revolution and The Revolutionary Ideal.* Cambridge, Mass, forthcoming.
Blanshard, Brand. "Morality and Politics," in Richard T. de George, *Ethics and Society.* Doubleday, 1966.
Bolnick, Joel. "An Examination of Class and Class Conflict in Neo-Colonial States," *Ufahamu,* Vol. VIII, No. 2, 1978.
Braundi, Emile. "Neo-Colonialism and the Class Struggle," *International Socialist Journal,* No. 1 (January-February, 1964).
Buell, R. L. *The Native Problem in Africa,* 2 vols. New York, 1928.
Cabral, Amilcar. "The Struggle in Guinea." *International Socialist Journal,* 4 (August, 1964).
Césaire, Aimé. *Discours Sur Le Colonialisme.* Presence Africaine, 1965.
Chodak, Szymon. "Social Classes in sub-Saharan Africa," *Africana Bulletin* (Warsaw), No. 4 (1966).
Cioffi, Frank. "Intention and Interpretation in Criticism." *Proceedings of the Aristotelian Society,* new series, Vol. LXIV (1963-1964).
Cohen, Robin. "Class in Africa: Analytical Problems and Perspectives," in Ralph Miliband and John Saville, *The Socialist Register, 1972.* The Merlin Press, 1972.
Coleman, James S. "Nationalism in Tropical Africa." *American Political Science Review,* Vol. XLVIII, No. 2 (1954).
Cranston, Maurice and Richard S. Peters. *Hobbes and Rousseau: A Collection of Critical Essays.* Doubleday, 1972.
Crowder, Michael. "Indirect Rule: French and British Style." *Africa.* Vol. 39, No. 3 (July, 1964).
————. *Senegal: A Study of French Assimilation Policy,* rev. ed. Methuen, 1967.
————. *West Africa Under Colonial Rule.* Northwestern, 1968.
Cumming, Robert D., ed. *The Philosophy of Jean-Paul Sartre.* Random House, 1965.
Dahrendorf, Ralf. *Class and Class Conflict in Industrial Society,* rev. ed. Stanford, 1959.
Dike, Kenneth. *Trade and Politics in the Niger Delta.* Oxford, 1956.
Downie, R. S. "Social Roles and Moral Responsibility." *Philosophy,* Vol. 39, No. 147 (January, 1964).
Dumont, René. *False Start in Africa,* 2nd rev. ed. Trans. by Phyllis Nautta Ott. Praeger, 1969.
Dunn, John. *Modern Revolutions: An Introduction to the Analysis of a Political Phenomenon.* Cambridge, 1972.

Easton, Lloyd D. and Kurt H. Guddart. *Writings of the Young Marx on Philosophy and Society*. Doubleday, 1967.
Eckstein, Harry. "On the Etiology of Internal Wars." *History and Theory*, Vol. 4, No. 2 (1965).
Emerson, Rupert. *From Empire to Nation*. Harvard, 1960.
Evans-Pritchard, E. E. "Some Collective Expressions of Obscenity in Africa." *Journal of the Royal Anthropological Institute*, Vol. 59 (1929).
Feraoun, Moulud. *Journal, 1955-1962*. Editions du Seuil, 1962.
Feuer, Lewis S. *Marx and Engels: Basic Writings on Politics and Philosophy*. Collins, 1969.
Finer, S. E. "The One-Party Regimes in Africa: Reconsiderations." *Government and Opposition*, Vol. 2, No. 4 (July-October, 1967).
Fortes, Meyer and E. E. Evans-Pritchard, eds. *African Political Systems*. Oxford, 1960.
Fraenkel, Herbert. *The Concept of Colonization*. Oxford, 1949.
Freeman, Michael. "Review Article: Theories of Revolution." *British Journal of Political Science*, Vol. 2 (July, 1972).
Fundamentals of Marxism-Leoninism. Moscow, 1961.
Gordon, David C. *The Passing of French Algeria*. Oxford, 1966.
————. *Women of Algeria: An Essay on Change*. Harvard, 1968.
Greenleaf, W. H. "Hobbes: The Problem of Interpretation," in Cronston and Peters, *Hobbes and Rousseau*.
Griewenk, Karl. "Emergence of the Concept of Revolution," in D. Mazlish, Arthur D. Kaledin and David B. Ralston, *Revolution: A Reader*. Macmillan, 1971.
Grundy, Kenneth. "The 'Class Struggle' in Africa: An Examination of Conflicting Theories." *The Journal of Modern African Studies*, Vol. 2, No. 3 (November, 1964).
Gurr, Ted. *Why Men Rebel*. Princeton, 1970.
Hodgkin, Thomas. *Nationalism in Colonial Africa*. New York University Press, 1957.
————. "A Note on the Language of African Nationalism," in Kenneth Kirkwood, ed. *African Affairs: St. Antony's Papers*, No. 10. Chatro and Windus, 1961.
————. *African Political Parties*. Penguin, 1961.
————. "The Relevance of 'Western' Ideas for the New States," in J. R. Pennock, ed. *Self-Government in Modernizing Nations*. Prentice-Hall, 1964.
Hospers, John. *An Introduction to Philosophical Analysis*, 2nd ed. Prentice-Hall, 1967.
Huxley, Elspeth. "What Future for Africa?" *Encounter* (January, 1961).
Jaspers, Karl. *The Question of German Guilt*. Trans. by E. B. Ashton. Capricorn Books, 1961.
Johnson, Chalmers. *Revolution and the Social System*. Hoover Institution, 1964.
————. *Revolutionary Change*. Little, Brown and Co., 1966.
July, Robert W. *The Origins of Modern African Thought*. Faber and Faber, 1968.
Kabwegyere, Tarsis B. "The Dynamics of Colonial Violence: The Inductive System in Uganda." *Journal of Peace Research*, 4 (1972).
Kautsky, John H. "The Appeal of Communist Models in Underdeveloped Countries," in Willard A. Belling and George O. Totten, *Developing Countries: Quest for a Model*. Van Nostrand Reinhold, 1970.
————. *The Political Consequences of Modernization*. Wiley, 1972.

Kedouri, Elie. *Nationalism in Asia and Africa.* The World Publishing Company, 1970.
Keita, Modeira. "Le Parti Unique en Afrique." *Présence Africaine,* No. 30 (February-March, 1960).
Kelly George Armstrong. "Notes on Hegel's 'Lordship and Bondage,'" in Alasdair McIntrye, ed. *Hegel: A Collection of Essays.* Doubleday, 1972.
Kerr, Malcolm. "Arab Radical Notions of Democracy," in St. Antony's Papers No. 16, *Middle Eastern Affairs, No. 3.* Chatto and Windus, 1963.
Khapoya, V. B. "African and Vietnamese Liberation Movements: A Comparative Study." *Pan African Journal* Vol. X, No. 1 (1977).
Kilson, Martin. "Nationalism and Social Classes in British West Africa." *Journal of Politics,* Vol. 20, No. 2 (1958).
————. "African Political Change and the Modernization Process." *Journal of Modern African Studies,* Vol. 1, No. 4 (December, 1963).
————. *Political Change in a West African State: A Study of the Modernization Process in Sierra Leone.* Harvard, 1966.
Kluckhohn, Clyde. "Ethical Relativity: Sic et Non." *The Journal of Philosophy,* Vol. LII, No. 23 (November, 1965).
Kopytoff, Igor. "Socialism and Traditional African Societies," in W. H. Friendland and Carl G. Rosberg, Jr., ed. *African Socialism.* Stanford, 1966.
Kramic, Isaac. "Reflections on Revolution: Definition and Explanation in Recent Scholarship." *History and Theory,* Vol. 11, No. 1 (1972).
Labedz, L. ed. *Revisionism: Essays in the History of Marxist Ideas.* Praeger, 1962.
Labricola, A. *Essays in the Materialistic Interpretation of History.* Monthly Review Press. 1966.
Larsson, Reiddan. *Theories of Revolution: From Marx to the First Russian Revolution.* Almquist and Wicksell, 1970.
Legum, Colin. "Socialism in Ghana: A Political Interpretation," in W. H. Friedland and Carl G. Rosberg, Jr., *African Socialism.* Stanford, 1966.
Lenin, V.I. *State and Revolution.* International Publishers, 1932.
————. *Left-Wing Communism: An Infantile Disorder,* rev. ed., trans. International Publishers, 1934.
————. *Imperialism: The Highest Stage of Capitalism.* International Publishers, 1939.
Lewis, Martin Deming. "One Hundred Frenchmen: The 'Assimilation' Theory in French Colonial Policy." *Comparative Study in Society and History,* Vol. IV, No. 2 (January, 1962).
Lewis, Sir W. Arthur. *Politics in West Africa.* Oxford, 1965.
Lloyd, Peter C. "The Political Structure of African Kingdoms: An Exploratory Model," in Michael Banton, ed., *Political Systems and the Distribution of Power.* Tavistock Publications, 1965.
————. ed. *The New Elites of Tropical Africa.* Oxford, 1966.
————. *Africa in Social Change.* Penguin, 1967.
Lonsdale, John. "Emergence of African Nations." in T.O. Ranger, ed., *Emergent Themes of African History.* Northwestern, 1968.
————. "Some Origins of Nationalism in East Africa." *Journal of African History,* Vol. 9, No. 3 (1968).
Lynch, Hollis R. *Edward Wilmot Blyden: Pan-Negro Patriot, 1832-1912.* Oxford, 1967.
Marcuse, Herbert: *Soviet Marxism: A Critical Analysis.* Vintage Books, 1961.
————. "Re-examination of the Concept of Revolution," in Raymond Klibansky, ed, *Contemporary Philosophy,* Vol. 4. Firenze: La Nuova,

Italia, 1968-71.
Martin, Guy. "Class Analysis and Politics in Africa: Some Observations on the Role of the Bourgeoisie in the Political Process in West Africa. *Ufahamu*, Vol. VII, No. 1 (1976).
Marx, Karl and Friedrich Engels. *Selected Works*. Moscow: Foreign Languages Publishing House, 1962.
———. *The Communist Manifesto*, with an introduction by A.J.P. Taylor. Penguin, 1967.
Memmi, Albert. *The Colonizer and the Colonized*. Beacon, 1967.
———. *Dominated Man*. Beacon, 1968.
Mitrany, David. *Marx Against the Peasant*. Collier, 1961.
Nettl, J.P. "The Study of Political Development," in Colin Leys, ed., *Politics and Change in Developing Countries: Studies in the Theory and Practice of Development*. Cambridge, 1969.
Nkrumah, Kwame. *Consciencism*, rev. ed. Monthly Review Press, 1970.
———. *Class Struggle in Africa*. International Publishers, 1970.
Nyerere, Julius K. *Democracy and the Party System*. Dar-es-Salam, 1963
———. *Uhuru Na Ujamaa: Freedom and Socialism*. Oxford 1968.
Nzongola, Georges. "The Bourgeoisie and Revolution in the Congo." *The Journal of Modern African Studies*, Vol. 8, No. 4 (December, 1970).
O'Connell, James. "The Inevitability of Instability, " *The Journal of Modern African Studies*. Vol. 5, No. 2 (September, 1967).
Ottaway, David and Marina Ottaway. *Algeria: The Politics of a Socialist Revolution*. California, 1970.
Plamenatz, John P. "The Place and Influence of Political and Social Philosophy." Paper read at the Rome Congress of the International Political Science Association, 1959.
———. *Man and Society*, 2 Vol. Longmans, 1963.
———. "The Use of Political Philosophy," in Anthony Quinton, ed., *Political Philosophy*. Oxford, 1967.
Quandt, William B. *Revolution and Political Leadership: Algeria. 1954-1968*. M.I.T. Press, 1969.
Ranger, Terrence. "Connexions Between 'Primary Resistence' Movements and Modern Mass Nationalism in East and Central Africa." *Journal of Africa History*, Vol. 9, Nos. 3 & 4 (1968).
Russell, Bertrand. *Human Society in Ethics and Politics*. Mentor Books, 1962.
Sartre, Jean-Paul. *What Is Literature?* Trans. by Bernard Frechtman. Methuen, 1950.
———. *Black Orpheus*. Trans, by S.W. Allen. Editions Gallimard, n.d.
Saul, John. "Africa," in Ghita Ionescu and Ernest Gellner, eds., *Populism: Its Meaning and National Characteristics*. Weidenfeld and Nicolson, 1969.
Schachter Ruth (Morgenthau). "Single-Party Systems in West Africa." *American Political Science Review*, Vol. 55 (June, 1961).
Seidman, Ann. "Class Stratification and Economic Development in Africa." *Pan-African Journal*, Vol. V, No. 1 (Spring, 1972).
Shanin, Teodor, ed. *Peasents and Peasant Societies*. Penguin, 1971.
Sharabi, Hisham. "The Transformation of Ideology in the Arab World." *The Middle East Journal*, Vol. 19, No. 4 (1965).
Shepperson, George. "The Politics of African Church Separatist Movements in British Central Africa." *Africa*, Vol. 24 (July, 1954).
Shils, Edward. "Further Observations on Mrs. Huxley." *Encounter* (October, 1961).
"Opposition in the New States of Africa and Asia." Government and Opposition, Vol. 1, No. 2 (January, 1966).

Skinner, Quentin. "Meaning and Understanding in the History of Ideas." *History and Theory*, Vol. 8, No. 1 (1969).
Sklar, Richard L. "Political Science and National Integration: A Radical Approach." *The Journal of Modern African Studies*, Vol. 5, No. 1 (May, 1967).
Smelser, Neil J. *Theory of Collective Behavior*. New York: Free Press, 1963.
Smith, Anthony D. *Theories of Nationalism*. London. Duckworth, 1971.
Sorel, Georges. *Reflections on Violence*. Trans. by T.B. Hulme. Collier, 1961.
Staniland, M. "The Rhetoric of Centre-Periphery Relations." *The Journal of Modern African Studies*, Vol. 8, No. 4 (December, 1970).
Stekloff, M. G. *History of the First International*. New York: M. Lawrence Ltd., 1928.
Stokes, Eric. "Traditional Resistence Movement and Afro-Asian Nationalism: The Context of the 1857 Mutiny Rebellion in India." *Past and Present*, Vol. 48 (August, 1970).
Stone, Lawrence. "Theories of Revolution." *World Politics*, Vol. 18, No. 2 (January, 1966).
———. *The Causes of the English Revolution, 1529-1642*. New York: Harper and Row, 1972.
Taylor, Paul W. "Social Science and Ethical Relativism." *The Journal of Philosophy*, Vol. LV, No. 1 (January 2, 1958).
Toulmin, S.E. *An Examination of the Place of Reason in Ethics*. Cambridge, 1950.
Ulam, Adam. *The Unfinished Revolution*. Random House, 1960.
Vidal-Naguet, Pierre. *Torture: The Cancer of Democracy, France and Algeria, 1954-1962*. Trans. by Barry Richard. London: Penguin, 1963.
Vollrath, Ernst. "Ross Luxemburg's Theory of Revolution." *Social Research*, Vol. 40, No. 1 (Spring, 1973).
Williams, Gavin. "The Social Stratification of a Neo-Colonial Economy: Western Nigeria," in C. Allen and R.W. Johnson, eds., *African Perspectives: Papers in the History, Politics and Economics of Africa Presented to Thomas Hodgkin*. Cambridge 1970.
Williams, Philip M. *Wars, Plots and Scandals in Post-War France*. Cambridge 1970.
Wolin, Sheldon. "The Politics of the Study of Revolution." *Comparative Politics*, Vol. 5, No. 3 (April, 1973).
Wolpe, H. "Some Problems Concerning Revolutionary Consciousness," in Ralph Miliband and John Saville, eds., *The Socialist Register, 1970*. The Merlin Press, 1970.
Wubnig, Judith. "Cultural Relativity and Disagreement," in *Proceedings of the XIVth International Congress of Philosophy*. Vienna, 1968.
Zagorin, Perez. "Theories of Revolution in Contemporary Historiography." *Political Science Quarterly*, Vol. LXXXVIII, No. 1 (March, 1973).
Zolberg, Aristide. *Creating Political Order: The Party States of West Africa*. Rand McNally, 1966.

INDEX